CHRIST'S

CHRIST'S

A Cambridge College Over Five Centuries

Edited by

DAVID REYNOLDS

MACMILLAN

First published 2005 by Macmillan

This edition published 2013 by Pan Books
an imprint of Pan Macmillan, a division of Macmillan Publishers Limited
Pan Macmillan, 20 New Wharf Road, London N1 9RR
Basingstoke and Oxford
Associated companies throughout the world
www.panmacmillan.com

ISBN 978 1 4472 6330 2

A CIP catalogue record for this book is available from
the British Library.

Typeset by SetSystems Ltd, Saffron Walden, Essex

Contents

Acknowledgements

The idea for this rather unconventional College history was conceived back in 1999. Since then a large number of people have helped bring it to fruition. Above all I am grateful to the individual contributors – all busy scholars – who spared time from more substantial academic projects for this exercise in *pietas*. They have endured editorial requests with great forbearance. I am particularly grateful to Quentin Skinner for much helpful comment and advice and to Barry Supple for guidance on economic statistics.

The project was warmly supported in its early days by Alan Munro and then by his successor as Master, Malcolm Bowie. I am greatly indebted to Toby Wilkinson, then Development Director, for much assistance on practical aspects. His successor, Elizabeth Norris, has also been very helpful, as has the Honorary College Archivist, Geoffrey Martin. The maps were researched by Toby Wilkinson and drawn by Kate Spence. On the publishing side, my thanks to Jason Cooper of Macmillan and to Peter Robinson of Curtis Brown.

Rachel Wroth has kindly shared her fascinating researches on College servants, to be published in greater detail in the *College Magazine*. My appreciation of the invaluable research assistance provided by several graduate students – Lucy Brown, Christopher Moore-Bick, Christopher Thompson and Rhiannon Thompson – is recorded more fully at the end of the Introduction.

DAVID REYNOLDS

Introduction

CAMBRIDGE IS OFTEN SEEN as a quintessential symbol of the British Establishment. Sunlit stone, manicured lawns, dons at High Table, undergraduates after a May Ball – the stereotypes are almost culturally ingrained. Carols from King's and the Boat Race are national events, the Oxbridge mafia in the corridors of power a media obsession. Yet Cambridge, though so familiar, is little known or understood. This book offers some snapshots from the album of one Cambridge college – looking at how it developed and why it has mattered in British life.

The fascination of Cambridge, like that of the monarchy or the Church, lies in its antiquity. The earliest colleges date from the thirteenth century. Christ's, founded in 1505, is therefore of middling age. From the outside its heavy wooden door, towered gatehouse and stone façade present a castle-like appearance to shoppers hurrying between the Post Office and the marketplace. Yet that medieval front is eighteenth-century make-up on the crumbling face of a Tudor redbrick. And, although the Porter's Lodge inside the gate also evokes the late-medieval world of castles and manor houses, its computer, closed circuit television and shortwave radios bring one firmly into the twenty-first century.

The great gate of Christ's serves as a metaphor for the

College's history – an apparently unchanging institution that, on closer inspection, has been continually transformed. These essays on College life show the story unfolding – how a Catholic foundation adapted to the Protestant Reformation, how a way-station for unmarried clerics en route to a comfortable rural parish became a secular society of academic researchers, how modern science was implanted in a religious foundation, how an all-male club finally opened its doors to women. In the process the College expanded physically across its nine-acre, wedge-shaped site, with a series of new buildings that run the gamut from seventeenth-century classicism to twentieth-century brutalism.

This is not merely a piece of local history. Recurrently Christ's has impinged on national life, notably in the sixteenth century as a seminary for Puritan clergy in the Reformation, and in the twentieth as a nursery for the bureaucrats of nation and empire. Two of its alumni, John Milton and Charles Darwin, are figures of international renown. At the time of writing the College boasts among its Old Members the Archbishop of Canterbury, the Secretary to the Cabinet, the Lord Chamberlain and the Commander-in-Chief of UK Land Forces – to name only the most 'Establishment' posts.

Christ's in context – the College in relation to the city, the country and, at times, the world is the history presented here. It is written by authors who are not primarily historians of education, let alone of Oxbridge, but who were asked to reflect on a moment of College history in the light of their own professional training and interests. These authors are part of the history they relate because Christ's since the Second World War has been renowned for historical study. This has owed most to J. H. Plumb, later Sir John but always 'Jack', a bachelor don and distinguished historian, who gave munificently of his time and wealth to the College and to young historians. Plumb was a Fellow of the College from 1946 until his death in 2001, and all the contributors to this volume were his students or colleagues. Although working in very different fields and periods of history, each owes something to Plumb's passionate belief that professional history should inform the public culture of a civilized society.

*

Each year hundreds of thousands of visitors enter the antechapel of King's College. Few who gawp at the fan vaulting know that they are standing over the remains of the original Christ's College. From 1436 William Byngham, a London priest, acquired several hostels on Milne Street but the college he founded there with a royal licence in 1439, God's House, survived only a few years. King Henry VI, intent on a college of his own, appropriated the site and the land stretching down to the river, clearing away the maze of streets, alleys and wharves that formed the commercial heart of medieval Cambridge. Milne Street disappeared, though its extremities still exist as Trinity Lane and Queens' Lane. In 1446 the king relocated God's House just outside the city walls on the south-east, on land next to the Barnwell Gate and the King's Ditch – a Saxon earthwork whose function by then was as a town dump (Hobson Street today).

God's House was a struggling enterprise throughout its half-century of obscure existence. Our story begins in 1505 with its refoundation as Christ's College by a remarkable woman, Lady Margaret Beaufort. She was the mother of Henry VII, the first of the Tudor dynasty, whose accession to the throne in 1485 marked the end of the Wars of the Roses. Her chaplain and collaborator was John Fisher, Bishop of Rochester. BARRIE DOBSON looks at their work with the eyes of a late-medieval historian, showing how Fisher's zeal for a trained clergy was balanced by the Lady Margaret's desire to ensure masses for the salvation of her soul. He also offers an intriguing glimpse into the life of a notable woman operating in a man's world.

England in 1505 was Catholic. A century later it was irrevocably, often paranoically, Protestant. Fisher had been burned at the stake for his allegiance to Rome; his college became the training ground for radical Puritans, dedicated to eradicating all relics of Popery from buildings, theology and worship. By the time John Milton arrived at Christ's in 1625, the religious frenzy of Elizabeth's reign had (temporarily) died down. QUENTIN SKINNER explores the place of Christ's in the 'generation' of John Milton – the influence exerted by the College on the great poet and what life was like there for him and his contemporaries. It was a college in which the official language was Latin, where chapel was compulsory twice daily, and in which studies centred on rhetoric, logic and philosophy. But it was also a place where top-up fees, student binge-drinking and a passion for sport (in this case tennis) offer striking similarities with today.

Milton left Christ's in 1632. A decade later the country was split asunder by a ruinous civil war, which saw the College purged first of Royalists in 1643–4 and then of supporters of Parliament when the monarchy was restored in 1660. Religion had been at the heart of that conflict and it was also central to a quieter but no less significant struggle in the years that followed. How should one square the findings of observation with the truths of revelation? In the long eighteenth century between the Glorious Revolution of 1688 and the First Reform

Act of 1832, several distinguished Christ's men addressed the increasingly problematic relationship between religion and science. ROY PORTER* looks especially at the Platonism of Ralph Cudworth, Master from 1654 to 1688, and the natural theology of William Paley, fellow and tutor in the 1760s and 1770s, whose *Evidences of Christianity*, published in 1794, remained compulsory reading in Cambridge until 1921. The clockwork universe of Paley's divine watchmaker became an Aunt Sally for Charles Darwin; the conservative polity pragmatically defended in Paley's pamphlets was a prime target for exponents of radical reform.

Christ's was still an Anglican foundation in 1828, when Darwin entered the College just over two centuries after John Milton, and it was only in the late nineteenth century that nonconformists and Jews were allowed into Oxbridge and College Fellowships opened to non-clergymen. These institutional changes coincided with the inclusion of experimental science in the university curriculum. This Age of Reform is the theme of JOHN BURROW's chapter. The College seems to have been sympathetic to liberal change – indeed if a majority of the Governing Body had had its way in 1838, Christ's would have been a pioneer of reform. But collegiality was the name of the game – as Burrow says, there was no blood on the carpet of the Combination Room. The nineteenth century also saw a growing sense of corporate student identity, measured by the growth of College sports (the Boat Club dates from 1829) and the birth of the *College Magazine* in 1886.

By the twentieth century Christ's, and Cambridge, had

---

* Roy Porter completed a draft of this chapter before he died. It has been revised by the editor.

returned to the centre of national life – but in a very different guise from the Puritan powerhouse of the sixteenth century. The new Triposes produced scientists for the national economy and civil servants to manage government and run the empire. Yet Christ's biggest contribution to the nation in the first half of the twentieth century, as BARRY SUPPLE's chapter notes, was unanticipated and tragic – the loss of 231 academic members in the two world wars. These conflicts had fall-out in many directions – in political and religious debate, for instance, as well as in the economic dislocations that challenged successive Bursars. Even so, the College had the money in 1937 to envisage a new building in Third Court – but not the nerve to go ahead with a modernist design from Walter Gropius. On the other hand, this period did mark a substantial improvement in plumbing – civilization, after all, is founded on drains. Probably the most significant long-term development was the growth of the student body from 176 in the spring of 1914 (comparable to Milton's day) to over 410 in the autumn of 1950. Of the latter, nearly 100 were graduate students – another sign of changing times.

For Christ's, as for higher education in Britain as a whole, the postwar years were an era of rapid and dramatic expansion. DAVID CANNADINE looks at three of the luminaries of Christ's from that generation – men of national and international distinction in their academic work and in public life. He relates the entangled stories of Alexander Todd, Nobel Prize-winning chemist; his long-standing antagonist, J. H. Plumb, the eminent historian; and Plumb's friend C. P. Snow, the scientist and novelist, who sought to mediate between what he dubbed 'The Two Cultures'. Todd was Master from 1963 to 1978, Plumb succeeded him until 1982, and Snow provided an immortal caricature of the prewar College in his novel *The Masters*. But this is a story not so much about the College itself as of three Christ's men trying to shape the culture and outlook of their era.

Finally, in more Proustian vein, SIMON SCHAMA reflects on life as a student and a Fellow in Christ's during the heyday of the Plumb era. He recounts the daunting ordeal of the entrance examination and evokes the jarring contrast between the ethos of the College and the home he had left. He depicts Plumb the teacher, presiding in formidable geniality over his after-dinner seminars of budding historians, and recalls the rich extra-curricular life of Cambridge in the 1960s, the friends and colleagues he made and lost. He also shows how, in outgrowing the College of his youth, he remained rooted in the teaching and experience of those formative years. This is the remembrance of one man, yet many others will surely catch echoes of their story in his. *Souvent me souvient*, the title of Schama's chapter, was the motto of Lady Margaret Beaufort. 'Often I remember'* also sums up the sentiments of many students over the centuries about the College she founded.

*

These essays are not, therefore, a heavy, chronological plod through five centuries of College archives. They offer, instead, a series of snapshots across time, sometimes with gaps in between. Like photographs, they also reveal much about the person behind the camera, for the historians who have written them range right across the professional terrain – from religious and intellectual history to biography, economics and the history of science. Some chapters focus on the College as an institution,

---

* Literally in the medieval French – 'Often it is recalled unto me'.

others concentrate on the thinkers and thinking it fostered – a variety of approaches that gives the book a distinctive texture. Coverage is deliberately weighted to the last century or so because the previous College history, by John Peile, was published in 1900. The editor has provided short linking passages between the chapters, to fill some of the chronological gaps and to mention topics not covered so fully (such as the work of College staff and the admission of women students). The cumulative effect is a vivid impression of five centuries of continuity and transformation.

A College history written by some of the distinguished historians who have studied and taught within its walls – in that sense this book celebrates a tradition. But the tradition is open-ended. Several of these chapters would have been impossible without the research assistance of a younger generation of Christ's historians. Lucy Brown, Christopher Thompson and Rhiannon Thompson – all of whom have been undergraduates and doctoral students at the College – undertook a preliminary survey of the relevant archives, extracting statistical and biographical data of use for all the chapters. Lucy also made a major contribution to the research for the chapter by Quentin Skinner, likewise Christopher for the one by John Burrow. Rhiannon and another Christ's doctoral student, Christopher Moore-Bick, helped locate material for the essay by Barry Supple. Their work is a reminder that Christ's history has a future as well as a past – that the community of teachers and students founded by Lady Margaret Beaufort and John Fisher in 1505 still flourishes five hundred years later.

PART ONE

BARRIE DOBSON

The Foundation

ON 1 MAY 1505 King Henry VII issued his formal Letters Patent officially licensing his most precious (*preciossima*) mother to enlarge and complete Henry VI's fifty-seven-year-old foundation of God's House into a community of up to sixty scholars, thenceforward to be known for ever as *collegium Christi Universitatis Cantabrigiensis*.[1] Located on a marginal but already crowded urban site just east of the Barnwell Gate and the King's Ditch, the members of this new academic fellowship have never been allowed to forget that their college was 'by Henry the Sixth, king of England first begun, and after his decease by Margaret of Richmond, mother of King Henry the Seventh, augmented, finished, and established'.[2] Although not a foundation charter in a formal sense (Christ's was only legally constituted as a corporation when its first statutes were presented and accepted by the last Fellows of God's House in the autumn of 1506), the prestige book copy of these Letters Patent of 1 May 1505 deserve their reputation as much the most precious item in the College archives. Appropriately enough for such a valuable document, it has recently been described as one of the few absolutely outstanding examples of early Tudor manuscript production in the country, although almost certainly illuminated not by an Englishman but by one of the attractively named 'Dutch Masters of the Dark Eyes'.[3]

Not that there can be any doubt that Lady Margaret herself chose the devices which embellished the splendid border of the opening pages of her son's Letters Patent. Within a few years the identical motifs of the Beaufort portcullis, the red rose of Lancaster and the queen mother's personal badge of the white daisy or marguerite were to adorn in profusion the façade of the main college gate and the oriel window above the door into the Master's Lodge. Whether or not Lady Margaret was able to admire – as seems likely – these sumptuous pieces of carved decoration before she died at Westminster on 29 June 1509, five centuries later they remain as not only the most exotic showpieces that Christ's College has to offer but also as the most enduring visual memorials to the artistic taste and wealth of the most formidable woman in early Tudor England. They are a memorial also to one of the most creative periods in the history of the University of Cambridge itself, for some historians its most 'phenomenal' age, when it finally achieved parity in numbers and academic esteem with the University of Oxford. During the last four years of Lady Margaret's life (1505–9) her new college rose above the ground against a background of more frequent formal royal visits to Cambridge than before or since.[4]

The origins of the pre-Reformation academic colleges of Oxford and Cambridge are rarely as simple as they have later seemed; and in the case of the new Christ's College the processes that led to its creation at the beginning of the sixteenth century were not only complex but also constitutionally unique. Indeed it has been argued that this apparently new college was never formally 'founded' at all. In the many documents that accompanied Lady Margaret's negotiations to establish Christ's College she was always at pains to state that her intention was not to create a new academic body but rather to fulfil the 'holy and devoute mynde of holy king henry the sext' who had been deposed in 1461 before he could endow his foundation of 'Goddeshouse' as adequately as he had originally intended.[5] It was on this assumption that A. H. Lloyd, the most learned historian of the early history of the College, concluded – somewhat dubiously – that 'Godshouse and Christ's College are one and the same body, the two names representing the stages of youth and man's estate respectively'.[6]

In practice, as opposed to theory, however, the Christ's College established on 1 May 1505 was very much a new foundation, with a new name and new buildings, so handsomely endowed that it rapidly became one of the largest and most influential of the colleges of the University of Cambridge by the time of the Reformation. In many ways the most interesting issue raised by Lady Margaret's dramatic intervention in English higher education is why she should have been content to revitalize two established Cambridge institutions (God's House and then St John's Hospital) rather than found the magnificent new academic college at either Cambridge or Oxford which her financial resources and royal connections would certainly have warranted.

The answer to that question probably lies in the peculiar circumstances of Lady Margaret's remarkable career. Born in May 1443 as the daughter and heiress of a father she never knew (John Beaufort, first duke of Somerset), the unique position held by Lady Margaret in public life stemmed from the fact that as early as January 1457 she had given birth – her only child – to the future Henry VII, son of the short-lived Edmund Tudor. Thereafter not one of her three subsequent husbands could shield her from the dangers and stresses of being a major prize or victim in the dynastic feuds of the Wars of the Roses.[7] It was only after her son's famous victory at the Battle of Bosworth in August 1485 (where the slain Richard III's Book of Hours was one of her personal trophies from the battlefield) that she had the opportunity, and indeed the obligation, to become the second most important fount of patronage in the kingdom. Within a few years of Henry VII's accession to the throne, she began to make the first of her many visits to the town of Cambridge, where she was solemnly received by the mayor and council in 1489 and presented with three pikes and six pounds of sweets or 'cowmfetts'.[8] Much more fateful was the first recorded meeting between the fifty-one-year-old countess and the thirty-five-year-old Cambridge graduate John Fisher, which took place in 1494 or 1495 at Greenwich, where the latter was a luncheon guest at the 'Queen Mothers', a title by which Lady Margaret was much less customarily addressed than as 'the King's Mother'.[9] Thus began the unlikely but extremely close partnership which, amidst much else, led to that explosion of new endowment which created the first properly funded professors of divinity at both Cambridge and Oxford in 1496–7, the provision of a university-based preacher in 1504, and the very substantial colleges of Christ's and St John's a few years later.

As her most recent biographers have been at pains to stress, Lady Margaret's commitment to the cause of higher education at Cambridge was 'almost certainly due to her relationship with John Fisher, who held office both in the university and as her confessor'.[10] So close was their relationship that it will always be difficult, perhaps impossible, to distinguish at all precisely between their respective contributions to the origins of Christ's. However, it is clear enough that their ideological and emotional commitment to their new college was in fact the result of a fusion of two fundamental if very different impulses within the practice of Christianity in early Tudor England. For Lady Margaret it seems overwhelmingly most likely that it was the commemorative nature of a college which appealed most, its role as a chantry establishment designed to maximize the recitation and singing (hence the word *cantaria*) of innumerable prayers and masses in intercession for the salvation of her soul. For John Fisher, much more committed to the religious regeneration of the realm, the primary purpose of a new academic college was more evangelical, to bring (in the words once applied to his labours by his friend Erasmus) 'the gospel of theology to the people'.[11] By the time of Bishop John Fisher's execution on Tower Hill on 22 June 1535, when this chapter comes to a close, it was already clear both that the chantry functions of Christ's College were already under threat and also – more ironically – that the pursuit of 'the gospel of theology' had been preached so vigorously and divisively that it had helped to bring the Bishop of Rochester himself to the scaffold.

The early history of Christ's College accordingly seems to present three major problems. First, how and why did Lady Margaret and John Fisher decide to transform a struggling little foundation, and very rapidly at that, into one of the largest and richest colleges of the University? Second, in what ways did Lady Margaret and John Fisher expect this transformed College to be religiously and educationally superior to its God's House predecessor? Third, how far did the new Christ's College fulfil Lady Margaret's and Bishop Fisher's ambitions and ideals during the tumultuous years of ideological conflict, which thirty years later were to annihilate Fisher himself?

That the successful foundation of Christ's College was the result of Lady Margaret's own formidable talents, energy and commitment is undeniable. She, like her confessor John Fisher, has never received more attention from historians than during the last thirty years.[12] Somewhat surprisingly perhaps, such intense critical scrutiny has positively enhanced their reputations as highly creative as well as sympathetic and charismatic figures. At the heart of their relationship was John Fisher's uncanny ability to recommend effective spiritual and practical remedies to his famous elderly patron. Despite her regal prestige and despite her ceaseless attention to detail (as witnessed, for instance, by her signature at the foot of so many pages of her household account books), Malcolm Underwood's recent penetrating analysis of her character rightly stresses the sense of alienation, of mental and physical pain, of foreboding indeed, which seems central to her personality during the final and best documented years of her troubled and often tortured career.[13] Certainly no one can read John Fisher's own famous and eloquent English *Mornynge Remembraunce had at the month's mynde of the Noble Princess Margarete, Countesse of Rychemonde and Darbye, emprinted by Wynkyn de Woirde* without being struck by the intense personal impact of Lady Margaret on him. No doubt allowances have to be made for Richard Rex's interesting suggestion that Fisher was deliberately trying to launch a campaign to transform his late patroness into a 'modern blessed woman Martha' and so into the canonized saint she never in fact became.[14] Still one can hardly deny that Fisher's memorial speech possessed the style, rhetoric and emotional power which all other tributes to English Queen Mothers have notably lacked. To quote the most often cited passage from Fisher's tribute, 'All Englonde for her death had cause of weeping ... the Students of both the universities, to whom she was as a Moder ... and All the lerned men of Englonde, to whom she was a veray patroness.'[15]

Perhaps no queen – or indeed king – of England has ever received such a fulsome tribute from an academic scholar. Did Lady Margaret deserve it? Well, both yes and no. In his emphasis on the austerity of his patroness's private life, Fisher underestimated Lady Margaret's very considerable political and administrative talents as well as her determination to cut an appropriately exalted figure in English national life. According to a herald's memoir of events at the royal court between 1485 and 1490, during those years Lady Margaret was quite extraordinarily prominent at all court occasions. Dressed in spectacular fashion, and often in her Garter robes, it is clear that she more or less consistently outshone her daughter-in-law, the king's new queen, Elizabeth of York.[16] Twenty years later, when her son Henry VII was buried at Westminster Abbey in May 1509, only a few months before her own death, she still enjoyed 'semi-regal status' and precedence over all the women in England.[17] Of the depth of her own religious beliefs there can be no doubt at all. Susan Powell's recent study of 'Lady Margaret and her Books' has certainly clinched the case that long before she met Fisher she was in close touch with printers (notably Caxton and Wynkin de Worde); that she supported the international book trade; that she bought books in large numbers; and that she actually read devotional works herself, always a difficult matter positively to prove.[18] Although Lady Margaret never learnt to read Latin (an incapacity, so Fisher alleged, that she much regretted), she was able to translate contemporary French texts into English, most famously the rare fourth book of the exceptionally popular *Imitatio Christi*, the central key to her own spiritual attitudes and – by extension – also one of the keys to the early spiritual programme at Christ's itself.[19] That Lady Margaret was a bookish woman is not in doubt, all the more impressively so indeed given her commitment (after 1485) to that exceptionally heavy round of public duties and acts of private religious devotion which occupied so many of her waking hours after she rose from her bed at five in the morning.[20]

Not the least of Lady Margaret Beaufort's claims to fame is accordingly that in many ways she is the first woman in English history about whose reading habits we have a quite detailed and reliable impression. But why and when she became interested in patronizing university learning at Cambridge is another matter entirely. As the most famous, wealthy and therefore most assiduously courted woman in England, it was no doubt inevitable that she should, like nearly all the most influential female members of the fifteenth-century English royal family, become a more or less compulsive patron of devotional enterprises. She must have been aware too that substantial endowment of an academic college was one such opportunity, not very often taken in fact but quite recently exploited at Cambridge by Elizabeth Woodville and Anne Neville in the case of their Queens' College.[21]

As already said, however, there is no doubt that it was John Fisher who harnessed Lady Margaret's lavish liberality to devotional causes to Cambridge at the expense of Oxford or Westminster Abbey. By the time the Countess and John Fisher first met in 1494 or 1495, the latter had already been a Cambridge student for a dozen years or so. How a merchant's son from Beverley School in the East Riding found his way to Michaelhouse (a college which disappeared when amalgamated into Henry VIII's foundation of Trinity College in 1546) at the age of fourteen in 1483 is perhaps the most mysterious feature of an otherwise exceptionally well-recorded career. His rapid promotion may well have been due to the patronage of

Dr William Melton, his tutor at Michaelhouse (under whose supervision 'he became well acquainted with the Greeke and Heabrew tonges') and also the first noted humanist scholar among the clergy of York Minster, where Melton was Chancellor for thirty years after 1496.[22] Fisher himself became the single most influential member of the growing 'northern clerical connection' of young scholars who from the mid-fifteenth century onwards preferred to study at Cambridge rather than Oxford. As Fisher understandably became an assiduous promoter of a large northern clerical presence in his own university, it is hardly surprising that the first statutes of Christ's College prescribed that six of its Fellows should always be from the nine most northerly English counties. As those statutes of 1506 make obvious, John Fisher was heavily influenced by the novel educational ideals of Erasmus; but – unlike that spiritual master – he was a congenital office-holder too.[23] Senior Proctor of the University at the age of twenty-three, Vice-Chancellor at thirty-two, the first Lady Margaret Professor in Divinity at thirty-three, two years later John Fisher became Bishop of Rochester and the Chancellor of the University of Cambridge in 1504, an office which he held until his execution thirty years later.[24] Fisher's long tenure as Chancellor proved critical in ensuring that the transition from God's House to Christ's College passed off with comparatively few constitutional or administrative obstructions – exactly the opposite of the case when God's House itself had come into tortuous existence half a century earlier.[25]

It can prove tantalizingly difficult, as in the case of nearly all collegiate foundations at all times, to be absolutely sure when the crucial decision to transform God's House into a larger college was actually taken. Although the tradition that Fisher wished to rescue God's House from obscurity because he had himself been a student at God's House is completely untenable, he is more likely than his royal mistress to have conceived such a project.[26] He was obviously well placed to interest Lady Margaret in so grand an enterprise after his appointment as her chaplain and confessor, almost certainly just before her ceremonial visit to Cambridge in the company of her son and daughter-in-law in the autumn of 1498.[27] Although Lady Margaret had employed a large number of Cambridge-educated clerks in her service, many of them inherited from the Yorkist kings, none of these seems to have had strong God's House connections.[28] On the other hand, as the primary purpose of the 1498 royal visitation was to celebrate the inauguration of Jesus College, recently converted from St Radegund's nunnery by Bishop John Alcock of Ely, it is tempting to believe that the prospect of a similarly large-scale act of collegiate foundation on her part may have been finding its way into her mind by that date.[29] It was probably even more significant that at the beginning of the following year and with the consent of her last husband, Lord Thomas Stanley, Margaret took an oath of chastity and transformed her now almost completely vanished manor house of Collyweston, four miles west of Stamford, into her palatial principal residence. The detailed accounts of her chamberlains, treasurers, cofferers and other officers leave no doubt that in all its essentials the creation and building of Christ's College was supervised and co-ordinated within her household at Collyweston.[30] Whether or not the valuable manor of Malton near Orwell in Cambridgeshire, bought by Lady Margaret in October 1503, was intended to endow a new academic college rather than her projected chantry at Westminster Abbey, by the following summer the king was certainly aware that his mother was planning to divert her patronage to some academic cause within the University of Cambridge.[31]

By this point of time the somewhat mysterious figure of John Syclyng, the last head (or Proctor) of God's House (1490–1505) and short-lived first Master of Christ's (1505–7), had stepped (too briefly) on to the stage. The evidence for the career of this obscurely born Suffolk clerk who appeared at Cambridge as a grammar student in 1482 can be problematic – presenting at one stage the alarming spectre of not just one but two contemporary John Syclyngs.[32] Many – if not all – of these biographical problems were much clarified sixty years ago by A. H. Lloyd, intent on arguing that Syclyng's election as the last Proctor of God's House was the most important event in the history of that college between the death of William Byngham in 1451 and its transformation in 1505. Understandably enough, Lloyd had a highly pious purpose in eulogizing what he called 'the labours of Syclyng working by divine influence in the heart of Lady Margaret'.[33] So enthusiastic a tribute is understandable enough in the case of the founding Master of Christ's, and the first to be buried in the new college chapel he never lived long enough to see completed. But the fact is that Syclyng emerges from the records as a difficult and perhaps truculent man, possibly once fined twenty shillings for breaking the peace in the town.[34] More certainly, Syclyng seems to have had few academic qualifications for the headship of a Cambridge college; he was also one of only two Masters of Christ's apparently never to have acquired a higher university degree. More ironically, to judge by the will he made on 25 September 1506, Syclyng did have some expertise in Canon Law, exactly the subject which Lady Margaret and John Fisher had no interest at all in promoting at Christ's.[35]

But then it was as an experienced businessman and accountant that Syclyng's services were of particular value to the University and God's House, to Lady Margaret and John Fisher. By 1492 Syclyng was already Fellow and Bursar-President of Corpus Christi College and the last Proctor (or head of house) of God's House as well as the University's Senior Proctor. A few years later he was working closely – often face to face – on university affairs with both Fisher and Lady Margaret. How could Syclyng not welcome – and indeed promote – the intoxicating prospect that his own college should be metamorphosed into one of the most distinguished academic *studia* in England?[36]

In 1505 and 1506 Lady Margaret rarely lost an opportunity to exploit Syclyng's own argument that Henry VI's foundation was no longer numerically or economically viable. To take a particularly important example, her supplication to the Roman Curia, later approved by Pope Julius II on 23 August 1505, argued 'that on account of lack of proper resources, due to the deficiency of lands, tenements, possessions, revenues and other goods, there has been in the college of "Goddeshouse" from its foundation to the present only a proctor and four scholars – and therefore the intention of the founder, King Henry VI, has not been – and is not being – fulfilled'.[37] It was on these grounds that the Pope agreed that Henry VII was justified in authorizing Lady Margaret's proposal to re-endow God's House, formally founded in 1448, and give it new statutes and a new name. But then the motives that benefactors announce to the world as the reason for their benefactions are rarely to be entirely trusted. Is Lady Margaret's well-publicized portrait of herself as a redeemer coming to the rescue of a God's House that had become rotten before it became ripe likely to be true or not? In some ways that central issue still remains remarkably open.

Nearly everything about the history of God's House during the half-century of its existence remains mysterious, not least its size, appearance and precise location. The most deeply considered and perceptive study, A. H. Lloyd's *Early History of Christ's College*, nearly always sees God's House through an optimistic haze of retrospective piety. At times Lloyd almost seems to be regretting that Lady Margaret had not left God's House well alone.[38] In fact, all the available evidence suggests that Syclyng and Lady Margaret were correct in their claim that God's House was in a highly precarious and vulnerable state, both economically and educationally, by the beginning of the sixteenth century. It has proved impossible to identify more than fifty individuals who were associated with that college during the fifty-seven years of its official existence between 1448 and 1505, of whom twenty-three were Fellows and six were Proctors.[39] So small a complement of scholars and students would certainly have disappointed and even scandalized the 'onlie begetter' and first Proctor of God's House, William Byngham. Nor did any of God's House's few alumni lead particularly distinguished careers in either academe or administration. The most obvious exception, that remarkable polymath from St Andrews, John Major, apparently only sought admission here (probably in 1491–2) because it behoved him as a Scot to attach himself to the only college in Cambridge within the parish of St Andrew's church.[40] Of the six Proctors of God's House, the sole Doctor of Theology was John Hurte, who retired from the Lodge after a few years and lived and died as the much more handsomely rewarded Vicar of St Mary's Church, Nottingham, from which he bequeathed two books to God's House Library on his death in 1476.[41] Apart from being much less active as teachers and scholars than their successors after 1506, these

Proctors seem to have spent much of their time away from disease-ridden Cambridge, often at the College's nearby living of Fen Drayton, which was to continue to fulfil its role of helping sustain the Master of Christ's for centuries to come.

Above all, as Lady Margaret fully appreciated, the annual revenues of her new college needed to be vastly increased. The initial endowments of God's House had always been inadequate, not least because Henry VI had failed to contribute at all substantially to the college William Byngham founded in his honour.[42] After the death of the indefatigable Byngham in 1451 the income of the college dwindled to only about £50 a year by the 1490s, when God's House seems to have been much the poorest secular academic college in Cambridge with the possible exception of Catharine Hall.[43] Towards the end of the century Bishop John Alcock of Ely regularly granted indulgences to all who supported God's House during its periods of indigence and distress.[44] Needless to say, the acquisition of new rent-generating estates and of spiritual income from churches in the college's patronage was an urgent matter, which had to be well in hand before the rebuilding and inauguration of the transformed college. As a result of a whirlwind campaign between 1503 and 1508 'for the buying of lyfelod' (the phrase employed by Lady Margaret's receiver), future Masters and Fellows of Christ's were to enjoy the revenues of a large if very miscellaneous agglomeration of properties dispersed erratically throughout southern England. According to the earliest surviving Master's annual accounts, the most significant of these were Kegworth and Diseworth in Leicestershire; the tithes of Manorbier in Pembrokeshire; and the dissolved abbey of Creke in Norfolk, granted by Henry VII to his mother for the purpose in 1507.[45] The manor of Malton, bought by Lady Margaret four years earlier, made a more direct contribution to the welfare of the Fellows of Christ's: its manor house, only nine miles south-west of Cambridge, was rapidly converted into a comfortable college bolt-hole at times of plague. Unfortunately, however, the most substantial of all Lady Margaret's purchases was the manor of Roydon in Essex, worth well over fifty pounds a year and therefore so valuable that fifteen years later the Master was reluctantly compelled to surrender it to Henry VIII in exchange for the priory of Bromehill in Norfolk. Without wishing to minimize the gravity of the short-term financial crisis that ensued ('without your help we are utterly undone,' wrote Master Henry Lockwood to Thomas Cromwell in 1532), by the late 1530s Lady Margaret's endowments still sufficed to sustain her ambitious objective of sixty members.[46]

Indeed, as early as 1509 (the year in which both Henry VII and his mother died), the College's total net income was already estimated at £250, quite sufficient to pay for the salaries and commons (living expenses) of the Master and twelve Fellows, the commons of the forty-seven pupil scholars, not to mention the wages and fees of the Master's servant, the manciple, two cooks, four servants, barber, washerwoman and (that special feature of Christ's) the *Lector Collegii*.[47] According to the first detailed Christ's College accounts to survive (for the years 1521–2), the total annual income of the college from its landed estates had stabilized at almost £300, of which only a tenth (£30 or so) derived from the old God's House properties. There is no more impressive tribute to Lady Margaret's success in placing her augmented college on an entirely new financial footing. Within fifteen years of its foundation Christ's could afford to maintain as many as sixteen Fellows, normally in residence and receiving twelve pence a week, as well as forty-seven scholars and the four servants at seven pence a week.[48] After Michaelmas 1530, when the long sequence of Master's account books becomes the major source for the income and expenditure on the College, both the revenues and numerical size of Christ's can be estimated with remarkable precision. In 1535, the year of John Fisher's execution and the first royal visitation of the University, Christ's was the fifth richest college in the University, only surpassed by King's, St John's, Queens' and King's Hall.[49] More significant still, these early account books give an impression of a high degree of numerical stability – as Lady Margaret and Fisher would have wished – with a regular complement of a Master, twelve Fellows and forty or so scholars or *discipuli*. Only fifty years later, during the reign of Elizabeth, did the numbers of undergraduates in residence at last begin to rise, often erratically but eventually to over one hundred.[50]

The speed with which Christ's College became a large and fairly prosperous institution is therefore one of the most remarkable features of its foundation. By the end of 1505 Lady Margaret had provided the College with its new common seal; and in the same year she was commissioning copies of both 'the statutes of godez howse in Cambrygge' (twenty pence) and 'my lady's boke of statutes of Cryst College' (six shillings and eight pence).[51] The latter were the statutes approved on 30 October 1506 by John Syclyng, the new Master, as well as by John Scott, Edward Fowke and Thomas Nunne (the last three Fellows of God's House and the first three Fellows of Christ's) and thereafter remained the constitutional basis of collegiate life and work in the College until 1860. Although they provide us with our best glimpse of the objectives of Lady Margaret and John Fisher, these statutes are not in fact easy to summarize. Most readily and accurately accessible in a privately printed edition of 1927,

The Fourteen Secular Colleges of Cambridge in 1535[52]

Names in order of foundation	Date of foundation	Approximate annual income	Approximate number of Fellows		
Peterhouse	1284	£125	Master	+	14
Michaelhouse	1324	£124	Master	+	6
King's Hall	1337	£211	Provost	+	41
Clare Hall	c.1340	£84	Master	+	12
Pembroke Hall	1347	£153	Master	+	15
Gonville Hall	1349	£99	Warden	+	9
Trinity Hall	1350	£72	Master	+	3
Corpus Christi	1352	£83	Master	+	8
[GOD'S HOUSE	1448–1505	c.£30	Proctor	+	4]
King's College	1441	£751	Warden	+	32
Queens' College	1448	£230	Master	+	18
St Catharine's Hall	1473	£39	Master	+	3
Jesus College	1496	£87	Master	+	6
CHRIST'S COLLEGE	1505	£190	Master	+	12
St John's College	1511	£507	Master	+	27

they consist of no less than forty-seven separate and substantial clauses or chapters, ranging over most aspects of College life – but not (with a few exceptions) raising many academic issues.[53] These statutes (at least one copy of which was signed by 'Nos Margareta' herself) were probably compiled by a clerk who may have worked under Fisher's personal direction; but they avoided the customary legal phraseology of such documents and were written in fluent late-medieval Latin. Although the statutes are invariably lucid and sometimes produce a striking phrase (for instance, *Nihil Iuveni Fugiendum est Magis Inerti Otio*: 'Nothing is to be more avoided by a young man than slothful idleness'), one finds few traces of the sub-Ciceronian Latin already being employed by Erasmus and about to be used by the young Thomas More.[54] All in all, a conservative literary style and format also convey a conservative and highly pious 'mission' statement.

The interpretation of late-medieval College statutes is a much more complex matter than one might imagine, partly because there was no generally accepted model of how to frame such documents and partly because the founders were nearly always relieved if they could copy or adapt the terms of available previous statutes.[55] That said, in some ways the most arresting feature of the 1506 Christ's statutes is how very disinclined they were to theorize. Admittedly, the first chapter employed a common, even hackneyed, medieval topos (also used at Balliol College Oxford) to liken the College – like a principality – to the human body so that 'the Master is the Head; the Reader is the member devoted to procreating new offspring; the Fellow Scholars are the principal members; and the college servants are the feet'.[56] Thereafter the statutes immediately plunged into a detailed description of the qualities needed in a Master, who was henceforth required to be either a Doctor or Bachelor of Theology, or at worst a Master of Arts studying for a higher degree in divinity. The twelve Fellow Scholars were preferably to be elected from the poorer of the College's scholar pupils; and they were required to dine and sup (*prandere et cenare*) at a separate table in Hall unless they fell ill or were obliged to leave Cambridge because of 'plague or any other contagious infection'. Unfortunately, little can be known about the way in which the forty-seven or so pupil scholars were selected for admission to the College; but although preference was supposed to be given to poor young clerks from the northern counties, they all had to be able to speak Latin. As a gesture towards the original ideals of William Byngham's God's House, six of these scholars were to be carefully chosen for specialized training in grammar so as to become qualified schoolmasters.

All the other young scholars were expected to follow the university's arts course – and to leave the College when they had qualified for the MA degree.[57] The practice of establishing a salaried lecturer to give lectures in arts and theology (the only quasi-professional teacher in the college) was borrowed from God's House. At Christ's after 1506 this *Lector* or Reader was required to give four lectures in hall a day, of two hours each ('one in sophistry, a second in logic, a third in philosophy, and a fourth on either the poets or orators'); but there is little suggestion in the statutes that teaching at the new college was intended to follow the most recent educational fashions in the so-called humanist 'New Learning'.[58] More significant for the future than any novel curricular features in Lady Margaret's statutes was a brief clause licensing the admission of fee-paying *pensionarii* or commoners into the community. Although increasing numbers of such fee-paying students had been making their way into Cambridge and Oxford colleges during the course of the fifteenth century, the word *pensionarius* makes its first appearance in any academic statutes within these Christ's statutes of 1506. Somewhat surprisingly, however, there are no references to the existence of such pensioners in the college accounts before 1545. Only during the late sixteenth century does a positive 'invasion' of commoners seem, at Christ's as elsewhere in Oxford and Cambridge, to have dramatically transformed the ranks of college society, above all by introducing laymen into what had previously been an overwhelmingly clerical community.[59]

However conventional and at times derivative, the Christ's statutes of 1506 convey a vivid impression of daily routine in the pre-Reformation College. It is no surprise that conditions seem to have been more spartan and discipline more rigorous than at any later stage of Christ's history. Drinking parties were completely prohibited, as was the use of dogs or hawks for hunting. Playing with dice or cards was also forbidden, except – rather curiously perhaps – in the Hall at Christmas.[60] Admirers of Lady Margaret have sometimes suggested that she exercised a moderating influence on these statutes, most particularly in permitting reasonably generous holidays to the Fellows and restricting the number of scholars in each College room to two. Somewhat unusually, the statutes also permitted – a little grudgingly – women of good reputation to enter the college as nurses at times of sickness. No doubt the severity with which Fellows were to be treated if they were found culpable of 'frequenting public taverns, suspect houses, drinking bouts and loose women, especially within any room of the said college' raises the strong suspicion that such offences were by no means unknown.[61] To state the obvious, early Tudor Cambridge was a violent town and university; and it need occasion no particular surprise that in 1529 John Pulter, not necessarily a member of Christ's, was pardoned for killing Edmund Wilson within the actual precincts of the College. Less seriously, four years later a group of rioting law students allegedly managed to lure one unfortunate Fellow of Christ's, Master Henry Pawley, out of his College into the street 'and so bette hym sore and also pulled off his hair'.[62] A more acceptable form of recreation was provided by the plays and musical entertainments performed in the Hall by the town waits and other minstrels from at least 1530, thus inaugurating Christ's long-standing reputation for dramatic productions.[63] By that date too the College library (one of whose windows needed re-glazing) was in regular use, although it is one of the more disappointing features of the early history of the College that we know so little of what a century ago M. R. James called 'the lost library' of Christ's manuscripts. However, the College's collection of early printed books, including many of Lady Margaret's own bequest of forty items, was thoroughly traditional – almost old-fashioned – in its academic character. As late as 1535 the library was dominated by standard medieval scholastic texts, notably works of Thomas Aquinas and editions of Aristotle and his commentators.[64]

From 1505 onwards the primary social function of Christ's College was what it remained until the nineteenth century – to educate young men (at this period usually admitted at the age of fourteen or fifteen) who would eventually proceed, if they were fortunate enough, to undertake the cure of souls in a parish far away from Cambridge. Such a conclusion emerges clearly enough from the careers of the one hundred and fifty or so individuals who are known to have been members of the College during the thirty years between 1505 and 1545.[65] Unfortunately, only a few of the pupil scholars who entered Christ's (although nearly all the Fellows) can be identified before 1545. Even the now most celebrated of all Christ's early alumni, Henry VIII's great antiquary and the godfather of English local history, John Leland, left only a casual reference in his voluminous writings to the fact that he had studied for an arts degree at Christ's: he graduated as a Cambridge BA in 1522 before continuing his studies in Paris.[66] But it has to be admitted that few of the first generations of Christ's Fellows and scholars were ever prominent figures outside Cambridge itself. The major exception was Nicholas Heath, a Fellow in 1523, who was later recommended to Thomas Cromwell as 'a most secret man' and went on to hold John Fisher's old see of Rochester from 1540 to 1544. A doctrinal conservative, he was promoted to both the archbishopric of York and the Lord Chancellorship of England during the reign of Queen Mary, thereafter paying the inevitable price of imprisonment and ejection from his see by Queen Elizabeth.[67]

The vicissitudes of Archbishop Heath's career illustrate on a grand scale the acute problems of spiritual allegiance and loyalty to which all Cambridge and Oxford college Fellows were exposed during the erratic progress of the religious revolution of the 1530s and 1540s. Before 1530 there is no evidence that any member of the Christ's community was at all discontented with the College's traditional religious practices. Indeed – rather surprisingly perhaps – the College was the most popular Cambridge residence of the last generation of English Carthusian monks, soon to be among the most notable opponents (and victims) of Henry VIII and Thomas Cromwell.[68] After 1531, however, when their most important episcopal patron, John Fisher, began to deny Henry VIII's claim to be the Supreme Head of the English Church, impartiality became increasingly impossible to maintain. Despite the atmosphere of secrecy and suspicion that descended upon the University, one can occasionally detect among the Christ's Fellows of the period advocates and opponents of the Protestant cause. John Mallory, an arts graduate at the College in the mid-1520s, was one of the circle of young men who first discussed Luther's heresies in Cambridge at the quasi-legendary 'White Horse' tavern between King's and St Catharine's Colleges.[69] Nor should one underestimate the genuine crises of conscience that must have afflicted so many members of Christ's as they heard that Bishop Fisher (for whom they regularly prayed in chapel) was being hounded towards his execution. According to a lurid and no doubt somewhat apocryphal story by the Protestant martyrologist John Foxe, one young scholar of Christ's called Randall was found in his study 'hanged by his own girdle, with his face turned towards his Bible and his finger pointing to a passage therein treating of predestination'.[70]

Like the members of most corporate bodies at most times, the spiritual and political attitudes of most Fellows of Christ's during the religious ordeals of the 1530s and 1540s were in any case directed and conditioned – as Lady Margaret had enjoined – by the opinions and personality of their superior, the Master. As again Lady Margaret would have approved, the first five Masters of Christ's were all Cambridge doctors of theology and almost all from northern England. Admittedly, the College seems to have been unfortunate in the choice of its first three heads. John Syclyng died in 1507 and so never lived long enough to see the new College in operation. His successor, Richard Wyott, was Master for only three years (1507–10) before returning to the north and the Precentorship of York Minster. Thomas Thompson, Master from 1510 to 1517, retired from his office

many years before his death: but although he later transferred
his allegiance to St John's College he presented Christ's with the
nearby property of the 'Brazen George', thereafter in heavy
demand for student accommodation.[71] A much more significant
figure was the fourth Master, John Watson (1517–31), who had
once been on pilgrimage to the Holy Land (in 1515) and was a
correspondent of Erasmus, a close disciple of John Fisher and
a leading defender of the religious status quo against radical
reformers. As Vice-Chancellor of the University in 1529–32, he
was faced with the unenviable task of handling the University's
response to Henry VIII's desire for a divorce from Catherine of
Aragon. His retirement – probably enforced – from both that
position and the mastership of Christ's marked the end of any
remote possibility that the College might try to resist the royal
will.[72] It accordingly fell to Watson's successor, Dr Henry
Lockwood (Master for seventeen years between 1531 and 1548),
to lead Christ's into the uncertain academic world of a Protestant future. As the personal tutor of Thomas Cromwell's son
('my loving pupill Gregory') who sent numerous obsequious
letters and a generous retaining fee to Cromwell himself, he was
hardly likely to do otherwise. By the time Lockwood retired in
1548 there can be no reasonable doubt that the great majority
of the Fellows of the College had come to accept the religious
changes of the previous fifteen years with a reasonable degree
of equanimity and sometimes positive enthusiasm.[73] Only a few
years later, after the succession of Queen Mary in 1553, at least
ten members of Christ's College (more than from any other
college except King's and St John's) expressed their opposition
to the re-imposition of the Roman religion by the extreme step
of leaving Cambridge for exile in such radical Protestant strong-
holds as Frankfurt, Geneva, Basle and Zurich. When they

returned five or more years later the stage would be set for Christ's to enter an era of greater religious influence within the university than ever before.[74]

Throughout the turmoil of these Reformation years, by far the most tumultuous in the entire history of the community, the Fellows and scholars of Christ's never forgot to remember Lady Margaret Beaufort. The celebration of the anniversary of her death was the most important ceremonial event in the College year. However by 1535, it was no longer true for the members of Christ's, as it had been for their foundress in 1505 that 'the college was seen primarily as a chantry for herself and her family, secondly as a house of devotion, and only then a place of study'. Chapter 29 of the 1506 statutes had made Lady Margaret's objectives absolutely clear: 'There are three things which we command all the Fellows of this College to cherish above all things, namely the worship of God, the increase of faith and the probity of morals.'[75] Only post-Reformation disenchantment with the idea of vicarious intercession for the souls of the dead by means of the mass has tended to conceal from later generations what was undoubtedly Lady Margaret's primary aim in founding Christ's College. Indeed, the statutes prescribe so many masses on more or less every day of the year that one may wonder whether the early Fellows had any time to do very much else. For Lady Margaret and John Fisher, the College chapel, consecrated in June 1510 and one of the largest and most handsome chapels in Cambridge at that date, was at the very heart of the purposes of the College. Above all, frequent masses were to be sung there for the salvation of Lady Margaret's own family, emphatically not forgetting the departed soul of Henry VI, formerly King of England. To an extent that deserves more emphasis than it has received, the King's Mother probably did see herself as a would-be saintly successor to a would-be saintly king. It is worth recalling too that the young Margaret had met and known Henry VI, the original titular founder of Christ's.[76] How better, after all, to demonstrate that the Tudor monarchs were indeed the legitimate spiritual heirs of the Lancastrian dynasty than to transform God's House into Christ's College?

There is perhaps a final moral to be drawn. The *collegium Christi universitatis Cantabrigiensis* came into existence in 1505 because John Fisher persuaded Lady Margaret Beaufort to share his almost obsessive concern that England should have a properly educated priesthood, able to face the challenges of heresy and maintain traditional theology. As has been seen, neither Margaret nor John Fisher ever envisaged the admission to their new college of any student incapable of a university course in arts – which whenever possible should lead to the supreme if arduous achievement of a bachelor's or doctor's degree in theology. Indeed the only members of Christ's, apart from the Master, who were allowed to live in a room of their own were doctors of theology. But the reasons for such emphasis on training in theology were not primarily academic but evangelical, not idealistic but vocational. At Christ's from 1505 onwards even pupil scholars, undergraduates, had to be intending priests. As for the Fellows of Christ's, they had either to be priests already or be ordained within a year, so making absolutely public their commitment to the celibacy which was then inextricably the consequence of an ecclesiastical career.[77] In that respect the 'new' Christ's College of 1505–6 could not have been more conservative. Perhaps no academic institution founded in the first decade of the sixteenth century turned its back so firmly against the promotion of higher education for laymen, a development so often vaunted as one of the most important novelties of the culture of early modern Europe. More intriguingly still, by creating – or trying to create – what was in effect a narrowly based theological seminary, Lady Margaret and Fisher took a leading role in ensuring that, for the next century and beyond, many of the cleverest young men in England would indeed become obsessed by theological debate. What this remarkable duo could not predict, let alone control, was the way in which that debate would turn.

NOTES

1. A. H. Lloyd, *The Early History of Christ's College, Cambridge* (Cambridge, 1934), pp. 288–91.
2. A. L. Peck, *The Lord King's College of God's-house, 1448–1948* (Cambridge, 1948), p. 13.
3. J. P. Carley and J. Backhouse, 'Remembrances of Lady Margaret Beaufort in the Archives: her Foundation Document and her Signatures', *Christ's College Magazine* 222 (1997), 14–17.
4. M. K. Jones and M. G. Underwood, *The King's Mother: Lady Margaret Beaufort, Countess of Richmond and Derby* (Cambridge, 1992), pp. 229–30. I am especially grateful to Malcolm Underwood, Archivist of St John's College, for his invaluable advice and assistance at all stages during the preparation of this chapter.
5. Ibid., p. 218. For the long established view that Christ's owes its very existence to the fact that Lady Margaret believed herself the 'heir to all king Henry's godly intentions', see, for instance, T. Fuller, *The History of the University of Cambridge*, ed. J. Nichols (London, 1840), p. 134.
6. Lloyd, *Christ's College*, p. 341.
7. Jones and Underwood, *The King's Mother*, pp. 35–65.
8. Cambridge Borough Archives, Treasurer's Accounts, 1488–9; E. M. G. Routh, *A Memoir of Lady Margaret Beaufort, Countess of Richmond and Derby, Mother of Henry VII* (Oxford, 1924), p. 111.
9. M. Bateson, ed., *Grace Book* B, part 1 [Cambridge Antiquarian Society, Luard Memorial Series, II] (Cambridge, 1903), p. 68.
10. Jones and Underwood, *The King's Mother*, p. 205.

11. H. C. Porter, 'Fisher and Erasmus', in B. Bradshaw and E. Duffy, eds, *Humanism, Reform and the Reformation: The Career of Bishop John Fisher* (Cambridge, 1989), pp. 81–101.

12. For instance H. C. Porter, *Reformation and Reaction in Early Tudor Cambridge* (Cambridge, 1958); Jones and Underwood, *The King's Mother*; R. Rex, *Henry VIII and the English Reformation* (London, 1993). For older biographies of Lady Margaret, see C. H. Cooper, *The Lady Margaret: a Memoir of Margaret, Countess of Richmond and Derby*, ed. J. E .B. Mayor (Cambridge, 1874) and E. M. G. Routh, *A Memoir of Lady Margaret Beaufort, Countess of Richmond and Derby, Mother of Henry VII* (Oxford, 1924).

13. Jones and Underwood, *The King's Mother*, pp. 256–9.

14. Rex, *Henry VIII and the English Reformation*, pp. 84–5.

15. J. E. B. Mayor, ed., *The English Works of John Fisher, part I*, Early English Text Society, e.s., 27 (London, 1876), pp. 300–1.

16. British Library, Cotton MS. Julius B XII, fos. 34–50. I am grateful to Professor Tony Pollard for this reference.

17. Jones and Underwood, *The King's Mother*, p. 92.

18. S. Powell, 'Lady Margaret Beaufort and her Books', *The Library*, 20 (1998), 197–240.

19. Ibid., pp. 222–3.

20. Mayor, ed., *The English Works of John Fisher, part I*, pp. 289–95.

21. D. R. Leader, *A History of the University of Cambridge, I; The University to 1546* (Cambridge, 1988), p. 229.

22. J. Raine, ed., *Testamenta Eboracensia*, vol. V (1884), pp. 251–63; A. B. Emden, *A Biographical Dictionary of the University of Cambridge to 1500* (Cambridge, 1963), pp. 400–1; J. K. McConica, *English Humanists and Reformation Politics under Henry VIII and Edward VI* (Oxford, 1965), p. 91.

23. Bradshaw and Duffy, eds, *Humanism, Reform and the Reformation*, pp. 1–24, 67–80.

24. Emden, *Biographical Dictionary*, p. 229.

25. Bradshaw and Duffy, eds, *Humanism, Reform and the Reformation*, pp. 47–66; Peck, *God's-house*, pp. 5–7.

26. Lloyd, *Christ's College*, pp. 200–1; Bradshaw and Duffy, eds, *Humanism, Reform and the Reformation*, pp. 24–30.

27. St John's College Archives, D. 91.17 (Cofferer's Account 1498–9), p. 36; Emden, *Biographical Dictionary*, p. 229; Jones and Underwood, *The King's Mother*, p. 213.

28. St John's College Archives, D. 91.21 (Cofferer's Account, 1505–7),

passim; J. Peile, *Biographical Register of Christ's College, 1505–1905* (2 vols, Cambridge, 1910–13), vol. I, pp. 1–3.

29. Leader, *History of the University of Cambridge*, pp. 270–5.

30. M. K. Jones, 'Colleyweston – an early Tudor palace' in D. Williams, ed., *England in the Fifteenth Century* (London, 1987), pp. 129–41. The remarkably detailed household accounts of Lady Margaret's household officials are at their most numerous and informative for the five years before her death (St John's College Archives, D. 91.16, 19, 20, 21, 22; D. 102.1). I am grateful to St John's College for permission to consult these accounts.

31. Jones and Underwood, *The King's Mother*, pp. 217–20.

32. Lloyd, *Christ's College*, pp. 203–8.

33. Ibid., p. 311.

34. The relevant entry in the University Grace Book for 1504–5 ('*Item a Magistro Suclyng pro pacis turbacione*') is admittedly ambiguous and may refer to the fines Syclyng had himself imposed on brawling students and other offenders in Cambridge. (M. Bateson, ed., *Grace Book* B, part I, p. 202; Lloyd, *Christ's College*, pp. 273–5).

35. Emden, *Biographical Dictionary*, p. 572. In his will of 24 September 1506 Syclyng mentioned only two books, copies of 'the Decreys and the Decretals', both of which he bequeathed to Christ's (Lloyd, *Christ's College*, p. 306).

36. St John's College Archives, D. 91.21 (Cofferer's Account, 1505–7) gives a vivid impression of Syclyng's close personal contacts with the foundress (including – at p. 14 – bringing 'apples and oranges unto my lady') during the eighteen months between the foundation of the new college and his own death.

37. M. J. Haren, ed., *Calendar of Papal Registers, 1503–13* (Dublin, 1989), pp. 34–5. I am most grateful to Dr David Yale for informing me that a bound photocopy of this confirmatory papal bull is now deposited in the College Library.

38. More justifiable is Lloyd's suggestion that the God's House statutes, only known to have been codified as late as 1495, were in many ways more educationally innovative than those of Christ's College eleven years later (Lloyd, *Christ's College*, pp. 242–4, 299–300).

39. Peile, *Biographical Register*, pp. 1–3; Lloyd, *Christ's College*, pp. 379–400.

40. Cambridge University Library, Adam Wall MS: Mm. 5.45, fo. 109; Leader, *History of the University of Cambridge*, p. 77, note 100.

41. Raine, ed., *Testamenta Eboracensia*, III, pp. 220–2; Emden, *Biographical Dictionary*, p. 222.

42. J. Peile, *Christ's College* (Cambridge, 1900), pp. 5–6. According to a valor of the properties of the new college made in 1509, its annual revenues already amounted to £250, of which however only £32 derived from endowments of God's House (*'de antiqua fundatione'*): Bodleian Library, Oxford, Bodleian Charter No. 39.

43. C. H. Cooper, *Annals of Cambridge* (5 vols, Cambridge, 1842–1908), vol. I, p. 370.

44. Cambridge University Library, Baker MS., Mm. 2. 24, p. 77.

45. Christ's College Archives, Master's Account Book B:1, fos. 1–4, 16–20, 36–9; cf. *Report of the Commissioners appointed to Inquire into the Property and Income of the Universities of Oxford and Cambridge and of the Colleges and Halls Therein* (London, 1874), III, pp. 300–61.

46. *Letters and Papers, Foreign and Domestic of the Reign of Henry VIII*, ed. H. S. Brewer and J. Gairdner, vol. 5 (London, 1880), nos. 766, 847, 1136.

47. Bodleian Library, Oxford, Bodleian Charter No. 39.

48. R. N. Swanson, 'The Finances of the New Foundation: Some Early Accounts', *Christ's College Magazine* 201 (1975), 9–16, is much the most informative guide to the complexities of the College's finances during its early years.

49. F. D. Logan, 'The First Royal Visitation of the English Universities, 1535', *English Historical Review* 106 (1991), 861–88; *Valor Ecclesiasticus* (Record Commission, 1810–34), III, pp. 505–6; cf. Fuller, *History of the University of Cambridge*, pp. 136–8.

50. Christ's College Archives, B:1, fos. 4v–8, 18–24, 39v–42v, 141–5, 283–6; Cambridge University Library, UA, Matr. 1 (Matriculation Book), fos. 8–17.

51. St John's College Archives, D. 91.21 (Cofferer's Accounts, 1502–5), pp. 37, 56; D. 91.19 (Treasurer's Account. 1507–8), p. 8.

52. Many of the items in this list (especially the financial details derived from the Valor Ecclesiasticus of 1535, a national survey of ecclesiastical wealth) pose complex problems of interpretation. See *Documents relating to the Universities and Colleges of Cambridge* (Queen's Commissioners, 1852) I, pp. 105–294; *Victoria County History of Cambridgeshire*, vol. III, *The City and University of Cambridge, passim*; D. Knowles and R. N. Hadcock, *Medieval Religious Houses: England and Wales* (London, 1971), pp. 449–51.

53. H. Rackham, ed., *Early Statutes of Christ's College, Cambridge* (Cambridge, 1927), pp. 44–121.

54. *Early Statutes*, pp. 106–7; H. Rackham, ed., *Christ's College in Former Days* (Cambridge, 1939), p. 430.

55. R. N. Swanson, 'Godliness and good learning: ideas and imagination in medieval university and college foundations', in *Pragmatic Utopias: Ideals and Communities, 1200–1630*, ed. R. Horrox and S. Rees Jones (Cambridge, 2001), pp. 46–7.

56. *Early Statutes*, pp. 45, 99; Swanson, 'Godliness and good learning', p. 47.

57. *Early Statutes*, pp. 107–8.

58. Ibid., pp. 99–103; A. Cobban, 'Commoners in Medieval Cambridge Colleges' in *Medieval Cambridge: Essays on the Pre-Reformation University*, ed. P. Zutshi (Woodbridge, Suffolk, 1993), p. 51.

59. *Early Statutes*, p. 115; Cobban, 'Commoners in Medieval Cambridge Colleges', pp. 49–52; A. Cobban, *English University Life in the Middle Ages* (London, 1999), pp. 97, 99.

60. *Early Statutes*, pp. 92–3.

61. Ibid., pp. 90–1.

62. *Letters and Papers, Henry VIII*, iv, no. 6135; Peile, *Biographical Register*, pp. 14–15.

63. A. Nelson, ed., *Records of Early English Drama: Cambridge* (2 vols., Toronto, 1989), II, pp. 748–9, provides the most useful introduction to early dramatic performances at Christ's.

64. M. R. James, *A Descriptive Catalogue of the Western Manuscripts in the Library of Christ's College, Cambridge* (Cambridge, 1905), p. 5; Rackham, ed., *Christ's College in Former Days*, pp. 290–1; Powell, 'Lady Margaret Beaufort and her Books', pp. 237–8; Peile, *Christ's College*, p. 191.

65. Peile, *Biographical Register*, pp. 4–22.

66. J. P. Carley, 'John Leland in Paris: The Evidence of his Poetry', *Studies in Philology*, 83 (1986), 7; J. G. Adami, 'John Leland', *Christ's College Magazine*, 18–19 (1892), 55–7; A. B. Emden, *A Biographical Dictionary of the University of Oxford, A.D. 1501 to 1540* (Oxford, 1974), pp. 350–1.

67. Peile, *Biographical Register*, p. 11; cf. Emden, *Biographical Dictionary of the University of Oxford*, pp. 278–9.

68. B. Dobson, 'The Monastic Orders in Late Medieval Cambridge', in *The Medieval Church: Universities, Heresy and the Religious Life: Essays in Honour of Gordon Leff*, ed. P. Biller and B. Dobson (Studies in Church History, Subsidia 11, 1999).

69. Peile, *Biographical Register*, p. 14; Porter, *Reformation*, pp. 4–7.

70. Porter, *Reformation*, p. 19.

71. Emden, *Biographical Dictionary of the University of Cambridge*, p. 572; J. and J. A. Venn, eds, *Alumni Cantabrigiensis to 1751* (4 vols, Cambridge, 1922–7), IV, p. 480; Peile, *Biographical Register*, pp. 4–7.

72. Cooper, *Annals of Cambridge*, I, p. 345; Emden, *Biographical Dictionary of the University of Cambridge*, pp. 622–3; Venn, *Alumni Cantabrigiensis*, IV, p. 348.

73. *Letters and Papers, Henry VIII*, iv, no. 619, 798, 847, 1136; Peile, *Biographical Register*, pp. 10, 15.

74. The 'Marian Exiles' from Christ's College are listed in Porter, *Reformation*, p. 91, a work which also (pp. 115–18) discusses the career of Anthony Gilby, an arts graduate of the College in the early 1530s who later returned from Frankfurt and Geneva to be the first of Christ's many vociferous ('roaring') Puritan critics of the Elizabethan church.

75. *Early Statutes*, p. 87; cf. Underwood, 'A Cruel Necessity? Christ's and St John's: Two Cambridge Refoundations' in Horrox and Jones, eds, *Pragmatic Utopias*, pp. 85–7.

76. Jones and Underwood, *The King's Mother*, pp. 35–9, 51–2

77. *Early Statutes*, pp. 80–1. For comments on the 'clerical conception of community' which permeated the statutes and early years of Christ's, see Swanson, 'Godliness and good learning', pp. 50–1.

PART TWO

THE COLLEGE IN 1515

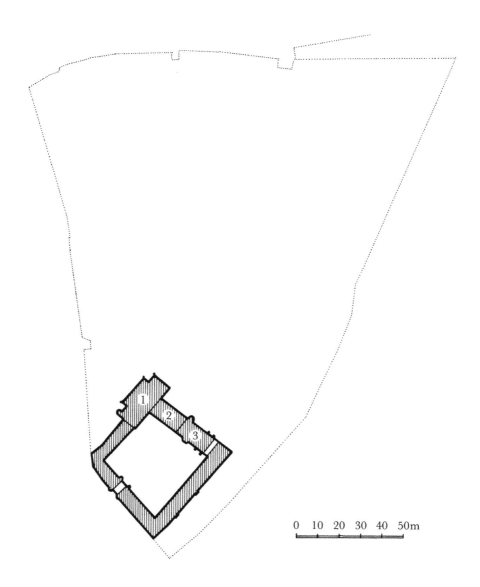

1 – The Chapel   2 – The Master's Lodge   3 – The Hall

ON 22 JUNE 1535, John Fisher – emaciated and 'a very image of death' after a year in the Tower – was taken out to the scaffold and beheaded. His naked body was left in the sun, his head impaled on London Bridge. Fisher's crime was his refusal to swear the nationwide oath affirming the monarch as head of the English Church. To succeed him as Chancellor, the University of Cambridge prudently chose Henry VIII's right-hand man, Thomas Cromwell. A series of royal injunctions that autumn brought the colleges under ultimate royal control. Over the next few years the monasteries were seized and sold by the crown in its search for cash and there was a real fear that the universities would be next on Henry's list. An Act of Parliament in 1545 gave the king the power to dissolve any college chantry at Cambridge or Oxford, and there were some at court, eager for future pickings, who urged a full survey of university wealth. In a shrewd pre-emptive move, Cambridge established its own commission, whose report in 1546 showed nearly all colleges to be operating on deficits. It is doubtful that the king was persuaded by such creative accountancy, but the universities had already proved their political utility by offering favourable advice on the theology of his divorce and he was himself a supporter of the New Learning – Cromwell's

1535 injunctions required daily lectures in Greek and Latin at every college. Henry's charter of foundation in 1546 for Trinity College, to match Christ Church at Oxford, set his seal of approval on Cambridge. The colleges would not go the way of the monasteries.[1]

This political reconstruction of the Church was intertwined in the larger patterns of Reformation and Counter-Reformation. The theological debate begun under Henry and intensified under his son Edward VI swirled back into traditional channels during the reign of Edward's half-sister Mary (1553–8), when scores of Cambridge reformers fled into exile. Christ's College was caught up in the ebb and flow of events. Richard Wilkes, Master from 1548 to 1553, was a moderate reformer; Cuthbert Scot, his successor until 1556, restored altars, candlesticks, vestments and other Catholic forms to the chapel and took the lead in imposing new doctrinal articles on the University. But when Mary died and Elizabeth became queen the pendulum swung again. Scot's successor, William Taylor, fled the Lodge in some haste in June 1559, 'leaving his chamber much disordered, his garments cast in corners' and 'the College writings scattered here and there'.[2]

By preference Elizabeth was a moderate Protestant, probably inclined to the Church settlement that had existed at her father's death. But her overriding concern was political – to find a position that would hold her fractious country together and avoid egregious provocation to the powers of Counter-Reformation Europe. To many the result was a church 'but halfly reformed' which still needed purifying of popish remnants in doctrine, liturgy and governance. For much of Elizabeth's reign Christ's was at the heart of the Puritan movement in the University and the nation. Leading lights at Christ's were Edward Dering, a

Fellow from 1560 to 1571; Laurence Chaderton (1568–77), who has been nicely called 'the pope of Cambridge puritanism';[3] and William Perkins, one of the best known Puritan theological writers, who came up to Christ's in 1577 and remained until 1595 when he resigned his fellowship on marriage. This was the heyday of the tutors, when a Fellow was responsible for up to twenty teenage boys, who lived in his chambers and paid him directly for their teaching. Puritan parents sought out godly tutors for their offspring and these 'pupil-mongers', particularly Chaderton, conspired to promote the supply of Puritan preachers for the church at large. Not education as we understand it today, but a project that was central to national life in the sixteenth century.

Chaderton went on to become Master of Emmanuel College, serving from its foundation by Sir Walter Mildmay (a Christ's man) in 1584 until 1622. But at Christ's the Elizabethan masters were not in the vanguard of the Puritan movement. Edward Hawford (1559–82), an associate of William Cecil, the queen's principal adviser, held the ring between various religious factions of the fellowship in a firm but discreet manner. Edmund Barwell (1582–1609) presided in a more easy-going way over College life as the flames of religious reform died down – at least for the moment. Perhaps Barwell's greatest claim to fame is that near the end of his mastership the College propitiated the new king, James I, who was keen to develop an indigenous silk industry, by purchasing three hundred mulberry trees. They were planted in 1608, the year in which one of Christ's most famous members was born.

NOTES

1. Damian Riehl Leader, *A History of the University of Cambridge: vol. I, The University to 1546* (Cambridge, 1988), ch. 13, pp. 330 and 333.
2. John Peile, *Christ's College* (London, 1900), pp. 60–1, quoting a letter to Cecil in the Calendar of State Papers.
3. Patrick Collinson, *The Elizabethan Puritan Movement* (London, 1969), p. 125.

QUENTIN SKINNER

The Generation of John Milton

ONE OF THE EARLIEST and most vivid accounts of John Milton at Christ's can be found in John Aubrey's *Brief Lives*. According to Aubrey, Milton 'was a very hard student in the University, and performed all his exercises there with very good applause'.[1] But he also seems to have cut an unusually dashing figure around the College. 'His harmonicall and Ingeniose Soul', Aubrey goes on, 'did lodge in a beautifull and well proportioned body', the most notable features of which were his 'exceeding faire' complexion and his 'abroun hayre'. Aubrey adds in a much-quoted aside that Milton's complexion was so very fair that 'they called him *the Lady of Christ's College*'.[2]

John Milton was admitted to Christ's College on 12 February 1625 and remained in residence for the next seven years, taking his BA degree in 1628 and his MA in 1632.[3] What was the University like at that time? What sort of life would Milton have led? What exactly were the academic exercises that he performed to such good applause? These are among the questions I want to consider as I focus on this celebrated moment in the College's history.

They are far from easy questions to answer, but the task of trying to do so is greatly eased by the existence of two remarkable sets of documents. One is the *Biographical Register* of the

College compiled by the philologist John Peile, who was Master of Christ's between 1887 and 1910. This source has been little exploited for the period I am discussing, but it is possible to glean from it a mass of information about the changing size and social composition of the College in its formative years. The other and even more enlightening source is the series of account books kept by Joseph Mead, a Fellow of Christ's who must have been well-known to the young John Milton, given that Mead served as one of the College Tutors from 1613 until his death in 1638.[4] Mead itemized virtually every charge that his pupils incurred, thereby making it possible to piece together an unusually detailed portrait of Milton's contemporaries and their daily lives.

John Milton was born in December 1608, and was thus admitted to Christ's shortly after his sixteenth birthday. His biographers have sometimes asked why he arrived at such a relatively late age, and have tried to explain what held him back.[5] But it is a myth to suppose that undergraduates in Milton's day were generally much younger than nowadays. There are no reliable statistics for the year of Milton's admission, but in his second year at Christ's the average age of those entering the College was seventeen. The figure then hovered between sixteen and seventeen for the next three years, stabilizing at seventeen in the early 1630s before rising to eighteen in the academic year 1633–4. If we examine the whole period between 1626 and 1640, we find that Milton was in fact slightly below the average age of those admitted to Christ's at that time.

All students entering the College in this period – and indeed in all periods up to the late 1970s – were of course male. They would have come from schools in which they had already received a good grounding in grammar, that is, in the Latin language. (Hence the name Grammar Schools.) The University Injunctions required all candidates for matriculation to be tested before their arrival to ensure that they knew Latin 'sufficiently'.[6] The need for this examination arose not merely from the fact that some university teaching was still conducted in Latin, but also from the fact that, in Christ's as in all other colleges, the statutes rather optimistically called for students to speak Latin at all times when they were within the College bounds.[7]

The town within which the colleges had begun to grow up in the closing decades of the thirteenth century was far more dominated by the University than it is nowadays. The population of Cambridge in Milton's time probably amounted to little more than five thousand,[8] but according to a near-contemporary estimate the presence of the University added three thousand more.[9] Christ's was one of sixteen colleges, the size of which – then as now – varied considerably. The largest, Trinity, had a total of four hundred and forty people living in it in the 1620s, while the smallest, Trinity Hall, contained only sixty.[10] Christ's in Milton's first year had thirteen Fellows, together with a hundred and fifty-six undergraduates and an unknown number of post-graduates studying for their master's degree. With the coming of the civil war in 1642 these figures suddenly declined, after which they recovered only very slowly and uncertainly. The number of students graduating from Cambridge in Milton's time was probably higher than at any period until the beginning of the twentieth century.[11]

The rhythm of the academic year when Milton was a student is still immediately recognizable even after an interval of nearly four hundred years. The year was divided into three terms, all of which carried the same names and lasted for much the same length of time as nowadays. The Michaelmas Term began on

10 October, the Lent Term on 13 January and the somewhat extended Easter Term ran from April until the beginning of July. The most obvious contrast with present arrangements was that entry to the colleges took place throughout the whole of this period. If we look, for example, at the Christ's *Biographical Register* for 1624–5, we find that seven undergraduates were admitted between October and December, and nine more – including John Milton – between January and March. But the usual time for coming into residence was the Easter Term, and in that academic year twenty-nine new undergraduates arrived at Christ's between April and early July.

Milton and his contemporaries were entering a college that had remained unchanged in many ways since its foundation in 1505. The main group of buildings – the modern First Court – would have looked much the same, although the brick and clunch walls were already beginning to decay, and were eventually to become almost ruinous before the ashlaring and a number of other major repairs were belatedly started in 1714.[12] The size of the Fellowship was likewise much the same, the sole addition to Lady Margaret's statutes of 1506 envisaging twelve Fellows being a deed of 1552 by which one further fellowship had been established. Nor had the College's basic purpose (or mission, as we are now urged to call it) undergone any significant modification, since its principal aspiration remained that of preparing young men for ecclesiastical careers.

As so often in the history of Cambridge, however, surface similarities masked deep processes of change. Although most students were still training for the Church, the Church itself had suffered a violent transformation as a result of the anti-papal reforms of the 1530s and the Protestant settlement of 1559. Cambridge had subsequently become a centre of Puritanism, and Christ's had emerged as perhaps the most radical college of all. One of its Fellows, William Perkins, had been summoned before the Vice-Chancellor's court in 1587 for preaching in the College chapel against the superstitious practice of kneeling to receive the sacrament.[13] Another Fellow, Francis Johnson, had been imprisoned two years later for declaring that the Church should be governed by elders, and that rule by bishops was not sanctioned by the scriptures.[14] These scandals were a thing of the past by the 1620s, but the College's Puritan reputation lingered on, and it may have been one reason why Milton's parents chose to send him there.[15]

A further important change lay in the social composition of the College. Christ's had been founded as an institution catering for poor scholars, and it was still taking a considerable number of these so-called 'sizars' in Milton's time. The term 'sizar' is obscure in origin, but it was probably used to designate undergraduates who were exempted from having to pay a charge (or 'size') for their food. Besides receiving this help from the College, sizars generally paid their way through university by waiting on other students and acting as servants to the Fellows. Early in the seventeenth century, however, we find the sizars beginning to be outnumbered for the first time in several generations by the so-called pensioners.[16] The term 'pensioner' was the name given to an undergraduate who (as Aubrey says of Milton) lived 'at his owne Chardge only', paying his fees in the form of a regular 'pension' to the College.[17] These students were invariably the sons of well-to-do parents, as in the case of Milton, whose father was a successful money-lender and scrivener.[18] After 1610, there is scarcely a year in which the pensioners were not in a large majority. If we look, for example, at the academic year 1627–8 – the year in which Milton took his BA – we find that thirty-four undergraduates were admitted as pensioners compared with only nine as sizars. The College was well on its way to entrenching, in defiance of its foundress's wishes, a social trend that has never subsequently been reversed.

Still more striking was the appearance during this period of the sons of the gentry and nobility among the ranks of the undergraduates. These students were admitted as Fellow-commoners, so-called because they had the privilege of 'taking their commons' (that is, of dining) with the Fellows rather than with the other undergraduates. They often came into residence with their own servants, and some of them lived very magnificently. There are no records of any such students at Christ's in the first generation of the College's existence, and even in the second half of the sixteenth century they appear only sporadically, with an average of not much more than one per year. After 1610, however, the situation suddenly changed. From that year until the outbreak of the Civil War in 1642 the average number of Fellow-commoners at Christ's remained at over four per year, and in some years there were as many as seven or nine. Among Milton's contemporaries, perhaps the most conspicuous was William Halford, who must have caused a considerable stir when he arrived from Oundle in May 1632. He began by tipping the College butler two shillings and sixpence for saving him the trouble of signing his name in the College register, and he went on to buy himself a gown costing £8, more than sixty times the normal price.[19] Halford stayed for less than two years, effortlessly maintaining the same level of extravagance, and left the College without taking a degree.

Most striking of all was the sheer growth in size of the student body at this time. The College in its first generation had been a very modest affair, with the number of undergraduates exceeding a total of forty on a regular basis only after about thirty-five years. Numbers began to rise sharply in the early 1560s – although there were still some large and mysterious dips – until a peak of over a hundred per year was consistently reached between 1575 and 1582. Then followed a catastrophic decline to less than seventy per year by the late 1580s and, after a brief rally in the mid-1590s, a similar figure at the end of the 1590s. With the early years of the new century, however, there was a sudden and dramatic improvement. From 1603 until the outbreak of the Civil War there was only one year in which the number of undergraduates in residence fell below a hundred, and during the years in which Milton was a student the size of the undergraduate body averaged one hundred and fifty-nine per year.

Given that Lady Margaret's buildings had been designed to house only twelve Fellows and forty-seven scholars, one consequence was that the College became intolerably overcrowded. The original statutes had called for each chamber to be shared by two students, but in Milton's day it was common for at least four undergraduates to be sleeping in the same room.[20] The problem was exacerbated by the fact that Fellow-commoners expected to have rooms of their own. When, for example, the son of Sir John Isham came into residence in April 1627, he was not only given a fine chamber but space for his servant as well. He immediately 'dressed' his rooms, as Joseph Mead laconically records, with carpets, hangings and 'a Canopie and Curtaines', all of course for his own exclusive use.[21]

One result of the overcrowding was that, in defiance of University statutes, a number of Christ's students lived outside the College. They usually seem to have lodged at the Brazen George Inn, which stood opposite the main gate, just south of

St Andrew's Church.[22] But the most obvious consequence was that the provision of extra accommodation within the College came to seem an urgent priority. The Fellows initially responded by running up a wooden building behind First Court in 1613. This appears to have been intended as a temporary structure, but it can still be clearly seen on the Loggan print of 1690 and it was not finally pulled down until 1731. It was known to the students of Milton's time by the revealing but somewhat discouraging name of Rats' Hall.[23] Rats' Hall was a substantial building, three storeys high and evidently containing twelve chambers. But it was still not enough, and in the 1630s the College resolved to launch an appeal in order to build on a much grander scale. The Fellows seem to have put one of their own number, Michael Honywood, in charge of the fund-raising, for it was he who sent out circular letters to potential donors and kept lists of those who responded favourably.[24] Milton did not subscribe, but two of his contemporaries contributed ten pounds apiece, and Honywood's lists show that the initiative as a whole raised over £3,600.[25] This enabled the foundations of the present Fellows' Building to be laid in 1640, and its sixteen chambers were largely fitted out and ready for occupation by 1642.

With so much overcrowding, it is perhaps not surprising that the College did not feel able to charge very high room rents. As Joseph Mead's account books reveal, the usual price for occupying a space in a sleeping chamber was one shilling and threepence per term. To this, however, you needed to add at least as much again for the cost of candles, together with two shillings a term for your bedmaker and up to three shillings a quarter in the winter months for coal. If, moreover, you felt the need for a study of your own in addition to a sleeping chamber, your costs began to rise very steeply indeed. Mead's pupil Zachary Wildbore slept in a room in Rats' Hall for which he paid the standard rent of one shilling and threepence per term, but he also had a study there for which he had to pay over twelve times that amount.[26]

The daily routine of student life was strictly regulated by the University and College statutes, and the resulting timetable was a forbidding and demanding one. The day began at five o'clock with prayers in Chapel, followed by the reading of a homily by one of the Fellows. (When in Chapel, incidentally, you had to wear a surplice, another item of high expense, the usual price being ten or twelve shillings.)[27] Following the morning service, breakfast was served by the sizars at around six o'clock, after which there were University lectures in the schools from 7 a.m. to 9 a.m. on Mondays to Thursdays. It would seem, however, that at Christ's there may have been some rivalry and even incompatibility between the College and University teaching arrangements. According to the College statutes, the Fellow holding the position of Domestic Reader was expected to deliver three lectures in Hall after breakfast, each lasting half an hour, an arrangement that would have precluded any member of Christ's from attending seven o'clock lectures in the Schools.

After lectures it was time for dinner, which must usually have been served at around 11 a.m., given that the College statutes called for the hour between noon and one to be devoted, at least on Mondays and Thursdays, to scholarly exercises. The afternoons were free,[28] although in Christ's the statutes prescribed some supplementary teaching between 3 p.m. and 5 p.m. on four days of the week. There was then a service in Chapel at 6 p.m., and this was followed by supper in Hall.[29] The University statutes required the College gate to be locked by 8 p.m., with an extension to 9 p.m. in summer. The key was thereupon handed over to the Master, and no one, including the Fellows, was subsequently allowed to go out.

The aim appears to have been to create a way of life virtually bounded by the College walls. Christ's even employed its own barber and laundry-women so that students would have no need to leave the College precincts for these services. If an undergraduate required for any reason to go out of College, he was enjoined by the University statutes to be soberly dressed, to be accompanied by at least one friend and to have gained permission beforehand. It was forbidden to loiter in the streets, to go to the market or to enter any tavern, although the statutes did permit undergraduates, when their parents were visiting, to accompany them to respectable hotels.

This was not perhaps a very healthy way of life, and there is a distressing amount of evidence in Joseph Mead's account books about student illnesses. During Milton's second year eight of Mead's pupils had to be permitted additional food during Lent because they were too weak to endure the fast. One of this group, John Higham, seems to have been seriously unwell, and we read of gargles, purgations, a medicine applied to the temples and the letting of blood under his tongue.[30] During the next year Robert Gray required gargles, purgations and suppositories, while in 1629 Charles Taysbrough was administered numerous plasters, unguents and special preparations of milk.[31] The saddest case was that of Joseph Browne, who suddenly fell ill in March 1632 after less than a year in College. Mead took him to a physician 'for Counsell & judgment' in the middle of the month, after which we read of copious blood-letting at the neck and a special payment to a butcher for sheep's entrails 'to lay to his head'. Despite these ministrations, and the services of a nurse who was paid eleven shillings for 'careful and laborious tending', Joseph Browne died before the end of the month at the age of only eighteen.[32]

As well as suffering from numerous ailments, everyone stood in constant terror of the plague. No sooner had Milton arrived in Cambridge than a devastating outbreak in London claimed some 35,000 lives.[33] Cambridge was largely spared, but the University had to shut down in the Easter Term, and it did not fully reopen until December. Far worse was the outbreak of 1630, in which Cambridge lost nearly 10 per cent of its population. The disease arrived in April, eventually killing over a hundred people in the parish of St Andrew's alone, and thus in the immediate vicinity of Christ's.[34] The University had to close for the remainder of the year and everyone was sent home.

John Milton spent these months of enforced vacation at his parents' house in Hammersmith, where he occupied himself in writing a number of his earliest poems. It was probably at this time that he completed his great ode 'On The Morning of Christ's Nativity', the first draft of which, he tells us, he had written on Christmas morning in 1629.[35] To this period also belong his earliest English sonnets and his first published poem, his sixteen-line epitaph on Shakespeare, which initially appeared in the second folio of Shakespeare's plays in 1632.[36] It is well worth quoting in full:

> What needs my Shakespeare for his honoured bones,
> The labour of an age in pilèd stones,
> Or that his hallowed relics should be hid
> Under a star-ypointing pyramid?
> Dear son of memory, great heir of fame,
> What need'st thou such weak witness of thy name?
> Thou in our wonder and astonishment
> Hast built thyself a live-long monument.

For whilst to th' shame of slow-endeavouring art,
Thy easy numbers flow, and that each heart
Hath from the leaves of thy unvalued book,
Those Delphic lines with deep impression took,
Then thou, our fancy of itself bereaving,
Dost make us marble with too much conceiving;
And so sepúlchred in such pomp dost lie,
That kings for such a tomb would wish to die.[37]

The confidence with which the young Milton here claims 'my Shakespeare' as his model is arresting, to say the least.[38] So too is the originality with which he reworks Horace's dictum that poets create their own most lasting memorials in the form of their works.[39] With Shakespeare, Milton suggests, it is the continuing wonder and astonishment experienced by his readers that provide him with his most enduring monument.

After this interlude Milton returned to his studies at some point towards the end of 1630. He was certainly back in residence by the time his younger brother Christopher arrived at Christ's in February 1631, and doubtless helped to introduce him to the somewhat daunting academic routines I have outlined. It would be a great mistake, however, to assume that the reality of undergraduate life – even in the case of so serious a student as Milton – closely mirrored the requirements of the statutes. To judge from the constant stream of remonstrations issued by the University, many of the more stringent rules and regulations were simply ignored. One repeated complaint was that undergraduates were failing to dress with appropriate frugality and soberness, a development blamed as early as 1578 on the fact that 'children of gentlemen and men of welth' were now entering the University, bringing with them 'very costly and disguised manner of apparrell and other attires unseemly for students'.[40] We hear of undergraduates growing their hair (as Milton did) to unsuitable lengths, sporting extravagant hats adorned with feathers and swaggering about with rapiers and swords. Still more frequently we hear of expensive silks and velvets being worn in riotously inappropriate colours and ostentatiously adorned with tassels and lace.[41]

Nor was student behaviour nearly as monkish as the statutes prescribed. Even when they remained in College the undergraduates seem to have smoked and gambled, and in Christ's they spent a remarkable amount of time playing tennis. A tennis-court had been erected in the College as early as 1565,[42] but it seems to have been repaired or brought back into use in 1630, when Joseph Mead's account books begin to show a sudden craze for the game. Despite the high costs involved, many of Mead's pupils played regularly, paying as much per term for the hire of the court as they did in many instances for their rooms.

From the point of view of the authorities, the gravest problem was that so many students contrived to spend so much of their time outside their colleges, entertaining themselves in a variety of disgraceful ways. They went to cock-fights and bear-baitings; they attended the plays performed at Stourbridge Fair; and they travelled to Chesterton to take part in football matches, where they got into serious fights with local youths.[43] They paid high fees to learn dancing and fencing, although both activities were punishable under the statutes by large fines. They roamed the town and frequented the three leading taverns – the Dolphin, the Rose and the Mitre – which came to be known as 'the best tutors in the University'.[44] There they gambled and smoked as well as drank, while many of them 'resorted' (in the words of the 1630 Injunctions) to the daughters of the innkeepers and other women with whom they contrived 'to misspend their time' and 'otherwise misbehave themselves'.[45]

The cloistered life envisaged by the statutes was further undermined by the fact that the rules about residence do not seem to have been strictly enforced. Milton provides a good example, for he tells us that he spent the spring of 1626, at the end of his second year, living in 'the Thames-watered city' rather than in Cambridge.[46] By this time, moreover, the ease with which students could move in and out of the town had been greatly improved by one of Cambridge's notable characters, the University carrier Thomas Hobson (after whom the street north of Christ's is still named). It was Hobson who had the idea of hiring out horses to students, and who added the ingenious proviso – to ensure that no one horse was over-exercised – that customers had to take whichever had been longest in the stable. (This came to be known as 'Hobson's choice'.) There is evidence in Joseph Mead's account books that the undergraduates at Christ's made good use of this facility, even though Hobson's services did not come cheap. Mead's pupil Charles Taysbrough had to pay four shillings in 1626 to travel to Suffolk, while John Roffey had to pay seven shillings in 1632 to hire a horse to take him to London.[47]

For those going to London, however, Hobson offered a less costly means of transport. He himself travelled to the city by wagon every week, and he accepted passengers for a fare of three shillings and fourpence.[48] Although he was over eighty by the time Milton was an undergraduate, Hobson was still making this weekly journey, which he gave up only when the outbreak of plague in 1630 led to a prohibition on such movements. The enforced leisure seems to have broken his spirit, and he died shortly afterwards.[49] Milton composed two verse epitaphs in his memory in 1631,[50] both of which are among the most affectionate and high-spirited of his early poems.

> Here lieth one who did most truly prove,
> That he could never die while he could move;
> So hung his destiny never to rot
> While he might still jog on and keep his trot . . .
> Rest that gives all men life, gave him his death,
> And too much breathing put him out of breath;
> Nor were it contradiction to affirm
> Too long vacation hastened on his term.
> Merely to drive the time away he sickened,
> Fainted, and died, nor would with ale be quickened;
> Nay, quoth he, on his swooning bed outstretched,
> If I may not carry, sure I'll ne'er be fetched . . .[51]

Milton pays witty tribute to Hobson's connections with the University and at the same time to his famously workaholic character.

So far I have said nothing about what one actually studied as an undergraduate in Milton's time. Some students, especially the Fellow-commoners, arrived at University with no intention of taking a degree, and most of them probably studied rather little. Among Milton's exact contemporaries there was one such Fellow-commoner, Henry Kendall, who resided in the College but was never even formally admitted as a student. A still larger number left the University without a degree because they came with the intention of moving on after a couple of years to train as lawyers at the Inns of Court. There were four such undergraduates in Milton's year, two of whom went on to Lincoln's Inn, one to Gray's Inn and one to the Middle Temple. Soon afterwards Milton's brother Christopher followed the same trajectory, leaving Christ's for the Middle Temple after only five terms and setting himself up in legal practice by the mid-1630s.[52]

Among Milton's contemporaries, however, virtually everyone else took the four-year course leading to the BA degree, and over half of them remained for an extra three years and proceeded to their MA. The outline of the BA course was clearly laid down in the University statutes, and formed a recognizable version of the medieval 'trivium' of grammar, rhetoric and logic. But by Milton's time this traditional arrangement had been altered in two crucial ways. One modification was that grammar (the study of Latin) was no longer taught, because students were assumed to have gained a sufficient knowledge of the language before coming up to University. The first year was accordingly earmarked for rhetoric, with the statutes further specifying that the main texts to be studied were Quintilian's *Institutio Oratoria* and one of the oratorical works of Cicero. Then came two years of logic, for which the recommended text was either Cicero's *Topica* or Aristotle's *Elenchi*. The other and more important modification to the traditional curriculum was that the fourth and final year was devoted to natural and moral philosophy. Moral philosophy was chiefly taught out of Aristotle, the two set texts being the *Politics* and the *Nicomachean Ethics*. Natural philosophy was taken to include physics, cosmology and a number of allied subjects, and in this case the recommended texts were Pliny's *Historia Naturalis* and Aristotle's *Problemata*, an apocryphal work mainly concerned with medical questions and assorted physical phenomena.

This, then, was the official syllabus, and it was taught by daily lectures in the University Schools. But did anyone go to these lectures? There are frequent complaints from the University about non-attendance, and there are several signs that the Colleges had begun to usurp the function of undergraduate teaching, although the examinations for the BA degree were still regulated by the University. Christ's had its own lecturers in logic and rhetoric by the 1620s,[53] and most teaching seems to have taken place within the College. Nor was this a surprising development. The new availability of relatively cheap printed books made it much easier for students to read the set texts for themselves and discuss them with their tutors at their own pace. This must have seemed a great improvement on trying to take notes (often by candlelight) while listening to lecturers expounding the same texts at inordinate length in the Schools.

What impact did these changes have on what was actually taught? This might seem an impossible question to answer, but in the case of Christ's we can discover from Joseph Mead's account books which particular texts his pupils bought, and at what exact stage in their academic careers. With this information we can work out the precise syllabus that Mead followed between 1625 and 1632, the years when Milton was in residence. Furthermore, we can make some plausible guesses about the order in which Mead taught the different parts of the course, and the extent to which he accepted, supplemented or ignored the official curriculum. Finally, we can determine (by some simple arithmetic) how much he charged for his services. The cost of tuition to a Fellow-commoner turns out to have been one pound five shillings per term, while to a pensioner like Milton the normal charge was fifteen shillings.

In the case of the Fellow-commoners under his care, Mead appears to have paid little attention to the official curriculum. Instead he concentrated on trying to ensure that they acquired some elegant and gentlemanly accomplishments. He adopted this approach most wholeheartedly in the case of the Tays-brough brothers, who came into residence in May 1626 and stayed for just over two years. They both took French lessons in their second year, for which a special teacher had to be found, and they spent a large amount of their time learning to play the viol. Both of them bought instruments in their first year, together with books of music, and thereafter they received regular lessons at the cost of six shillings and eightpence per month.[54]

If we turn to Mead's more academic students, we find that in their case he liked to make a number of substantial additions to the official curriculum. Sometimes he taught some mathematics, using as a textbook either Thomas Blundeville's *Exercises* in arithmetic and geometry or Bartholomew Keckermann's *Systema Totius Mathematices*. Still more frequently, he introduced his pupils to a wide range of religious questions, although the University curriculum normally reserved these subjects for those who had already taken their BA. To judge from the stage at which Mead asked his pupils to buy the relevant books, he generally seems to have squeezed these studies into their second year.

One of Mead's assumptions appears to have been that, for those not taking the BA, the most important subject on which they needed to acquire at least a smattering of knowledge was Christian theology. Noticeably, of the nineteen undergraduates who bought the basic theological textbook favoured by Mead – Bartholomew Keckermann's *Systema Theologiae* – fifteen left the College without a degree. Mead also took care to ensure that those following the prescribed curriculum received a great deal more in the way of religious instruction than the regulations required. No less than sixteen of his students in the period between 1625 and 1632 bought the so-called Heidelberg Catechism, the most popular statement of the Protestant faith to emerge from Reformation Germany. Ten of them also bought the complete Bible, presumably in the authorized version of 1611, although this was an expensive book to acquire, usually costing them at least seven or eight shillings.

Mead appears, moreover, to have encouraged some of his students to carry their biblical studies much further. We find ten of his pupils buying lexicons to help them understand the Greek New Testament, including four copies of Johann Scapula's great Greek–Latin dictionary, an enormous folio costing as much as fifteen shillings. At the same time seven of his pupils bought the Greek New Testament itself. Yet more impressively, six of them bought Hebrew lexicons for use with the Old Testament, while seven bought the Hebrew version of the Psalms and three more the Hebrew version of the Book of Samuel. With his habitual modesty, however, Mead appears never to have drawn the attention of any of his students to his own important work of biblical criticism, the *Clavis Apocalyptica*, which was first published in Cambridge in 1627.

Apart from emphasizing these religious studies, Mead seems to have been content to follow the prescribed curriculum, concentrating as required on rhetoric, logic and philosophy. But whereas the University statutes called for the first year to be spent on rhetoric, Mead had a strong preference for starting his students off on logic, whether or not they were reading for a degree. The textbook he liked to use was some version of the *Systema Logicae* of the ubiquitous Bartholomew Keckermann, for whose works Mead had a particular fondness. Keckermann had been a schoolmaster in the Gymnasium at Danzig, and had managed in the course of a brief lifetime (1573–1609) to produce a series of highly successful textbooks on logic, rhetoric, theology, philosophy and mathematics, each unerringly aimed at the burgeoning undergraduate market.[55] Mead generally asked his pupils to buy the 'lesser' version of Keckermann's *Systema*, but many of them acquired the 'greater' version as well, and Mead seems to have lost no time in telling them to make these essential purchases. In at least a dozen cases, the first item that appears on an undergraduate's account – often before the fee for matriculating as a member of the University – is a charge for one or another version of Keckermann's logical works. The *Systema* even in its 'lesser' form was a book of considerable size, but the fact that it was possible to acquire it so cheaply – the average cost being about ninepence – makes one suspect the existence of a second-hand market, possibly organized by Mead himself.

Mead's attitude to the University regulations about the teaching of logic seems to have been an ambivalent one. As we have seen, the recommended texts were Cicero's *Topica* and Aristotle's *Elenchi*, his study of fallacious reasoning. Mead completely ignores the *Topica*, a book he never once asks his students to buy, but he seems to have carried the study of Aristotle's logic much further than the University statutes required. It is particularly impressive to find him requiring a considerable number of his pupils to buy the complete edition of Aristotle's *Organon*, the system of which the *Elenchi* forms the final part. If Mead really took his students through the whole of that complex work, he provided them with a training in syllogistic reasoning of the most comprehensive kind.

After this grounding in logic, Mead's pupils were next introduced to the study of rhetoric. To judge from the pattern of their book-buying, they normally turned to this subject early in their second year. The aim of this part of the course was to show students how to speak and write persuasively, and at the same time how to 'ornament' their speech with elegant figures and tropes. Mead occasionally seems to have taught this subject out of a textbook, but it is striking that he never required any of his pupils to buy Quintilian's *Institutio Oratoria*, the text specifically recommended by the University. He preferred Cicero's *De Oratore*, and among modern authorities he sometimes added Gerard Vossius's *Rhetorices Contractae* or Keckermann's *Systema Rhetoricae*, two of the most up-to-date surveys of the subject.

Generally, however, Mead seems to have agreed with Erasmus that the best means of teaching students to speak and write well is to introduce them to the finest literature. It was chiefly with this end in mind that undergraduates in Milton's day were asked to study poetry and history, and a large number of literary and historical works duly appear in the lists of books that Mead's students purchased for this part of the course. Among the poets, Mead seems to have had a special fondness for Juvenal, and several of his pupils also bought a popular anthology of ancient Greek verse. But Mead's overwhelming favourite was Homer, whose *Odyssey* was regularly acquired by his students throughout these years, sometimes as early as their second term. Among the historians Mead recommends, we find most of the leading Latin writers, including Sallust, Caesar, Livy and Tacitus. But here too he had a special favourite, although in this case a markedly eccentric one. He constantly recommends Johann Sleiden's *De Quatuor Summis Imperiis*, a brief survey, originally published in 1556, of the histories of Babylon, Persia, Greece and Rome.[56] It is not clear why Mead so much admired this rather elementary work, but it is one of the books that he most frequently told his pupils to buy.

With students in their third and fourth years Mead continued to follow the official curriculum, focusing as required on natural and moral philosophy. When teaching natural philosophy he ignored the statute enjoining the study of Aristotle's *Problemata*, and only very occasionally recommended any of Aristotle's texts at all. He preferred to teach the subject almost entirely from modern textbooks in which his students could hope to find a synthesis of current views about cosmology, psychology and physics. He tried out various of these compendia at different times, including Eustacius's *Summa*, Burgersdijck's *Ethica et Physica* and Keckermann's *Systema Physicum*. But his favourite was Johannes Magirus's *Physiologiae Peripateticae*, originally published in Frankfurt in 1600, a text bought by at least a dozen of his pupils during these years.

To judge from the pattern of their book purchases, the final subject that Mead's students were asked to tackle was moral philosophy. By contrast with his method of teaching the physical sciences, Mead made little use of textbooks for this part of the course and appears to have concentrated on a small number of well-known primary works. As we have seen, the two texts officially recommended were Aristotle's *Politics* and *Ethics*. Mead never read the *Politics* with his students, but he certainly taught the *Nicomachean Ethics*, and a considerable number of his pupils bought the book. However, his own view of ethics seems to have been out of line with Aristotle's emphasis on the virtues and the nature of the good life. Mead was evidently more interested in inculcating an essentially practical ideal of good manners and civility. Of the two works he recommends most frequently, one was Henry Peacham's *The Compleat Gentleman*, which had appeared as recently as 1622.[57] This was chiefly concerned with the proper 'carriage' of a gentleman and the sort of studies that give the right polish to life. The other was Giovanni della Casa's *Galateus, seu de morum honestate, et elegantia,* first published in Italian in 1558.[58] This was even more straightforwardly a book about elegant deportment, with detailed instructions on how to eat, dress, speak and generally conduct oneself in a noble yet affable style. The *Galateus* was by far Mead's favourite work on moral theory, and he never ceased to urge it on his pupils throughout his teaching career.

After finishing this course, the student was ready for the examinations leading to the conferment of the BA degree.[59] These took the form of public disputations, and the University statutes called for undergraduates to prepare for these occasions by performing at least two similar exercises in their colleges. Candidates for the BA were required to appear twice in the Schools as Opponents and twice as Respondents. The task of a Respondent was to defend a given proposition put forward for debate, while that of an Opponent was to raise objections to it. Of these two 'Acts', the more challenging was that of the Respondent, and in playing this role the student became the centre of a highly ritualized event.

As soon as they felt ready to undertake their Responsions, students began by proposing three subjects for debate, fixing them to the door of the Schools three days before their disputation was to take place. The statutes required that the questions should be both 'decent' and 'disputable', and that they should be approved beforehand by the Vice-Chancellor, on pain of a fine of £2. The requirement of decency was evidently introduced to counter undergraduate levity, while the requirement of disputability alluded to the fact that some questions were held to be beyond argument. For example, in theological disputations one often encounters questions about such matters as the applicability of the Mosaic Law, but never about such matters as the existence of God or the divinity of Christ.

Once the questions had been agreed, the Respondent presented himself in the Schools at one o'clock in the afternoon to wrangle with his Opponents. The proceedings were opened by a Moderator, who declared which specific topic was to be discussed. The surviving evidence about the range of propositions that were debated is unfortunately somewhat fragmentary. But among the disputations in moral philosophy around this time we find such propositions as 'Equality in a state is dangerous' and 'The middle way is the safest means of conserving a state', while among disputations in natural philosophy we find 'Our senses never deceive us' and 'Gold can be produced by chemical art'.[60]

After the specific topic had been announced, a figure known as the Father of the Respondent stepped forward. He would normally be a Fellow of the candidate's college, and it was his duty to introduce his pupil and offer a preliminary outline of his argument. Then came a licensed interruption – which often caused a great deal of trouble – from a figure known as the Prevaricator. He sat on a three-legged stool known as the Tripos, and had the congenial job of satirizing the proceedings. For example, when the proposition 'Gold can be produced by chemical art' was put forward for debate in 1631, James Duport as Prevaricator proved syllogistically that this must indeed be the case. If gold can be produced, he reasoned, it can only be by science or by art. But it can easily be produced without science, because doctors often produce a great deal of gold for themselves without having any science at all. Therefore they must produce it by art.[61]

Following this interruption, the Respondent rose to present his case. If he was a candidate for a higher degree, this was the moment at which the University ushers (known as Bedells) handed out copies of the printed Latin verses in which he was already expected to have summarized his argument in the grandest rhetorical style. One of the Fellows of Christ's had to act as a Respondent for such a degree in 1628, and had the clever idea of persuading the young John Milton to write the requisite verses for him.[62] The proposition under debate was that nature is liable to old age, and Milton argued the contrary case, producing in the process one of his most spectacular Latin poems.[63]

Once the Respondent had presented his case, the Father rose to restate his pupil's position and to counter some possible objections to it. Then the Moderator called on the Opponents to refute the Respondent's argument. Usually there would be three Opponents, also candidates for the BA degree, but still at the stage of propounding objections rather than having to resolve them. After they had stated their objections in turn, it was up to the Respondent, mustering as much extempore Latin as possible, to reiterate their arguments and dispose of them one by one in proper syllogistic style. This could be a daunting exercise even for senior members of the University, as is clear from a report of the disputation staged for the visit of King James I to the University in 1615. On this occasion the Respondent was William Roberts of Queens', later Bishop of Bangor, and one of his Opponents was William Chappell of Christ's, John Milton's first tutor. Roberts found himself so overwhelmed by Chappell's objections that he fainted. King James, a great admirer of his own skills in disputation, thereupon took up the case on Roberts's behalf, but Chappell proceeded to refute his sovereign no less unmercifully, and appears to have basked for years in the glory of that day.[64]

After the Respondent had done his best to reply to his Opponents, the Moderator brought the proceedings to a close by offering the right measure of praise to all involved. Once this ordeal was over, the chief requirement for the BA degree had duly been met. It only remained for candidates to become 'Quaestionists', that is, to submit to a final examination in which they were asked about the nature of syllogistic reasoning. When they had given satisfactory answers they were said to be 'Determiners', after which they were declared by the Proctors to have attained the standing of full Bachelors of Arts.

One might finally ask what became of Milton's contemporaries after they had taken their degrees. Of the fifteen other students admitted in the same half-year, four have left no trace on the historical record at all. Two more left without degrees to go to Inns of Court, and one of these, Richard Earle, went on to have a prominent public career, becoming a baronet in 1629 and Sheriff of Lincoln in 1647. All the rest became clergymen, and all but one eventually sank into decent obscurity in country parsonages. Only Robert Pory, a friend of Milton's at St Paul's School as well as at Christ's, carved out a more imposing place for himself in the Church. Although he suffered in the Civil Wars, he later flourished mightily as a rich pluralist under the restored monarchy after 1660.

Milton likewise sank into obscurity for some years after graduating, returning to live with his parents in Hammersmith and moving with them three years later to their country retreat at Horton. He was by no means vegetating, however, but was systematically working his way through a self-imposed course of reading in history, theology and philosophy, and at the same time trying out his vocation as a poet. One outcome was the composition of his masque *Comus*, which was first performed at Ludlow Castle in September 1634 and was published in 1637. But by far the most important product of these years was *Lycidas*, which has come to be regarded not merely as the finest of Milton's early poems but as one of the greatest lyrics in the English language.

Although nothing is known about the circumstances in which *Lycidas* was composed, it is possible that Milton was commissioned to write it by some of the Fellows of Christ's. The poem was occasioned by the death of Edward King, a junior contemporary of Milton's who had become a Fellow of the College. King was shipwrecked and drowned in 1637 at the age of twenty-five while crossing to visit his family in Ireland, and his colleagues decided to issue a volume of poems in his memory. The resulting collection was published in 1638 under the title *Justa Edouardo King Naufrago, ab Amicis Moerentibus*. The first part of the book consists of encomia in Latin and Greek, while the second part contains thirteen English poems, among which *Lycidas* appears over the initials 'J. M.'

While most of the contributors limited themselves to conventional expressions of admiration and grief, Milton used the opportunity to produce an immortal meditation not merely on the death of his friend but on lost youth, unfulfilled gifts and the futility of ambition in the face of the fates.

> Alas! What boots it with uncessant care
> To tend the homely slighted shepherd's trade,
> And strictly meditate the thankless Muse?
> Were it not better done as others use,
> To sport with Amaryllis in the shade,
> Or with the tangles of Neaera's hair?

Fame is the spur that the clear spirit doth raise
(That last infirmity of noble mind)
To scorn delights, and live laborious days;
But the fair guerdon when we hope to find,
And think to burst out into sudden blaze,
Comes the blind Fury with th'abhorrèd shears,
And slits the thin-spun life.[65]

Milton's long poem – nearly two hundred lines – brings the volume to a close, as if in acknowledgement of its unsurpassable qualities.

After the 1630s Milton maintained no further links with Cambridge, and in later life he always spoke disparagingly of the training he had received there. He complains in his *Reasons of Church Government* about the 'monkish and miserable sophistry' encouraged by the system of disputation, and he claims in his treatise *Of Education* that the curriculum generally gave rise to an active 'hatred and contempt of learning' in those subjected to it.[66] Nevertheless, he seems to have retained a warm affection for his College, as he makes clear in his *Apology* of 1642. He is very glad, he writes, to have the opportunity 'to acknowledge publickly with all gratefull minde, that more than ordinary favour and respect which I found above any of my equals at the hands of those curteous and learned men, the Fellowes of that Colledge wherein I spent some yeares'.[67]

Milton even hints that he could have stayed at Christ's as a Fellow had he wished. When he left the College, he goes on, the Fellows 'signifi'd many wayes, how much better it would content them that I would stay; as by many Letters full of kindnesse and loving respect both before that time, and long after I was assur'd of their singular good affection towards me'.[68] Despite his contempt for the curriculum, he accordingly feels able to bring this section of his *Apology* to a close by bidding his teachers a fond farewell: 'To those ingenuous and friendly men who were ever the countnancers of virtuous and hopefull wits, I wish the best, and happiest things, that friends in absence wish one to another.'[69] Seldom can the Fellows of Christ's have been thanked in such elegant terms.

NOTES

1. John Aubrey, *Brief Lives*, ed. Oliver Lawson Dick (Harmondsworth, 1962), p. 272.
2. Ibid., p. 273.
3. John Peile, *Biographical Register of Christ's College, 1505–1905* (2 vols, Cambridge, 1910–13), vol. 1, p. 363.
4. On Mead see John Peile, *Christ's College* (London, 1900), pp. 133–6. His account books are to be found in Christ's College Muniments Room, T. 11.
5. Donald L. Clark, *John Milton at St Paul's School: A Study of Ancient Rhetoric in English Renaissance Education* (New York, 1948), pp. 29–30; cf. Harris F. Fletcher, *The Intellectual Development of John Milton* (2 vols, Urbana, Ill., 1956–61), vol. 2, p. 44.
6. Here, as in all subsequent references to the statutes and injunctions of the University in force in Milton's time, my information comes from the *Collection of Statutes for the University and the Colleges of Cambridge* (London, 1840).
7. Here, as in all subsequent references to the Christ's College statutes in force in Milton's time, my information comes from H. Rackham, ed., *Early Statutes of Christ's College, Cambridge* (Cambridge, 1927).
8. J. Willis Clark and Arthur Gray, *Old Plans of Cambridge 1574 to 1798* (Cambridge, 1921), pp. 137–8; cf. Fletcher, *Intellectual Development*, vol. 2, p. 13.
9. [Gerard Langbaine], *The Foundation of the Universitie of Cambridge* (London, 1651), p. 17.
10. [Langbaine], *Foundation*, pp. 7, 15.
11. John Venn, *Biographical History of Gonville and Caius College 1349–1897* (3 vols, Cambridge, 1897–1901), vol. 1, p. xxi.

12. Robert Willis and John W. Clark, *The Architectural History of the University of Cambridge* (4 vols, Cambridge, 1886), vol. 2, p. 223.

13. H. C. Porter, *Reformation and Reaction in Tudor Cambridge* (Cambridge, 1958), pp. 180–2.

14. Ibid., pp. 141–2, 157–63.

15. Barbara K. Lewalski, *The Life of John Milton: A Critical Biography*, (London, 2000), p. 18.

16. There is some evidence, however, that the College took more pensioners than sizars from an early stage in its history, and it is possible that it was only during the period from *c.*1570 to *c.*1610 that the sizars regularly outnumbered the pensioners.

17. Aubrey, *Brief Lives*, p. 271.

18. Lewalski, *Milton*, pp. 2–3.

19. Peile, *Biographical Register*, vol. 1, p. 419; cf. Christ's College MS T. 11. 3, fo. 179ʳ.

20. Rackham, *Early Statutes*, pp. vii, 110.

21. Peile, *Biographical Register*, vol. 1, p. 382; Christ's College MS T. 11. 3, fo. 89ʳ.

22. For some instances see Peile, *Biographical Register*, vol. 1, pp. 382, 402.

23. Peile, *Christ's*, p. 36.

24. Cambridge University Library MSS, Mm. v. 46, fos. 181ʳ–188ᵛ.

25. The list in Christ's College MSS, Shelf 85: *A catalogue*, fo. 12ʳ gives a figure of £2,589. 17s. 2d. and this is quoted in Peile, *Christ's*, p. 157, but the fuller list in the University Library (note 24) totals £3,622. 11s. 7d. For further discussion see *Christ's College Magazine* 119 (1929), 26–37.

26. Christ's College MS T. 11. 3, fo. 24ᵛ.

27. I have worked out the average cost from numerous entries in Mead's account books.

28. It would appear that at least some of the weekend was free time too.

29. David Masson, *The Life of John Milton: Narrated in Connexion with the . . . History of his Times* (7 vols, 1877–96), vol. 1, p. 136.

30. Christ's College MS T. 11. 3, fos. 38ᵛ, 39ᵛ.

31. Christ's College MS T. 11. 3, fos. 72ᵛ, 73ᵛ, 97ᵛ.

32. *Christ's College Magazine* 8 (1888), 1–7.

33. William Riley Parker, *Milton: A Biography* (2 vols, Oxford, 1968), vol. 1, p. 29.

34. James Heywood and Thomas Wright, *Cambridge University Transactions*

during the Puritan Controversies of the 16th and 17th Centuries (2 vols, London, 1854), vol. 2, p. 390.

35. For Milton's account see Lewalski, *Milton*, pp. 37–8.

36. Lewalski, *Milton*, pp. 39, 41.

37. John Milton, *The Complete Poems*, ed. John Leonard (London, 1998), p. 19.

38. A point well noted in Lewalski, *Milton*, p. 41.

39. Milton's poem is built around a series of allusions to Horace, *Carmina*, III. XXX.

40. Heywood and Wright, *Cambridge University Transactions*, vol. 1, p. 217.

41. Ibid., vol. 1, p. 219, 397–405. There are frequent references to the purchase of silk, lace and velvet in Mead's accounts.

42. The court (for the playing of real rather than lawn tennis) can be seen behind the Fellows' Building in the Loggan print of 1690; it was not dismantled until 1711. See Fletcher, *Intellectual Development*, vol. 2, p. 26.

43. Heywood and Wright, *Cambridge University Transactions*, vol. 1, pp. 305–6 and vol. 2, pp. 33–8, 212–14. Cf. also John Venn, *Early Collegiate Life* (Cambridge, 1913), pp. 118–20.

44. Fletcher, *Intellectual Development*, vol. 2, p. 59.

45. Heywood and Wright, *Cambridge University Transactions*, vol. 2, p. 377.

46. Masson, *Milton*, vol. 1, pp. 163–7.

47. Christ's College MS T. 11. 3, fos. 65^v, 161^v.

48. Christ's College MS T. 11. 1, fo. 5^v.

49. Masson, *Milton*, vol. 1, pp. 134–5, 240.

50. For this dating see Lewalski, *Milton*, pp. 41–2.

51. Milton, *Complete Poems*, pp. 20–1.

52. Lewalski, *Milton*, p. 55.

53. Masson, *Milton*, vol. 1, p. 130; Peile, *Biographical Register*, vol. 1, p. 267.

54. Christ's College MS T. 11. 3, fos. 81^v–85^v, 97^v–98^v.

55. Fletcher, *Intellectual Development*, vol. 2, p. 150. On Keckermann's importance see William T. Costello, *The Scholastic Curriculum at Early Seventeenth-Century Cambridge* (Cambridge, Mass., 1958), pp. 85–6, 90–100.

56. See Johann Sleiden, *De Quatuor Summis Imperiis, Libri Tres* (n. p., 1556).

57. See Henry Peacham, *The Compleat Gentleman, Fashioning him absolute in the most necessary & commendable Qualities concerning Minde or Bodie* (London, 1622).

58. See Giovanni della Casa, *Galateus, seu de morum honestate, et elegantia,*

trans. Nathan Chytraeus (Hanover, 1619). Fletcher, *Intellectual Development*, vol. 2, pp. 577–9 shows that this was the version used by Mead's students.

59. My ensuing account draws on Masson, *Milton*, vol. 1, pp. 140–2 and Parker, *Milton*, vol. 1, pp. 52–3.

60. Heywood and Wright, *Cambridge University Transactions*, vol. 2, p. 155.

61. Christopher Wordsworth, *Scholae Academicae: Some Account of Studies at the English Universities in the Eighteenth Century* (reprinted London, 1968), p. 282.

62. Parker, *Milton*, vol. 1, pp. 43–4.

63. See Masson, *Milton*, vol. 1, pp. 199–203; for the poem see Milton, *Complete Poems*, pp. 567–9. But Lewalski, *Milton*, pp. 29–30 thinks that Milton's contribution may have been his briefer and more lighthearted *De Idea Platonica*, for which see Milton, *Complete Poems*, pp. 571–2.

64. Masson, *Milton*, vol. 1, p. 128.

65. Milton, *Complete Poems*, p. 43.

66. For a discussion of Milton's hostility to the Universities see Lewalski, *Milton*, esp. pp. 28, 555.

67. [John Milton], *An Apology Against a Pamphlet Call'd A Modest Confutation of the Animadversions upon the Remonstrant against Smectymnuus* (London, 1642), p. 12.

68. [Milton], *Apology*, p. 12.

69. [Milton], *Apology*, p. 12.

PART THREE

THE COLLEGE BY 1642

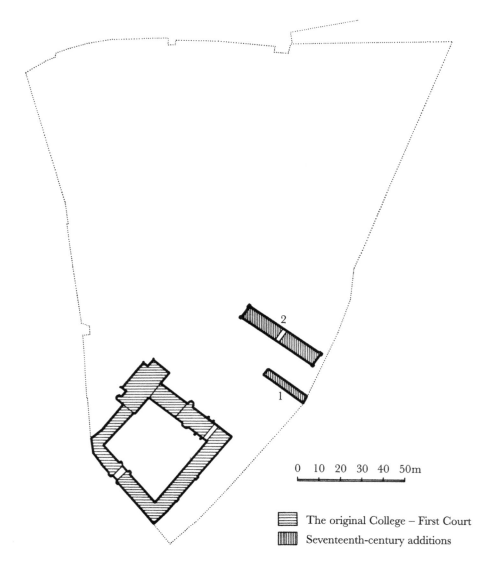

0 10 20 30 40 50m

▦ The original College – First Court

▨ Seventeenth-century additions

1 – Rats' Hall, 1613 (demolished 1731)

2 – New Building, 1642 (known today as The Fellows' Building)

THE MOST STRIKING ADDITION to the College in the seventeenth century was the 'New Building' constructed between 1640 and 1642, on the eve of the Civil War. Although there is no evidence to support the tradition ascribing it to Inigo Jones, it may have been designed by Thomas Grumbold, who was responsible for some of the contemporaneous work at Clare College.[1] The money was raised through an appeal to old members and we still have the text of the circular letter that was sent out in 1638. This translation from the original Latin shows that the language of importunity has changed a little over the centuries but the message remains essentially the same.

> Although we value discretion in private matters (as is proper), since this is a public matter we have come forward without shame, considering it better to incur a short-lived charge of audacity than the long-lived penalty of indigence. Silence would certainly be inopportune in this age rich in beneficence, and discretion would bear no fruit.
>
> This is the state we are in, most excellent sir. We are saddened that a college illustrious for its royal founders and (may my words not incur envy) for its own merits should lack the advantages and splendour that it is easy to long for, yet anything but easy to deliver.

The College's great age has undermined it, and the additions that necessity has brought about are no less damaging, with abundance lessening beauty. For the lodgings of our students have been reduced to dire straits, and when the muses sweat they are being denied the sweetness of fresh air.

We do not envy others their wealth or grandeur. We desire only a certain grace, salubrious rooms and appropriate elegance. It must be said that we have not failed ourselves: for what funds were available we have spent on the decoration of the chapel, library, hall and other places, when practical need demanded it. But we are collapsing under the great burden that oppresses us, and although our minds aspire to a finer establishment, poverty is weighing upon them. All that keeps our spirits up is the hope of support.

Among others we approach you, great philanthropist that you are, sure of your affection and good will. We are confident that you will not let down the honour of those buildings in which you drew the seeds of that virtue and erudition that still adorn you as a man. Those buildings to which you see fit to extend just a helping hand will recognize that their restoration is owed among others to you.

Our successors, to whom we shall take care to pass on the names of those responsible for such beneficence, will honour the memory of your name with grateful remembrance through every age.[2]

Over £3,600 was needed to pay for the building (equivalent to more than £5 million today) and the list of those who subscribed makes interesting reading.[3] Some of the money came from the Master and Fellows, either out of their own pockets or from the profits of vacant fellowships and windfalls such as fines from the College estates. Among the Fellows, Edward King (Milton's 'Lycidas') left £112 in his will and Joseph Mead (or 'Mede' as spelled here) gave £143. But about two-thirds of the money came from old members, as the researches of Lucy Brown make clear. Of about one hundred and forty such donors, sixty gave £10 and twenty-eight gave £5 – at a time when the 'average' Englishman's earnings for a whole year were roughly £16. But there were a number of larger donors, including a mysterious Henry Wilson, who gave £500, and Henry Montagu who contributed £100.[4]

Montagu came up to Christ's as a Fellow-commoner in 1583 and then enjoyed a lucrative career as a lawyer and royal counsellor, for which service he was created First Earl of Manchester. When he died in 1642, his son Edward (educated at Sidney Sussex) inherited the title. But whereas the father was an ardent Royalist, who gave much of his fortune to the king, the son became one of Parliament's leading generals of the Civil War. He was also charged with the purge of Royalist sympathizers and anti-Puritans from Cambridge in 1643–4. Although Christ's fared better than many colleges, keeping its Master, eleven Fellows were ejected.[5]

The contrasting story of the two Montagus is a reminder of how the English Civil War, like all such conflicts, pitted father against son and brother against brother. It also severed other bonds of community. Among those giving £10 to the 1638 College appeal were Thomas Hurst, later a chaplain to Charles I, and Miles Corbet, one of the regicides who signed the king's death-warrant in 1649. Those who gave £20 included William Boteler, who died fighting for the Royalists at Cropredy Bridge in 1644, and Denzil Hollis, a leading Parliamentarian early in the war who later turned against Cromwell and helped restore Charles II in 1660. College, crown and country – allegiances were by no means simple for the men of Christ's in the 1640s.[6]

NOTES

1. See the discussion in Arthur Oswald, 'Christ's College – II', *Country Life*, 2 May 1936, esp. p. 461.
2. Translation from the original Latin kindly provided by Penny Sarginson and Professor David Sedley.
3. The essay in *Christ's College Magazine* 119 (1929), 26–37, uses the list in the University Library to correct the figure of £2,589 in John Peile, *Christ's College* (London, 1900), p. 157, which seems to have come from the less complete version of Honywood's list in College archives.
4. Contemporary values, which can only be very rough, have been calculated using National Income statistics and the historical series for average earnings on the Economic History Services website at http://www.eh.net/hmit
5. See figures in John Twigg, *The University of Cambridge and the English Revolution, 1625–1688* (Woodbridge, Suffolk, 1990), pp. 97–8.
6. This discussion follows the database provided by the research of Lucy Brown.

Roy Porter

Science versus Religion?

THE SEVENTEENTH CENTURY proved an era of epoch-making, perhaps unsurpassed, scientific and intellectual change, in which, though the question remains contentious, universities played a key role. Cambridge's part in the rise of modern science was crowned, of course, by the presence in Trinity College for over thirty years of Isaac Newton – 'a mind for ever / Voyaging through strange seas of thought alone', in Wordsworth's resonant phrase[1] – and by the subsequent incorporation of 'Newtonianism' into the emergent mathematical Tripos.[2]

Before the supremacy of Newton, however, there was no single, united scientific front in the University, but rather many strands competing for intellectual primacy, and the value of scientific studies to academe remained to be proved. Indeed, as I shall suggest in the final pages, even after the triumph of Newtonianism, the authorized version of the philosophy of Nature then cast into the disciplines of 'natural philosophy' and 'natural theology' remained contestable. In such debates over science's role in what would eventually be called the 'two cultures', *alumni* of Christ's have played a quite disproportionate part. That is in large measure due to Charles Darwin but others, such as Charles Raven and C. P. Snow, also figure in later chapters of this volume. Yet Darwin's predecessors at Christ's –

men such as Henry More, Ralph Cudworth and William Paley
– had also wrestled with the same issue – not surprisingly since
it was central to the raison d'être of a religious foundation
increasingly dedicated to the advancement of knowledge. It is
with their efforts during the 'long eighteenth century' from the
end of the Civil Wars to the Victorian 'Age of Reform' that this
chapter is concerned.

*

The 1640s saw a collapse of religious authority, as upholders of
godly rule struggled against those on the antinomian fringe –
Ranters, Fifth Monarchists and others convinced that the 'saints'
were beyond the decrees of ecclesiastical discipline. Symbolic
occasions such as the swearing of the Solemn League and
Covenant and other oaths brought allegiances into the open
and exacerbated divisions of doctrine and conscience. During
the Civil Wars and Interregnum, such subscription and loyalty
tests were dramatized in Cambridge by the quartering of troops
upon the University, and by successive waves of expulsions and
intrusions of masters and fellows. Rival doctrinal camps spied
on the teachings of their foes. 'Witch hunt' would be too strong
a term, but mistrust and rancour ran deep, as is evident in the
bitter battle in Christ's waged by the Puritan Ralph Widdrington
against More and Cudworth.[3]

In the teeth of rebellion and potential anarchy – doctrinal,
social and political – 'rational' philosophies and theologies had
a strong potential appeal for scholars minded to promote
'reasonableness' as an antidote to dogmatism and sectarianism.
'Latitude men' – initially a sneer against those urging a middle
way based upon reason and inclusiveness – gained and retained
a foothold, though often precarious, in Cambridge during the

disruptions of the Interregnum and then through the renewed waves of ejections and intrusions of the Restoration, when the once Puritan university was made markedly High Church. Important in establishing and sustaining that latitudinarian presence was the patronage and protection offered by John Tillotson, a Fellow of Clare College until driven out at the Restoration. Shortly afterwards, on account of harbouring 'Latitude men', Christ's was accused of being 'a seminary of Heretics'.[4]

These Latitude men embraced 'the reasonableness of Christianity', to quote the title of John Locke's classic of 1695. For them modern science (the 'new philosophy') held out particular promise. As expounded by thinkers from Bacon to Gassendi and Descartes, the mechanical philosophy, with its model of Nature as a system of atoms or corpuscles, seemed infinitely preferable to the Aristotelianism so long ensconced in the universities. Repudiating such scholasticism as mere rhetoric, full of meaningless 'virtues', 'substances' and other 'quiddities', the mechanical philosophers claimed to replace words with things. They championed investigation and observation, experiment and measurement, and sold the results as a fruitful utilitarian philosophy of works not words. With Bacon's 'knowledge is power' dictum in mind, Henry Power, a Christ's-educated champion of experimentalism, was one of many who proclaimed how the new science would generate progress. 'This is the Age in which all mens Souls are in a kind of fermentation', he wrote in 1664, 'wherein (me-thinks) Philosophy comes in with a Spring-Tide' and 'all the old Rubbish must be thrown away with so powerful an Inundation. These are days that must lay a Foundation of a more magnificent Philosophy.'[5]

With scholasticism thus under fire, the doctrines of Descartes initially won a warm welcome among progressive thinkers in England, not least the Cambridge Latitude men and 'Platonists', a loose connection including John Worthington (of Jesus), Benjamin Whichcote (of King's), Ralph Cudworth (initially of Clare Hall) and, easily the most prolific, Henry More (a Fellow of Christ's from around 1639 until his death in 1687).[6] These thinkers voiced their fears that the doctrinal mudslinging then endemic was sure to undermine true Christian charity. They expressed particular distaste for the Calvinism dominant both within the University and beyond, and countered its predestinarian denial of free will with an appeal to a Christian Humanist ideal of human dignity and in particular a faith, derived from Psalm Twenty, in reason as 'the candle of the Lord' in man. The Cartesian elevation of the *cogito* ('I think therefore I am') seemed entirely supportive of this Christian Platonism. In 1653, More thus hailed Descartes, with whom he had been corresponding, in fulsome terms as 'a man more truly *inspired* in the Knowledge of Nature, than any that have professed themselves so these sixteen hundred years', and said he was 'ravished with admiration' at Descartes and his 'transcendent *Mechanical* inventions'.[7]

On further reflection, however, More and others concluded that, despite the attractions of its bold espousal of the autonomous, immaterial soul as the seat of reason and free will, the tendency of Cartesianism was pernicious. Following from its obdurate insistence that Nature was but matter in motion, it threatened to banish God from His Creation, thus providing a Trojan horse for atheism. Rationalism was desirable no doubt, but its Cartesian version allowed only for mechanistic materialism, and so was, on due consideration, blinkered, shallow and debasing. 'I oppose not rational to spiritual', declared Benjamin

Whichcote, 'for spiritual is most rational.'[8] This conviction, fundamental to the Cambridge Platonists, clinched the anti-Cartesian case. By 1665 More himself was insisting to Robert Boyle, founder member of the Royal Society and the country's leading experimentalist, 'that the phaenomena of the world cannot be solved merely mechanically, but that there is the necessity of the assistance of a substance distinct from matter, that is, of a spirit, or being incorporeal'. In his *Enchiridion Metaphysicum* of 1671, More severed himself completely from the 'upstart Method of Des Cartes'.[9]

This revised and negative Cambridge verdict on Cartesianism should primarily be understood as a reaction against the rampant notoriety of the home-grown mechanist (and, by inference, atheist) Thomas Hobbes – though, following the rhetorical strategies of the time, the 'Monster of Malmesbury' was rarely accused by name. Their teachings could not have been further apart. Hobbes was a naturalist, the Cambridge Platonists were idealists; he posited a universe permeated by matter, they celebrated a spirit-saturated world; he postulated determinism in a mechanical universe driven by inflexible laws, they portrayed man as a free agent operating within a vital, dynamic, 'plastic' nature. Hobbes accepted nothing transcendental; they relished 'the delicious sense of the divine'.[10]

In their mature writings, the Cambridge Platonists and Christ's Latitude men thus expounded doctrines which, while stubbornly discrediting scholasticism, equally distanced themselves from Cartesian mechanism and its alleged atheistic drift. True study of Nature was called for, since that would prove not only that God existed but that His Creation was spiritual through and through.

What exactly did More and his associates have in mind

when insisting that study of Creation would disclose the 'Spirit of Nature'? Nature's workings, More maintained in his polemical *Antidote against Atheism* (1653), could not be explained by Descartes' passive billiard-ball model of matter. Given that the body was 'not *Self-moveable*', something else must coexist besides so as to account for Nature's operations, and this was an opposite entity – spirit. Since spirit generated activity, More considered it 'plain that a *Spirit* is a notion of more perfection than a *Body*, and therefore the more fit to be an Attribute of what is *absolutely perfect*, then a *Body is*'.[11] Spirit thus pointed towards God. It was, moreover, a fundamental neo-Platonist conviction that the higher could never be engendered by the lower, nor explained in terms of something inferior. That granted, spirit could not possibly be a product of matter. For the same reasons, the soul could not be an emanation of a body, nor *pace* Descartes, a function of the brain.

Ralph Cudworth, Master of Christ's from 1654 to 1688, in his *True Intellectual System of the Universe* (1678), offered a more comprehensive and sober version of More's anti-mechanism polemics in defence of the real presence of the spiritual, all set in the context of the Great Chain of Being. Claiming in his subtitle that his was a work '*Wherein, All the Reason and Philosophy of Atheism is Confuted: And its Impossibility Demonstrated*', Cudworth set out to prove the existence of a God defined as 'a perfect conscious understanding Being (or Mind) existing of it self from eternity, and the cause of all other things'. Since Hobbes professed himself a Christian, Cudworth felt obliged to distance himself from the degrading Hobbesian caricature of the Supreme Being. An incorporeal deity, he stressed, 'moves Matter not *Mechanically* but *Vitally*, and by *Cogitation* only', just as our souls 'move our Bodies and Command them every way, meerly by *Will* and *Thought*'. Cudworth explained that God presided over Creation not immediately but indirectly, through an intermediary 'plastic nature', a subordinate agent executing his designs. The claim (popular with radical Protestants and mischievously adopted by Hobbes) that 'God himself doth all *immediately*, and as it were with his own hands, form the body of every gnat and fly, insect and mite' was therefore demeaning to the Deity.[12] The intervention of this 'executive instrument' moreover allowed the anti-Calvinist Cudworth to resolve to his satisfaction the old theodicy problem: how was it that the Almighty was not the author of evil? Creation's apparent imperfections and paradoxes were due not to His direct will, but arose from the inadequacies of this subaltern plastic nature when faced with the 'indisposition' of matter. (Did Cudworth have in mind the analogous problems of running a college?)

While principally a metaphysician, steeped in book-learning, Cudworth was not indifferent to empirical evidence. Among the Cambridge Platonists, however, it was More – as befitted a fellow of the Royal Society, in touch with Boyle and the scientific elite – who energetically pursued 'matters of fact', so as to establish the limits of mechanism and thus prove the actuality of spirit through scientific inquiry. In the third book of *An Antidote against Atheism* and throughout *The Immortality of the Soul* (1659), More expatiated on accounts of miraculous cures, on witchcraft, and on apparitions and poltergeist phenomena, including such 'extraordinary effects' as 'speakings, knockings, opening of doores when they were fast shut, sudden lights in the midst of a room floating in the aire, and then passing and vanishing'.[13]

In pursuit of such spiritual manifestations, good and evil, More collaborated with Joseph Glanvill, an Oxford graduate and West Country clergyman, who was determined to promote the new philosophy and its methods. Initially entitled *A Philosophical Endeavour towards the Defence of the Being of Witches and Apparitions*, Glanvill's demonology was greatly expanded with More's aid and published posthumously in 1681, under the latter's editorship, as *Saducismus Triumphatus* – literally 'Agnosticism Overcome'.[14] The first part canvases the theory of witchcraft, the second musters evidence for witches themselves. Attacking Hobbes and associating his denial of witches with atheism, Glanvill and More denounced materialism as crude, dogmatic and implausible. Were not many things beyond human reason? And was not belief in spirits reasonable in the light of attested experience, the weight of opinion, and the gradated nature of the Chain of Being, with its implication of cosmic plenitude? Glanvill also attacked Descartes – whom, much as More, he had initially admired – as a two-faced sophist who affirmed the existence of spirit but denied that it was anywhere in the world. Descartes was thus a covert Hobbist, and Hobbes a closet atheist.[15]

This hope, entertained by the Cambridge Platonists, of proving the spiritual and the supernatural through scientific investigation must not be seen, therefore, as some eccentric foible. As pointed out, however, by Boyle – sympathetic but more cautious than More – it was a precarious enterprise. Judge everything by human reason, and would not materialism follow? Concede too much to that which was beyond reason, and would not superstition run riot?[16] These two Christ's men, Henry More and Ralph Cudworth, valiantly strove to bridge the cultures, but their conceptions dated rapidly and were quickly forgotten after their deaths.

*

One reason for their eclipse was that many pressing issues of science and religion were resolved by the breakthroughs and formulations of Isaac Newton, resident at Trinity from 1661 until 1696 when he left to take charge of the Royal Mint. His *Principia Mathematica Philosophia Naturalis* (1687) established a dazzling and compelling scheme of universal order on the basis of a few elemental natural laws, notably those of mechanics and of gravity. Although not directly influenced by Cambridge Platonism, Newton's general amenability to it is clear.[17] The Newtonian variant of the new philosophy gave prominence not to mechanical determinism but to immaterial forces, notably gravity, and infinite void space and so could be represented by Newton and his followers alike as championing Christian idealism over mechanistic materialism and atheism.

It was also providential that Newton's *Principia* was published on the eve of the Glorious Revolution of 1688. A staunch Whig and Member of Parliament for his university, Newton was soon rewarded under William and Mary with high office, and his science was enlisted to promote the new political, religious and moral order. A prestigious platform for this was provided by the Boyle Lectures – a sermon series, endowed by Robert Boyle, to be preached annually from London pulpits 'for proving the Christian Religion against notorious infidels'. Delivering the first series in 1692, published as the *Confutation of Atheism*, Richard Bentley, Master of Trinity, used the *Principia* with Newton's approval to demonstrate God's providential design for the universe and His miraculous interventions. For Newtonians, God was no mere First Cause but a personal Creator who continually sustained Nature and, once in a while, applied a rectifying touch. Samuel Clarke (a Fellow of Clare Hall), William Whiston (also of Clare) and other early lecturers likewise drew on Newton to bolster latitudinarian Anglicanism, and to hammer home the alliance between empirical inquiry, intellectual freedom and rational religion.[18]

It was not only the Christian faith, however, which was boosted through these lectures and other vehicles of popular Newtonianism; the new regime was legitimated too. The affinities between the Newtonian cosmos and the national polity were widely proclaimed after 1688 and especially following the Hanoverian transition of 1714, with science recruited as political propaganda. In the year after Newton's death, his disciple J. T. Desaguliers produced an explicit application of physics to politics in *The Newtonian System of the World: The Best Model of Government. An Allegorical Poem* (1728), which celebrated the British monarchy as the guarantor of liberty and rights: 'attraction is now as universal in the political, as the philosophical world':

> What made the Planets in such Order move,
> He said, was Harmony and mutual Love.[19]

The *Principia* thus provided an explanatory model not just for Nature but also for the booming, if widely suspected, Hanoverian commercial society (freely-moving individuals regulated by law).

Whereas skulking Oxford proved a den of spleen for Jacobitism, Cambridge eagerly embraced the new Whig and Hanoverian politics, and Newton's mathematical cosmology was quickly assimilated into the curriculum at his *alma mater*. It is, however, intriguing that Christ's, the college at the cutting-edge of so much seventeenth-century debate on natural philosophy and theology, played virtually no part in the formulation and dissemination of Newtonianism. The one exception was Nicholas Saunderson, Lucasian Professor from 1711 to 1739. Blind from childhood, after leaving school he studied mathematics at home until the age of twenty-five. In 1707 one Joshua Dunn came up to Christ's, and brought Saunderson with him as a private tutor. The blind mathematician was kindly received by Whiston, with whose permission he lectured in the University, and when Whiston was ejected for his heretical beliefs, Saunderson was the obvious successor. On 19 November 1711 he received the MA degree to qualify him for the Professorship, and next day was elected to the Chair.[20]

Saunderson aside, Christ's lacked distinguished Newtonian disciples, tutors and popularizers. This may be symptomatic of the general decline of the College during the Georgian era. In the decade 1671–1680, when Cudworth was Master, Christ's was admitting an average of thirty-six students a year; by the 1680s the figure was nineteen, falling to ten in the 1730s and seven in 1751–60. There was a slight increase until the late eighteenth century and then another sharp fall during the era of the wars against France (1792–1815). In October 1784, when Henry Gunning came up to Christ's, he was one of only three entrants – two 'professed not to read and I was ignorant of the first Proposition of Euclid'. His tutor, Thomas Parkinson, though an accomplished mathematician, was engaged to a young lady of wealth who lived eighteen miles away in Suffolk. Parkinson usually rode over to see her three times a week, often lecturing with a gown barely concealing his boots and spurs. Gunning also records taking his father to the College's annual feast around Christmas, where the post-prandial combination of the Fellows degenerated into a rowdy drinking bout. The Master, guests and senior members of the University were seated at one table, from which the Master 'at intervals made the standard toasts', but the lower table, full of Fellows, soon became 'quite uproarious' with jokes, applause and raucous laughter. At one point Parkinson was seized and promised his liberty only after consuming a bumper of port. 'Make him drink it! Force it down!' they cried, and the Master had to intervene to restore order. Gunning notes that his father was astonished by such behaviour – and he was a member of St John's, 'a college more remarkable for its cordial hospitality than for the refinement of its manners'.[21]

The University as a whole was in decline during this period, with only about one hundred and fifty entrants a year for much of the eighteenth century, and nearer one hundred around 1750. In part the malaise reflected the mounting expense of university education and the irrelevance of much that was studied. In so far as Cambridge showed an even sharper decline in admissions than Oxford, this may have reflected, ironically, a side-effect of the Latitude men's passion for Newtonianism – namely the predominance of mathematics in the examinations. This gave the Cambridge curriculum a counterbalance to classics that was not available at Oxford, but it was a discouragement to many students. The young Horace Walpole, for instance, received special tutoring from Nicholas Saunderson, but declared after two disastrous weeks that studying mathematics had reduced his letters to parallelograms and his paragraphs to axioms. Although sterile for many 'pass men' in the ordinary examinations, mathematics could be very challenging to candidates for honours – a gruelling combination of oral disputations and a week of written examinations, held in January in the unheated Senate House. The first twelve students on the class list (known because of their skill in disputation as Wranglers) became the cult figures of their year and also guaranteed themselves college fellowships.[22]

But while mathematics eclipsed theology as the supreme discipline, the University remained an essentially clerical institution and those Fellows interested in the sciences still had to make their peace – intellectually and politically – with the

Anglican order. Here the career of William Paley, the most distinguished Christ's don of the second half of the eighteenth century, is revealing about the relations between science, religion and reform in the late Georgian era.

*

A Yorkshire schoolmaster's son, born in 1743, Paley came up to Christ's in 1759 and, after a distinguished undergraduate career, was made a Fellow of the College in 1766. Six years later he was appointed joint tutor with John Law, who taught mathematics and natural philosophy, while Paley took charge of metaphysics (which meant Locke), ethics and the Greek Testament. With his informal and relaxed personality, Paley's teaching was strikingly successful. 'I was a constant attendant on his lectures', recalled one of his star pupils, William Frend:

> You should have seen him, as we did, when he stept out of his little study into the lecture room, rolled from the door into his arm chair, turned his old scratch over his left ear, and his left leg over his right, buttoned up his waistcoat, pulled up a stocking, and fixed a dirty, cover-torn, ragged Locke upon his left knee, moistened his thumb with his lip, and then turned over the ragged leaves of his books, dogs eared and scrawled about, with the utmost rapidity.[23]

In 1775 Paley left Cambridge to marry, and he spent the remainder of his life as a parish clergyman in Westmorland, then Carlisle, and finally in Durham and Lincoln from 1795 until his death in 1805. It was after leaving Cambridge that he produced the books by which he is remembered: *The Principles of Moral and Political Philosophy* (1785), *Horae Paulinae* (1790), the *Evidences of Christianity* (1794), and the *Natural Theology* (1802).[24]

Paley is central in this discussion of the integration of natural science into humanistic learning because his *Natural Theology* produced a formulation of natural order which proved exceptionally cogent and durable, serving its own and succeeding generations as effectively as the Boyle lectures a century earlier. Its argument was mechanistic through and through. 'In crossing a heath', it famously opens,

> suppose I pitched my foot against a stone, and were asked how the stone came to be there; I might possibly answer, that, for any thing I knew to the contrary, it had lain there for ever: nor would it perhaps be very easy to show the absurdity of this answer. But suppose I had found a watch happened to be in that place; I should hardly think of the answer which I had before given, that for any thing I knew, the watch might have always been there. Yet why should not this answer serve for the watch as well as for the stone? Why is it not as admissible in the second case, as in the first? For this reason, and for no other, viz. that, when we come to inspect the watch, we perceive (what we could not discover in the stone) that its several parts are framed and put together for a purpose, e.g. that they are so formed and adjusted as to produce motion, and that motion so regulated as to point out the hour of the day; that, if the different parts had been differently shaped from what they are, of a different size from what they are, or placed after any other manner, or in any other order, than that in which they are placed, either no motion at all would have been carried on in the machine, or none which would have answered the use that is now served by it.[25]

Nature was thus like a watch, and every watch must have its watchmaker.

Turning to Nature's myriad 'adaptations' – particularly bones, muscles and organs – and showing each to be subservient to some necessary function, Paley piled up abundant evidence of 'design', and hence of the divine Designer:

> Were there no example in the world, of contrivance except that of the eye, it would be alone sufficient to support the conclusion which we draw from it, as to the necessity of an intelligent Creator.[26]

And in creating all these perfectly crafted adaptations, the divine watchmaker was pursuing a utilitarian end: from the creature's point of view 'it is a happy world after all' – as was abundantly visible. The 'sportive motions' of new-born flies, for instance, 'their wanton mazes, their gratuitous activity, their continual change of place without use or purpose, testify their joy, and the exultation which they feel in their lately-discovered faculties'.[27] Paley thus had no qualms at all about parading and blessing a mechanical, indeed a hedonic, universe: it was not for him, as it had been for More, the path to materialism or atheism.[28] Paley's clockwork universe did not, in the short term, stir the anxieties expressed by the Cambridge Platonists and even by the Newtonian apologists, that mechanism would drive God out of Nature and prove the thin end of the atheistic wedge.

How should this insouciance be interpreted? It is surely, in large measure, a vote of confidence by the Georgian Anglican elite in the holy alliance of natural philosophy and Christianity.[29] Paley does not seem to have felt he was on the back foot when countering the Epicurean doctrines of Nature as the product of chance, or the early evolutionism of Buffon, Erasmus Darwin and perhaps Lamarck, and he dispatched them all with coolness and conviction. Mechanism, as embodied in his philosophy of adaptations, contrivances and design, seemed a sure bulwark against the sophistries of speculative atheism: not even Hume, after all, gave credence to the possibility that the order of Nature had just happened.[30]

Paley, it must be remembered, while seeing mechanism as the best confirmation of the divine in Nature, was certainly not indifferent to supernatural intervention. His *Evidences of Christianity* (1794) – prescribed reading in Cambridge until 1921! – upheld the New Testament miracles against Deist naturalism, though it did so not on the basis of explicating the workings of divine agency but by vindicating the probity of their witnesses. Yet his espousal of mechanism was read by more jaundiced eyes as symptomatic of how much defenders of the faith had been forced, or had opted, to concede to the dominant secular, scientific and rationalist orthodoxy – to Georgian worldliness. This was in effect the verdict of treason passed on Paley and his rationalist ilk by preachy Evangelicals and lofty Victorian dons. In *A Practical View of Christianity* (1797) William Wilberforce had in his sights the Christian utilitarian philosopher whose bland and blanket optimism seemed offensive. It ought to be the grand object of every moral writer, declared Wilberforce,

> to produce in us that true and just sense of the intensity of the malignity of sin . . . and of the real magnitude of our danger, which would be likely to dispose us to exert ourselves to the utmost to obtain deliverance from the condemnation and emancipation from the power of sin. Now, here, Dr. Paley appears to me to fail.[31]

Adam Sedgwick, one of the prime educationalists in early Victorian Cambridge, likewise deplored Paley's factual and mechanical approach to religion, preferring the Romantic, muscular, living faith of Wordsworth, and arguing that Paley had reduced virtue to matters of calculation, mere profit and loss. In short, religion was moving on, as well as science. The Georgian middle way did not satisfy the evangelicalism of what has been called the Age of Atonement.[32]

Apart from helping craft a new synthesis for science and religion, Paley applied his utilitarianism to social and political life. He was, for instance, an active supporter of moves to make the degree system more efficient. To counter what was generally recognized to be the shambolic state of undergraduate studies, annual exams had been introduced by St John's College, and their desirability was urged by the young Richard Watson (a progressive who went on to become a bishop) and the energetic John Jebb, a former fellow of Peterhouse and private tutor. For two years from 1772 Jebb proposed a variety of schemes for annual exams; all were rejected. But in February 1774 he successfully moved in the Senate to establish a syndicate to scrutinize undergraduate studies. The committee included a number of dons sympathetic to change, among them Paley who was in favour of broadening the curriculum and making all undergraduates subject to examination. The syndicate recommended that noblemen and Fellow-commoners (then exempt from the Senate House Tripos examination) be examined annually in classics, algebra, geometry, natural philosophy, Locke's *Essay*, natural law and modern history. Other undergraduates – those taking the Tripos – were also to be examined in their second year in classics and mathematics. These proposals were narrowly defeated in the Senate – not only did they infringe college autonomy but it was also feared that such regulations would drive away the gilded youth.[33]

Paley's reformism embodied the philosophical utilitarianism

expounded in his first book, *The Principles of Moral and Political Philosophy* (1785), a work dedicated to Edmund Law, which immediately became a Cambridge set text. Paley's espousal of the greatest happiness of the greatest number paralleled Bentham's, but in a Christian garb, with God ordaining and sanctioning the utility principle. Paley does not seem to have derived it from Bentham, however – nor, for that matter, from Hume – but from the heroes of his own Cambridge schooling: the sensationalist psychology and associationist epistemology of Locke, Gay and Hartley, and the progressive vision of human history set out by Edmund Law.[34] Paley the utilitarian was thus a modern churchman espousing a practical faith shorn of the learned theology of Cudworth's times and adapted to the enlightened outlooks of a rapidly changing polite and commercial society.

The Principles of Moral and Political Philosophy propounded a courageous radicalism on many points. Slavery was 'abominable tyranny' – the trade, Paley believed, called into question Britain's fitness to hold a great empire. Inequality of property was *per se* an evil; and 'it is a mistake to suppose that the rich man maintains his servants, tradesmen, tenants and labourers: the truth is, they maintain him'.[35] There should, he argued, be a complete toleration of all dissenters from the established church, while the oath of allegiance 'permits resistance to the king, when his ill behaviour or imbecility is such, as to make resistance beneficial to the community'. Paley related the parable of the pigeons, which mocked the 'paradoxical and unnatural' distribution of property, ninety-nine out of a hundred birds 'gathering all they got into a heap' and keeping it for 'one, and the weakest, perhaps worst pigeon of the flock'.[36] Strong stuff from an Establishment divine, and small wonder that the *Anti-Jacobin*

Review remarked in 1802 that in it 'the most determined Jacobin might find a justification of his principles, and a sanction for his conduct', or that George III conspicuously declined to elevate 'Pigeon Paley' to the episcopate.[37]

Despite these radical touches, Paley's utilitarianism argued for acceptance of the established order on the grounds that it broadly worked for the general happiness. The distribution both of property and of the franchise were, admittedly, full of anomalies, but each could be defended on the grounds of public utility at large. By the 1790s, Paley's political voice had an unambiguously conservative ring. Rebutting the French Revolution, his *Reasons for Contentment Addressed to the Labouring Part of the British Public* (1793) lauded 'the divine spirit of dependence and subordination' and urged obedience. He reminded his readers that the pleasures of the rich were balanced by the gratifications of common life, the routine toil that brought fitness, the comforts of plain food, rest after hard labour, and freedom from the destructive ambition that fretted the mighty. On account of such sentiments William Hazlitt dubbed Paley a 'shuffling Divine'.[38]

Paley's pragmatic propensities and utilitarian principles left him equivocal towards what proved the most strident reform campaign in the Cambridge of his day. Opposition rose during the 1760s to compulsory clerical subscription to the Thirty-Nine Articles of 1559 – the theological linchpin of the Reformation church settlement. Since such subscription requirements kept the universities exclusively Anglican, they became targets for radical Dissenters like Joseph Priestley. Liberal and rationalist Anglicans were also increasingly hostile to the tyranny of the Articles. Their inspiration was Paley's old hero, Edmund Law, presiding genius of the liberal tendency in Cambridge divinity.

A national campaign was mounted for the abolition of subscription and for the modification of the Articles. In 1772 a petition was presented to the House of Commons, proposing to replace subscription with a profession of belief in the Scriptures. It was rejected.[39]

Meanwhile, at Cambridge, graces were proposed abolishing subscription for the various degrees offered by the University. They were all rejected in the Non-Regent House – that for the BA by only eight votes. A grace was granted, however, substituting a declaration by BAs that they were '*bona fide* members of the Church of England as by law established' – a concession then extended to bachelors of law, physic and music, and to doctors of music. The door to full membership of the University, however, was to remain officially shut to Dissenters for many years yet.[40]

What was Paley's part in this agitation? Predictably, this admirer of Locke's *Reasonableness of Christianity* was in favour of relaxing the subscription requirements. Indeed, he proved the inspiration for radical ex-pupils, above all William Frend, who became leader of a subsequent movement against enforced subscription in the late 1780s. Paley himself, however, declined to sign the anti-subscription petitions, with characteristic self-deprecating humour declaring that 'he could not afford to keep a conscience'.[41] Was this pusillanimous timeserving? Or was it his way of saying to more zealous friends that they were making a mountain out of a molehill? Did he find something a touch laughable about subscribing to anti-subscription documents?

Paley did, however, discuss subscription in his *Moral and Political Philosophy* of 1785. The reasoned defence offered there of a modified orthodoxy typifies his philosophical personality. Tests ought to be made as simple as possible, since 'they check inquiry; they violate liberty; they ensnare the consciences of the clergy, by holding out temptations to prevarication'. Many who could not accept all Thirty-Nine Articles might nevertheless subscribe with a clear conscience provided that they were not among those – Paley meant Roman Catholics and Anabaptists – whom the Articles had been framed to exclude. Thus, while the Church would be best served by abolition, its requirement was harmless enough, since subscription did not demand 'the actual belief of each and every individual proposition contained in them'.[42]

While Paley sounds like a tergiversating casuist, it would surely be a mistake to paint him as an ambitious man who trimmed his sails in hopes of promotion. After all, the radical-ism of some of his published views had effectively disqualified him from high ecclesiastical elevation. In any case, he himself always saw 'reasons for contentment' with one's lot, as part of a utilitarianism which regarded happiness as the product of 'engagement', meaning freely chosen activity.[43] Asked once what made him happy, he replied: 'I will tell you in what consists the *summum bonum* of human life: it consists in reading *Tristram Shandy*, in blowing with a pair of bellows into your shoes in hot weather, and roasting potatoes under the grate in cold.'[44] Better, surely, to regard Paley as a level-headed pragmatist, fighting shy of the self-aggrandizing humbug of self-inflicted martyrdom, the taste for political moralizing which left the talented Frend ineffective and exposed the sublime Coleridge first as a windbag and then as a turncoat.[45] Paley's position may perhaps mirror Henry More's studied silence as to whether he swore the Solemn League and Covenant.

*

From the Cambridge Platonists via Newton and his disciples to the utilitarianism of William Paley, the 'long eighteenth century' saw various efforts to find a balance between religion and science. This mattered particularly in a university that was supposed to be at once a fellowship of clerics and a community of scholars, and Christ's College had played a leading part in the story. At the end of the Georgian age, Paley's utilitarian natural theology lay at the heart of a Cambridge education. Charles Darwin, who came up to Christ's in 1828, noted in his autobiography that he found the mathematical and classics curricula tedious. But, he added,

> in order to pass the BA examination it was, also, necessary to get up Paley's *Evidences of Christianity* and his *Moral Philosophy*. This was done in a thorough manner, and I am convinced that I could have written out the whole of the Evidences with perfect correctness, but not of course in the clear language of Paley. The logic of this book, and as I may add of his Natural Theology, gave me as much delight as did Euclid. The careful study of these works, without attempting to learn any part by rote, was the only part of the Academical Course which as I then felt and as I still believe, was of the least use to me in the education of my mind. I did not at that time trouble myself about Paley's premises; and taking these on trust I was charmed and convinced by the long line of argumentation.[46]

But there was no steady state. Science, religion and society were all in flux and Paley's eirenic balance came under attack from religious evangelicals and political radicals. In time, Darwin did turn his mind to Paley's premises and ended up refuting Paleyan natural theology through a version of evolutionism which uniquely privileged 'adaptation' or 'fitnesses'. Just as Newtonianism was much more than a set of physical theories, so Darwinism, in both its biological and social forms, would become the scientific paradigm and almost secular religion of the modern age.

NOTES

1. William Wordsworth, *The Prelude: Or Growth of a Poet's Mind (Text of 1805)*, eds Ernest de Selincourt and Stephen Gill (Oxford, 1970), p. 35.
2. John Gascoigne, *Cambridge in the Age of the Enlightenment: Science, Religion and Politics from the Restoration to the French Revolution* (Cambridge, 1989); Peter Searby, *A History of the University of Cambridge, vol. III: 1750–1870* (Cambridge, 1997); Roy Porter, 'The Scientific Revolution: a Spoke in the Wheel?', in R. Porter & M. Teich (eds), *Revolution in History* (Cambridge, 1986), 290–316. The best history of that revolution remains that by the Christ's College historian of science, A. Rupert Hall: *The Scientific Revolution, 1500–1800* (London, 1954).
3. Marjorie Hope Nicolson, 'Christ's College and the Latitude Men', *Modern Philology* 27 (1929), 36–53.
4. Gascoigne, *Cambridge in the Age of the Enlightenment*, p. 44.
5. Quoted in Marjorie Hope Nicolson, *The Breaking of the Circle: Studies in the Effect of the 'New Science' upon Seventeenth-Century Poetry*, rev. edition (London, 1960), p. 203.
6. See Frederick J. Powicke, *The Cambridge Platonists: A Study* (New York, 1971); C. A Patrides, ed., *The Cambridge Platonists* (London, 1969). More began publishing in the year of Newton's birth (1642), and died in the year that his *Principia* appeared (1687).
7. Quoted in A. Rupert Hall, *Henry More and the Scientific Revolution* (Cambridge, 1990), pp. 149–50.
8. Quoted in Patrides, ed., *Cambridge Platonists*, p. 10.
9. Quotations from Patrides, ed., *Cambridge Platonists*, p. 30.
10. Patrides, ed., *Cambridge Platonists*, p. 28.
11. Quoted in Patrides, ed., *Cambridge Platonists*, p. 221.
12. Ralph Cudworth, *True Intellectual System of the Universe* (London, 1678), pp. 888, 129. On his philosophy see J. A. Passmore, *Ralph Cudworth: An Interpretation* (Cambridge, 1951).

13. Patrides, ed., *Cambridge Platonists*, p. 32, and generally Hall, *More*, ch. 7.

14. Hall, *More*, pp. 137–8.

15. R. D. Stock, *The Holy and the Daemonic from Sir Thomas Browne to William Blake* (Princeton, NJ, 1982), p. 88.

16. For the similar ambition in Robert Boyle see Michael Hunter, *Robert Boyle (1627–91): Scrupulosity and Science* (Woodbridge, 2000), pp. 25 ff.

17. See generally R. S. Westfall, *Never at Rest: A Biography of Isaac Newton* (Cambridge, 1980).

18. Margaret C. Jacob, *The Newtonians and the English Revolution, 1689–1720* (Hassocks, 1976); Simon Schaffer, 'Newtonianism', in R. C. Olby, G. N. Cantor, J. R. R. Christie and M. J. S. Hodge, ed., *Companion to the History of Modern Science* (London, 1990), pp. 610–26.

19. Quoted in Margaret Jacob, *The Radical Enlightenment: Pantheists, Freemasons and Republicans* (London, 1981), p. 124. See also see Larry Stewart, *The Rise of Public Science: Rhetoric, Technology, and Natural Philosophy in Newtonian Britain, 1660–1750* (Cambridge, 1992).

20. John Peile, *Christ's College* (London, 1900), p. 219.

21. Peile, *Christ's*, p. 217; Henry A. Gunning, *Reminiscences of the University, Town, and County of Cambridge from the Year 1790, vol. 1* (2nd ed., London, 1855), pp. 5–11, 45–6. [This paragraph and the next two were added by the editor.]

22. Searby, *History of the University of Cambridge*, vol. 3, pp. 60–3, 158–63, 184–5.

23. Obituary in *Universal Magazine*, 4 (1805), assumed to be by Frend, quoted in M. L. Clarke, *Paley: Evidences for the Man* (London, 1974), p. 16.

24. For discussion, see D. L. LeMahieu, *The Mind of William Paley: A Philosopher and His Age* (Lincoln, Nebraska, 1976).

25. William Paley, *Natural Theology* (1802), in Edmund Paley, ed., *Works of William Paley* (4 vols, London, 1838), part 1, ch. 1, p. 25. The watch argument comes from Bernard Nieuwentyt's *The Religious Philosopher*, translated into English in 1710.

26. Edmund Paley, ed., *Works of William Paley*, p. cxcvi.

27. William Paley, *Natural Theology*, chapter 26. See discussion in LeMahieu, *The Mind of William Paley*, p. 82.

28. For this natural theological tradition, see John Gascoigne, 'From Bentley to the Victorians: The Rise and Fall of British Newtonian Natural Theology', *Science in Context*, ii (1988), 219–56.

29. On this theme see A. M. C. Waterman, 'A Cambridge "Via Media" in Late Georgian Anglicanism', *Journal of Ecclesiastical History* xlii (1991), 419–36; B. W. Young, *Religion and Enlightenment in Eighteenth-Century England: Theological Debate from Locke to Burke* (Oxford, 1998).

30. Ernest Campbell Mossner, 'The Religion of David Hume', in John W. Yolton, ed., *Philosophy, Religion and Science in the Seventeenth and Eighteenth Centuries* (Rochester, N.Y, 1990), pp. 111–21.

31. W. Wilberforce to Ralph Creyke, 8 Jan 1803, *The Correspondence of William Wilberforce*, ed. R. I. and S. Wilberforce (London, 1840), vol. 1, pp. 247–53.

32. Adam Sedgwick, *Discourse on the Studies of the University* (Cambridge, 1833), pp. 11–28. See generally Boyd Hilton, *The Age of Atonement: The Influence of Evangelicalism on Social and Economic Thought, 1795–1865* (Oxford, 1988).

33. G. M. Meadley, *Memoirs of William Paley* (2nd ed., Edinburgh, 1810), pp. 62, 99; Gascoigne, *Cambridge in the Age of the Enlightenment*, p. 202. On Jebb see Anthony Page, 'Enlightenment and a "Second Reformation": The Religion and Philosophy of John Jebb (1736–86)', *Enlightenment and Dissent* xvii (1998), 48–82.

34. Virtue is 'the doing good to mankind, in obedience to the will of God, and for the sake of everlasting happiness'. These words form the epigraph to Book I, chapter seven of Paley's *Moral and Political Philosophy* and are a quotation from Edmund Law. For Law's progressive view of history see D. Spadafora, *The Idea of Progress in Eighteenth Century Britain* (New Haven, 1990).

35. For Paley on property see *Moral and Political Philosophy*, book 3, part 1, ch. 2 and book 3, part 2, ch. 2, and on slavery book 3, part 1, ch. 3.

36. For the pigeons and the oath of allegiance see *Moral and Political Philosophy*, book 3, part 1, chs 1 and 18 respectively.

37. Waterman, 'A Cambridge "Via Media"', p. 423; Searby, *History of the University of Cambridge*, vol. 3, p. 307.

38. William Paley, *Reasons for Contentment addressed to the Labouring Part of the British Public* (London, 1793), p. 12; Catherine Macdonald Maclean, *Born Under Saturn: A Biography of William Hazlitt* (London, 1943), p. 194.

39. Martin Fitzpatrick, 'Heretical Religion and Radical Political Ideas in Late Eighteenth-Century England', in Eckhart Hellmuth, ed., *The Transformation of Political Culture: England and Germany in the Late Eighteenth Century* (Oxford, 1990), pp. 350–2.

40. Searby, *History of the University of Cambridge*, vol. 3, 407–10; cf. Waterman, 'A Cambridge "Via Media"', pp. 421–5.

41. Gascoigne, *Cambridge in the Age of the Enlightenment*, p. 241. On Frend and the later anti-subscription movement in Cambridge see Frida Knight, *University Rebel: The Life of William Frend (1757–1841)* (London, 1971).

42. Paley discussed 'Subscription to Articles of Religion' in *Moral and Political Philosophy*, book 3, part 1, ch. 22.

43. LeMahieu, *The Mind of William Paley*, p. 25. According to Paley, 'happiness does not consist in greatness'.

44. H. Digby Beste, *Personal and Literary Memorials* (London, 1829), p. 209. I owe this quotation to Michael Neve.

45. On this see Seamus Deane, *The French Revolution and Enlightenment in England 1789–1832* (Cambridge, Mass., 1988).

46. Nora Barlow, ed., *Autobiography of Charles Darwin* (London, 1958), p. 59.

PART FOUR

THE COLLEGE BY 1800

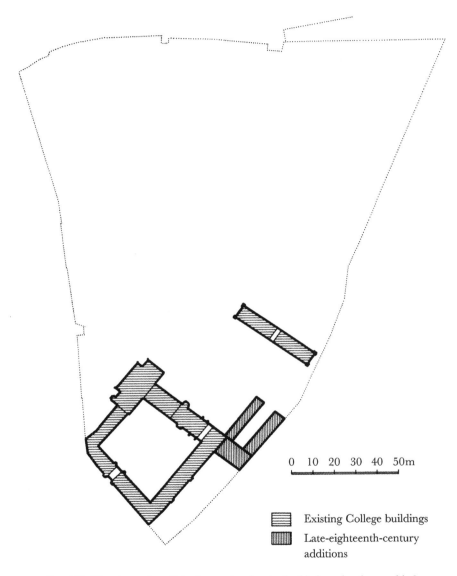

0 10 20 30 40 50m

▤ Existing College buildings

▥ Late-eighteenth-century
   additions

Rats' Hall has been demolished, an extension to the kitchens has been added,
and two temporary wings jut out into Second Court.

CHARLES DARWIN, OF course, deserves a volume to himself because *On the Origin of Species* (1859), published when he was fifty, proved one of the most influential books in modern Western history. But the question for our purpose is what Darwin and Darwinism owed to his time at Christ's.

On the face of it, not much at all. Born in 1809, the son of a Shrewsbury doctor, Charles was sent to Edinburgh University to learn his father's profession but dropped out after two years. So he was packed off to Christ's, where his brother Erasmus had studied, to take an Ordinary Arts degree as the first step to Holy Orders. Arriving in January 1828, he lived in rooms in First Court that had once been Paley's and, as Roy Porter noted in the previous chapter, the young Darwin read Paley's philosophy with much admiration. That said, neither Darwin's head nor heart were in his academic studies and he spent much of his time in the fashionable pursuits of riding, hunting and shooting.

It might seem, then, as if Darwin's years at Cambridge contributed little to his subsequent career. But that would be a superficial judgement. Like many undergraduates, he profited hugely from the broader culture of the College and University, not least in his case by pursuing his passion for entomology in company with like-minded bug hunters – the nerds of their day.

Even more important, he became the protégé of two senior academics – John Henslow, the Professor of Botany, whose death he later lamented as being like the loss of 'a parent', and the geologist Adam Sedgwick, whom he accompanied on field trips to North Wales. It was Henslow who secured Darwin a place on the round-the-world voyage of the *Beagle*, and what has been called the 'Cambridge Network' also smoothed entry into London scientific society on his return to England. As Darwin's biographer, Janet Browne, has put it, 'Darwinism was made by Darwin *and* Victorian society' – with Cambridge a vital part of that larger social context.[1] Intellectually, Charles Darwin may have been exceptional, but the benefits he derived from Cambridge outside the classroom mirrored the experience of countless others before and since.

Darwin also owed something to Christ's in a narrower intellectual sense. He noted in his *Autobiography* that on the *Beagle* and other journeys his inseparable companion was a copy of Milton's *Poetical Works*. These exerted a profound influence, particularly *Paradise Lost*, which celebrates the diverse fecundity of nature. Darwin was not 'merely' a scientist – he grew out of the romantic materialism of the early nineteenth century – and his revolution was as much one of language as of evidence. The move from natural theology to natural selection – a phrase 'poised on the edge of a metaphor', to quote Gillian Beer – represented a total paradigm shift, from Paley's vocabulary of 'design' and 'creation' to a new language of 'prediction' and 'mutation'.[2] John Milton and Charles Darwin are the two most celebrated alumni of Christ's – one a literary giant, the other a founder of modern science – but they have more in common than simply this academic affiliation.

The College Darwin entered in 1828 was beginning to awake

from its eighteenth-century torpor and the long agony of the French wars. Admissions were running at over twenty a year, part of a surge across the University which now welcomed more than four hundred new undergraduates annually. In the late eighteenth century two temporary wings had been erected, jutting out into Second Court. After 1815 rising postwar incomes permitted the College to replace them with a more substantial block of twenty-one sets of rooms adjacent to Christ's Lane. No architect was employed and the builder did little to harmonize the new block (1823–5) with the older buildings, but the whole project still cost over £7,400. Of this nearly £1,000 came from the Master and Fellows; the rest being borrowed and then repaid in little more than a decade.[3] The lack of an appeal is perhaps instructive: in contrast with 1638, the College could not expect much support from its old members. And the jerry-built character of this new block symbolizes the ethos of the College and of Cambridge in the 1820s – a patchwork of ancient and add-on, turned in on itself, that looked more and more unappealing as the nineteenth century progressed. In the Victorian Age of Reform, Cambridge would change more profoundly than at any time since the Tudor Reformation.

NOTES

1. Janet Browne, *Charles Darwin* (2 vols, London, 1995–2002), esp. vol. 1, introduction, quoting p. xi, and chapters 4–6; also vol. 2, p. 152.
2. Gillian Beer, *Darwin's Plots: Evolutionary Narrative in Darwin, George Eliot and Nineteenth Century Fiction* (2nd edn., Cambridge, 2000), esp. xvii– xviii, 5–6, 29–32, 37.
3. John Peile, *Christ's College* (London, 1900), p. 278; also Peter Searby, *A History of the University of Cambridge, vol. III* (Cambridge, 1997), p. 61.

John Burrow

The Age of Reform

IN 1838 A LARGE majority of Christ's Fellows agreed to a remarkable set of proposals. They would have altered the statutes to allow marriage of Fellows, the substitution on weekdays of prayers in Hall, open to all creeds, for College Chapel, and Dissenters would have been allowed to benefit from College endowments. If implemented these proposals would have made Christ's an altogether exceptional society in both ancient universities. Oxford and Cambridge and their colleges were at the time strictly Anglican corporations for Fellows, and compulsory chapel according to the rites of the established church was fiercely defended as an essential aspect of their Anglican and clerical character. The dissident minority in Christ's appealed to the Visitor and the measures were stalled. It would be a generation and more before they were revived, on a university-wide basis.[1]

The Master at this time was John Graham. After resigning the Mastership in 1848 on his elevation to the see of Chester (where he irritated the High Church party by his conciliation of Dissenters), Graham re-emerged in the history of university reform in Cambridge as chairman of the Royal Commission on Oxford and Cambridge set up in 1850.[2] Its report in 1852 advocated, among other things, the appointment of university lecturers financed by college contributions. Christ's was one of only a trio of colleges in Cambridge (with Trinity and Peterhouse) to declare willingness to accept a 5 per cent tax on revenues for the purpose and was apparently the only one to be willing to open its fellowships to general university competition;[3] whether the latter was a sign of confidence or modesty is unclear.

These proposals were not immediately implemented and the most far-reaching reforms had to wait until the Oxford and Cambridge Act of 1877, but Christ's part in the early pressure for university reform is striking. The College's historian, John Peile, says it had in the 1830s a reputation as a 'radical' society;[4] its recent tradition, epitomized by Graham, certainly seems Whig and tolerant. Sheldon Rothblatt, in his classic 1968 study of reform in Cambridge, *The Revolution of the Dons*, places Christ's in a bracket with Trinity and King's as the reforming colleges. In the second half of the century, Peile (Fellow from 1860, Master from 1887 to his death in 1910, and also for a time Vice-Chancellor) was the most prominently placed and one of the most energetic university reformers of the period, with a special though thwarted interest in the admission of women to degrees.[5] He played a leading part in the foundation of Newnham College, where he is commemorated by Peile Hall. As historian of Christ's and compiler of its valuable *Biographical Register* (to 1905) this chapter is much indebted to him.

The years of Peile's Fellowship saw the greatest institutional changes in the University's history, above all in the aftermath of the 1877 Act.[6] They witnessed the transformation of the colleges from Anglican, largely clerical corporations, with celibate Fellows (apart from professors), daily compulsory chapel and an undergraduate curriculum restricted to mathematics and classics, into institutions which, despite the changes of the twentieth century, most notably the increase in numbers, especially of Fellows, and the admission on equal terms of women, are essentially those of the modern university. In the later nineteenth century there were instituted a number of new Triposes: natural sciences and moral sciences from 1851, followed by history and law in the 1860s, and medieval and modern languages in 1878. These brought with them, though painfully at first, university laboratories and university lectureships and demonstratorships. Religious tests and compulsory chapel were eased and then abolished and, without celibacy restrictions on fellowships, lay academic careers became normal. No longer were fellowships, often without significant duties, mainly staging-posts between success in Tripos and the acquisition of a parish and a wife.

Harder to pin down but evident too is an enhanced sense of college identity, epitomized in Christ's by the foundation of the *Christ's College Magazine* in 1886, continuous from that date to now and a valuable source for the informal history of the College. Much of the new spirit may be attributed to the development of collegiate sports. The Boat Club dates back to 1829, two years after the first 'Bump' races on the river. In the first year Christ's shared a boat with Magdalene; then in Michaelmas 1830 some club members drew the successful ticket in a raffle selling off a spare St John's boat. For the price of a sovereign, Christ's rowing was truly launched. But competitive sport really got going in Cambridge in the 1850s, paralleling its development in the public schools and with much the same object of exercising body as well as mind. By the last third of the century inter-collegiate competition was in full swing, with rowing as the pinnacle, and there was already debate about whether sport had become an impediment to scholarship, not its complement. A 'Critical Enquiry into the After Health of the Men who Rowed in the Oxford and Cambridge Boat Race, 1829–1869' included this comment from F. J. Young, a Christ's Blue of 1869: 'during the time of training, and for some time afterwards, all study is impossible. Although the body is in an apparently perfect state of health, and capable of any exertion, the mind is incapable of doing anything. I do not know whether this proceeds from exhaustion or excitement, perhaps both.'[7]

On the academic front, this period saw the introduction of written examinations (though most undergraduates took the pass degree). It is often the fate of educational reforms to become abuses and by the middle of the century the written exams were coming to be seen as a problem and an obstacle. In Cambridge, though not Oxford, the classical as well as the mathematical class lists were individually ranked. To aid exact marking the curriculum was on the whole kept rigidly grammatical and philological.[8] Ranking seems to have had rather the same effects as ticked boxes at lower levels in the educational system in our own day. Individual ranking of Wranglers in the Mathematical Tripos ended only in 1906. Defenders of the system cited exactness of marking as a merit and in denigration of the newer humanities Triposes such as moral sciences and history. The new subjects lacked the lucrative prizes established for the older ones, and moral sciences, in particular, remained small and without cachet throughout the period. The natural sciences began to flourish from the 1870s, despite the formidable problems of laboratory provision.

The greatest prizes were of course, fellowships, on which the bulk of endowments were concentrated. They were usually embellished with teaching duties only by agreement. Hence most teaching for the older Triposes was by private coaching, which added significantly to the costs of an honours degree. To reformers it seemed essential that coaching be superseded by teaching Fellows and that the new subjects be supported by university posts which would spread the rather meagrely available expertise more widely. All these points were taken up in the 1877 Act. In 1853, after the Graham Report, Christ's had again been so eager to be modern that it had petitioned to be allowed to change its statutes immediately, but had been bidden to wait. So it is from the statutes of 1882, though sometimes revised, that the modern College, apart from the admission of women, essentially dates.[9]

Christ's in the 1850s and 1860s was not only a society of unusually liberal views. It also admitted a number of exceptionally able undergraduates, of whom a good many became Fellows, mainly nurtured, apparently, by a remarkable tutor, William Gunson. He achieved no wider note but in these years was the central College figure, to whom contemporary tributes abound, dwelling on his excellence as a teacher and his broad Cumberland speech.[10] The Senior Combination Room wine books testify to his sociability, often presenting bottles of wine in settlement of bets, on events of national or local interest – which was the custom of the Room. In a small society – undergraduate admissions in these decades ran between twenty and thirty, while the Fellowship remained static throughout the whole period up to 1910 at thirteen to fifteen – such a man could be highly influential.[11]

Of those matriculated in the mid-century only John Seeley (1852) achieved wide national recognition, but the generation of friends, mostly subsequent Fellows, to which he belonged clearly formed an unusually lively intellectual society, which gave a character to the College in these years; several were to be presences for much longer. The one who made most impression on his contemporaries by his wit, social talents and conviviality and his academic gifts, was Charles Stuart Calverley. Seeley called him a genius[12] and he was foremost in all his contemporaries' recollections. He was a migrant from Balliol College, Oxford, itself becoming famous as a place of intellect and liberal opinions. Balliol's liberalism, however, had been strained to breaking point by what Leslie Stephen, Calverley's obituarist in the *Dictionary of National Biography*, calls 'offences against discipline proceeding from mere boyish recklessness'; one instance has passed into Balliol folklore.* Calverley was also a notable athlete, his speciality being jumping, apparently of the vertical variety.[13] He graduated second classic and became a Fellow in 1858, but left to read for the Bar and died prematurely. He has left no memorial except some once popular light verse and the testimonies of his friends, but like Gunson he was clearly, for a while, a key figure, socially and intellectually, in College. One example of this, which became much talked about, was the examination he set his contemporaries on Charles Dickens's *Pickwick Papers*, sat in Hall in 1857, for which he produced a ranked list of candidates. *Optime* was (Sir) Walter Besant, who reproduced the exam paper in his autobiography – it is hard.[14]

After this flying start Besant became a popular novelist and an historian and topographer of London. Like another of this Christ's group, (Sir) Walter Sendall, who, after a colonial career, became Chairman of the Charity Organization Society – that

---

* On one occasion Calverley, showing a visitor around the College, pointed to a window and said: 'That is the study of the Master of Balliol.' Picking up some gravel he threw it at the window and, when the predictably irate and august figure appeared at it, he added: 'And *that* is the Master.'

characteristic product of the middle-class conscience combined with strict book-keeping – Besant was a prominent philanthropist. He had an agreeable inclination to get people what they wanted rather than what it was thought they should have, epitomized by the project for a 'People's Palace of Delights', a sort of combined library and leisure centre, in the Mile End Road. He was disappointed rather than gratified when it subsequently became East London College and part of the University of London. It is pleasing, however, still to find the name 'People's Palace' on direction signs on the Queen Mary College campus. The runner-up (*proxime accessit*) in the Pickwick exam was William Walter Skeat, who remained at Christ's as a Fellow until his death in 1910. As the leading authority of his day on Anglo-Saxon and Early English language and literature he was probably, in terms of pure scholarship, the best known of the College's Fellows. As an undergraduate he seems to have encouraged Seeley in learning German; they read Goethe's *Faust* together. His first College post was as lecturer in mathematics, but this left him, as he explained in an autobiographical fragment, ample leisure to develop the scholarly interest that led to his appointment in 1878 to the newly created chair of Anglo-Saxon.[15]

Another who came up in the same year as Besant, 1856, was Peile, at whose later career we have already glanced and to whom we shall return later. But if Peile became the most prominent figure from the group within Cambridge and the College, the one who achieved national celebrity, as imperialist publicist and historian of Empire, was John Seeley, who became Regius Professor of History in 1869. He is commemorated most famously in Cambridge by the glasshouse Seeley Historical Library on the Sidgwick Site. As Regius Professor when history was establishing itself in the University, he more than anyone can claim to be the father of the History Tripos. For this reason and because his extensive writings – polemical and hortatory rather than contributions to technical scholarship – offer a portrait of his mind fuller than that of any other Christ's figure of the period, he calls for some extended attention, even though there is no indication he exercised any particular influence within the College, either institutionally or ideologically. Though his was an austere, professorial voice, not a vulgar one, it was as a spokesman for empire that Seeley achieved fame, and for which he was knighted in 1894, the year before his death.[16] The book entitled *The Expansion of England*, based on lectures given to candidates in Cambridge for the Indian Civil Service, sold over 80,000 copies in the two years after its publication in 1883, was still selling 10,000 in 1919 and only went out of print in the year that symbolizes the end of Empire, 1956. Seeley was also president of the Cambridge branch of the Imperial Federation League. In the time of his celebrity, though he lived in Cambridge, his connection with the College was no longer close.

But earlier in his career Seeley had several other literary identities, through which he expressed ideas more congruous with the society to which, as a Fellow from 1858 to 1869, he then belonged. He initially achieved recognition as the proponent, in his *Ecce Homo* (1865), of a highly humanistic version of Christianity, and as a vigorous critic of unreformed Cambridge and its colleges. He also became known, as Regius Professor, as a strong advocate of what he called 'political science', under the guise of history. As one attempts to understand his mind one comes to see that these roles formed for him a coherent whole. Didactic and unremittingly serious, Seeley is easier to respect than to warm to – perhaps he always was.[17] People spoke admiringly of the power and lucidity – in retrospect it can look like rigidity – of his mind and of his dedication to teaching. It seems characteristic, however, that he achieved no distinction in the Pickwick exam. Perhaps he did not sit; he disapproved of competitive examinations as anti-educational. He appreciated his undergraduate circle, however, describing it as 'a remarkable society', though he added, typically, that it was united by no 'powerful idea'.[18] Seeley liked powerful ideas and entertained several. He provides, in fact, a kind of conspectus of English intellectual attitudes in the second half of the nineteenth century and in him, at least, intellectual life at Christ's is linked visibly to them.

Seeley's connection with the College, initially close, as undergraduate, Fellow and College lecturer in Latin (which entailed teaching), was curtailed when in the mid-1860s he took up the Chair of Latin at University College, London, though without resigning his fellowship. It is odd to modern eyes that a fellowship should be compatible with a post elsewhere but not with marriage, which enforced his resignation in 1869. In the same year he accepted the Regius Chair of History. The two events were in the wrong order. Since professors were exempt from the celibacy requirement he could perhaps have been translated into a professorial fellowship but he had already resigned. In the ensuing years, when he was a prominent Regius Professor resident in Cambridge, there was no move by the College to re-elect him. Caius elected him in 1882, perhaps under their revised statutes, and Christ's made him an Honorary Fellow in the following year. There are signs that Seeley was rather a heavy presence in the Senior Combination Room. As a Fellow the only times he figures in the SCR wine book are when fined for lateness or when, as junior for the evening ('Mr Nib'), he committed some misdemeanour in noting the wine drunk. He never bets, at a time when betting was clearly an important part of conviviality, arising from the conversation, usually parochial, on examination results, presentations to College livings, and their corollary, marriages. Rarely the outside world impinges, though the projected fall of Sebastopol was worth a flutter in the mid-fifties as was the future fate of Miss Gwendolen Harleth in 1874. Seeley seems not to have felt the lack of a collegial attachment in the 1870s.

Seeley's guiding ideas came from several directions. The most obvious is the Broad Church sympathies which supplanted the family Evangelicalism. Among leading Broad Church spokesmen were the theologian F. D. Maurice, the headmaster and historian Thomas Arnold and Seeley's predecessor in the Regius chair, the novelist Charles Kingsley. Seeley came to exemplify both of the two main dimensions of the Broad Church movement. One was a desire to make the Church of England truly national by playing down doctrinal differences which were repellent to Dissenters in particular, and also to the educated who were alienated by biblical literalism and dogmatism. The aim was above all inclusiveness. To this end tolerance, and a certain paring away of dogma, seemed essential. The other dimension, correlative to this, was an urgent concern with education, including calls for a reallocation of educational endowments to provide the basis for an extended system of national education. The aim was the nation as an inclusive spiritual community, tended by a corps of educators whom the intellectual founding-father of the Broad Church, Coleridge, had referred to as the clerisy.

Seeley shared these ideals. It is characteristic that in the early 1860s he followed Maurice and Kingsley in teaching for the

London Working Men's College and also for the companion women's college. Though women's education was never as central to his concerns as it was to Peile's, he was always a sympathizer. The published result of his urge to theological inclusiveness was the book by which he first attracted attention, *Ecce Homo*. It is an exposition of the moral teachings of Christ which is neither New Testament scholarship nor sceptical critique, nor a sentimental biography in the manner of its exact literary contemporary, the even more famous *Vie de Jésus* by the oriental scholar and failed priest Ernest Rénan. It simply presents what Seeley takes to be the ethical core of Jesus's teachings, devoid of reference to the supernatural, which he, like others, had come to regard as an impediment. He did not, like Renan, explicitly reject the supernatural, or like David Friedrich Strauss, seek to re-interpret it; he simply left it out.

There was another strand in his intellectual biography that merits attention, to which he was most probably drawn through his connection with University College, London, where it was a significant presence in the mid-century. This was the Positivist creed of Auguste Comte and his English disciples. There was a certain concordance with Broad Church principles and where there was not Seeley straddled the two. Both were humanistic and reconciliatory but Comtism made much of scientific method and the scientific laws supposedly discernible in human society; so did the later Seeley. Conversely Comtist Positivism, in its aspiration to universality, discountenanced the nation. But both preached social harmony and co-operation, promoted by a kind of priesthood of education, in Comte's case a corps of scientist-priests of the Religion of Humanity. Seeley did not follow him so far, but 'science' became a key word for him and a sense of the potential social role of political science – like many English academics he avoided Comte's term 'Sociology' – a key part of his message.[19]

To the idea of a modern and inclusive system of education, analogous to the Prussian, ministering to the creation of the national community, he added his conception of science as the discovery and demonstration of social laws, as an instrument of social harmony and, when seen in historical terms, as the key to understanding the national destiny. This was the way his social, educational and historical concerns cohered. In his contribution of 1867 to *Essays on a Liberal Education*, edited by the Broad Church cleric and author of derided school stories F. W. Farrar, Seeley was something of a firebrand. He held the common view that the chief obstacle to university reform was the colleges and their fellowships without duties. Their endowments must be diverted to the University, which must become the central provider of teaching at all levels as well as, through its professors, subsidizing research (he seems to have taken it as axiomatic that only they would do research). Seeley also had a particular detestation of examinations, which he saw as narrowing the curriculum and confining teaching to utilitarian ends. For him Germany was the model, particularly the modernization, which included education, undertaken in Prussia after the defeat of Napoleon, under Freiherr von Stein, the statesman of whom he wrote an admiring biography. One has the impression that Seeley thought that Oxford and Cambridge should become as like the universities of Berlin and Jena as possible, as soon as possible, and in this vision there was no room for colleges.

In German scholarship Seeley's *Life of Stein* broke no new ground, but in his own mind it seems to have figured, imperceptibly to everyone else, as the sequel to *Ecce Homo*. This was because for him the nation was the vehicle for the purposes of God in the nineteenth century, the modern form of the spiritual community, and Stein was its minister. This was not at the time an uncommon, certainly not an illiberal, view. Those who preached the ideal of realized nationhood throughout Europe, like the darling of English liberals, Giuseppe Mazzini, said much the same. But, like Hegel and Ranke, Seeley also accepted the power politics entailed by the existence of nation states as a kind of moral discipline. It was good for nations, as for individuals, he wrote, to live 'in society', sounding rather like Squire Brown – another product of the Broad Church imagination – deciding to send his son Tom to Rugby.[20]

When Seeley was offered the Regius Chair of History in 1869 he had no particular achievement in historical writing to his name. The most he could show was an edition of the first book of Livy; he was, we remember, at the time a Professor of Latin. To qualify oneself in a subject after obtaining a chair in it was not an uncommon nineteenth-century practice; it showed conscientiousness. Seeley's predecessor in the Regius chair could not be described as an historian. Charles Kingsley was apparently given the chair because his preaching appealed to Prince Albert. Seeley's successor, Lord Acton, was the first established historian to be offered the chair, and even he had never held a university post. The first appointee to be both an historian and already an academic was Acton's successor J. B. Bury. Seeley's inaugural lecture caused irritation to practising historians by treating history as raw material illustrating the laws to be discovered by political science. The Oxford historian John Richard Green called it 'a half ignorant, half contemptuous fling at his own chair'.[21] The story, though doubtful, is too good to lose of the old don emerging from the Senate House after the lecture expressing wonder that 'we should so soon be regretting poor Kingsley'.[22]

But if Seeley did not support or really practise historical research, as Regius Professor the new Historical Tripos owed him a good deal. Initially it was regarded as a soft option and its examinations as a test merely of memory. Seeley's notion of 'a science of politics' escaped at least that reproach, and has left, though barely recognizably, a residue of a kind in the now esteemed 'History of Political Thought' component in the present Tripos. Seeley's other phrase for the history degree, 'a school of statesmanship', was, however inflated, a brilliant piece of public relations.[23] By the time of Seeley's death in 1895 the Tripos was reputable and attracting candidates in significant numbers, assisted, notably from King's (and not from Christ's) by the creation of lectureships for its teaching. As professor, Seeley himself, in addition to his lectures, gave a well-regarded weekly conversation class in his own home, open to women as well as men.

Seeley's imperialism, which accounted for the greatest part of his reputation, had some specific features. 'Empire' was for him always the 'white' colonies. India was the result of conquest, not colonization. It was to be lived with because it was there, but it never evoked from him pieties about the white man's burden. Africa, and the scramble for it, did not interest him at all. But race was not emphasized either; Seeley's Empire was not particularly Anglo-Saxon. For him 'Greater Britain' and the possibility of Imperial Federation were constituted, if at all, by community of sentiment, not ethnicity. It was his fundamental idea of the inclusive national community written across the globe.[24]

Seeley's long-term influence in his subject is at best question-able. His dislike of party strife prompted him to dismiss the ideological continuity of the historic parties, Whig and Tory, half a century before Sir Lewis Namier, though the guild of political historians seems to have given him no credit for this. His Germanic emphasis on power politics in international affairs, in contrast to Gladstonian moralism, has drawn favour-able attention.[25] But in general his enthusiasms remain locked in their period. The same need not be said of possibly the most creative scholar possessed by the College in this period – though he had nothing like the public renown of Seeley and in so far as his name was known to a wider public it was a case of notoriety rather than fame. This was William Robertson Smith, who was elected a Fellow in 1885. The circumstances of his arrival in Christ's, interesting in themselves, also prompt some wider reflections on the intellectual lives of some of the College's most prominent members, including Peile, in the first half of our period, for they in a sense paved the way for Smith's election.

A number of Fellows, classically educated, of course, in the traditional fashion, but feeling the quickening pulse of intellec-tual life in Britain, and in Cambridge, in the third quarter of the century, chose to broaden and focus their philological expertise, on their own initiative, in the direction of non-classical languages and literatures, Slavonic, Anglo-Saxon, and oriental, and of the newly fashionable – in England – science of compar-ative philology. The first of such cases is Albert Wratislaw, a Fellow who left early in the 1860s, after having been Seeley's tutor, to become Headmaster of Bury St Edmunds Grammar School. Of Czech extraction, Wratislaw, elected a Fellow in 1844, cultivated his roots and became a leading authority on medieval Slavonic texts and Bohemian medieval history. He was also one of the first academically respectable Fellows of the Royal Historical Society after its murky beginnings in the 1870s, and contributed to its *Transactions*.[26] We have already noted Skeat's turn towards Anglo-Saxon and to medieval English literature. Peile, whom we have only considered so far as Master and University reformer, took up Sanskrit – preparing himself by the almost obligatory period of study in Germany – and became University Reader in Comparative Philology in 1884.

The most original of them, however, Robertson Smith, was an acquisition. His election followed his acceptance in 1883 of the University Chair of Arabic; he also became University Librarian. Already distinguished but also controversial, he was an academic refugee who had been ejected from his Chair in Old Testament Exegesis at the Free Church College of Aberdeen for heresy. The credit for the offer of his Fellowship at Christ's, and also possibly of his chair, seems most plausibly to belong to Peile, shortly to be Master. Peile was a comparative linguist and orientalist; so was Smith. Peile had studied at Göttingen in the 1860s; so had Smith. Smith was associate editor of the ninth edition of the *Encyclopaedia Britannica* to which Peile was a contributor. It certainly begins to look as though among the College's many debts to Peile was the addition of Robertson Smith to its Fellowship. Peile in his history of the College speaks of Smith as 'one of the very ablest men ever numbered in this society'. It is a defensible view. Smith's academic concerns were, of course, remote from those of undergraduates, but he seems to have been a good College man, not too aloof to oversee the *College Magazine*, and he left his splendid collection of oriental books to the College rather than to the University Library where he was Librarian. He died, aged only forty-seven, in 1894, in the Fellows' Building.

Smith was an orientalist but he won a wider reputation in a new subject coming to the fore in Cambridge and in the country in the 1890s, social anthropology. Late Victorian anthropology is usually associated chiefly with another Scot, James Frazer, Fellow of Trinity and author of *The Golden Bough*. When Smith first came to Cambridge he resided in Trinity and he and Frazer were friends, but it is clear from Frazer's acknowledgements – too many to quote – that Smith's was the dominant influence. Frazer dedicated *The Golden Bough* to him. The subsequent consensus in anthropology has found inspiration in Smith's ideas rather than Frazer's.[27] While Frazer, with his theory of religion as emerging from magic, and of magic as a kind of incompetent technology, soon came to be regarded in the profession as superseded, Smith's pioneering work on totemism in his two major works, *The Religion of the Semites* and *Kinship and Religion in Early Arabia*, with their insistence on the essentially collective character of religion and on the priority of ritual to myth, became more and more influential. Emile Durkheim, whose own work on totemism lay behind the revolution in anthropology in Britain in the 1920s, paid ample tribute to the seminal character of Smith's ideas.[28] Radcliffe Brown, who dominated British anthropology between the wars, constantly cited him, and he was still a felt presence for the Professor of Anthropology in Cambridge in the 1950s, Meyer Fortes.[29] Only the greatest scholars have so long and so powerful an influence.

It is no more than a coincidence, though a gratifying one, that the other 'Father of British Anthropology' in this period for quite different reasons was also a Christ's man. Alfred Haddon (elected a Fellow in 1901) owes his place at the head of the fieldwork tradition in British anthropology to his initiation and leadership of the Cambridge expedition to the Torres Straits in

1898. It included such subsequently illustrious names as James McDougall, the social psychologist, W. H. R. Rivers, later eminent in both psychology and anthropology, and Charles Seligman, who became Professor of Anthropology at the LSE. But Haddon, who had graduated from Christ's in the natural sciences in the 1870s and subsequently become a zoologist, was the moving spirit and leader. There was no established senior post in anthropology in Cambridge at the time but Haddon became Reader in Ethnology in 1909. Not all his remarks about the inhabitants of the Torres Straits would meet modern standards of political correctness, but it is clear that in general his sympathies were with them rather than their imperial masters. He spoke of the world's map as covered with 'the red paint of British aggression'.[30] He died in 1940 and was until recently a living memory.

It is time to return, in conclusion, to the College as an institution. It was one thing to accept or welcome reform in principle and also its negative provisions: the abolition of religious tests, compulsory chapel and the celibacy requirement for Fellows. It was another to find the means to support the new Triposes, with their need for university and college lectureships, demonstratorships and laboratories. Inevitably the lead was taken by the richer colleges, notably Trinity, particularly in physics, and King's for history, for which it became particularly noted. Christ's contribution, except in botany and zoology, seems to have been modest and in some cases non-existent. It elected no fellows in moral sciences or modern history during the period and the histories are silent on its possible contribution to the development of experimental physics. Some physics continued, of course, to be taught as part of the Mathematical Tripos, including the lectures of one Fellow of Christ's at least,

THE FOUNDERS

Lady Margaret Beaufort (*left*)
and Bishop John Fisher (*above*)
– both oil portraits, on wood.

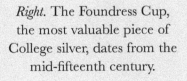

Right. The Foundress Cup,
the most valuable piece of
College silver, dates from the
mid-fifteenth century.

John Milton (shown *left* in a bust of *c.* 1660) was a student at Christ's from 1625 to 1632. A decade after he left, the College completed the New Building (*opposite*), which is also depicted in the right background of David Loggan's 1690 engraving (*below*). 'Rat's Hall' stands between it and the main court. A page from the list of subscribers to the New Building (*opposite, bottom*) shows donations from the Master and Fellows, including Joseph Mead (spelled here as Mede), and from alumni, among them Henry Montagu (Mountague), Earl of Manchester.

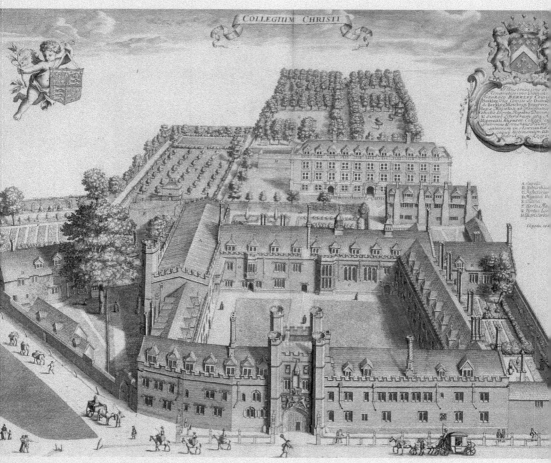

COLLEGIUM CHRISTI

M

		£	s	d
Mr Ralph	Minors Scholmaster of Hartford ———	10	0	0
Dr Otway	Meverill, a Physitian of London ———	30	0	0
Henry	Mountague E. of Manchester so Privy Seal	100	0	0
Sr Sidney	Mountague of Hinchinbroke in Huntingd. kn	20	0	0
Sr Mr Humphry	Monaux of in Bedfordshire ———	20	0	0
Mr Joseph	Mede, Fellow of Chris: Coll: (besydes what given in Common) in his lyfe, and by his Will	143	4	0
Mr Nicolas	Mason V. of Freeston in Northampton sh ——	8	0	0
	Master & Fellowes of Chris: Coll: gave in common (viz: the Mr 20, each Fellow 10)	150	0	0
Drayner	Maskingbird of Bratoft in Lincolnshire Esq —	20	0	0
George	Manours Earl of Rutland ———	40	0	0
Mr Alexander	Mors, Alderman of Grantham ———	40	0	0
Dr Gabriel	Mors Pa of Barton in the clay in Bedf. and Prebendary of Westminster —— and Fellowes.	20	0	0
	Master gave also in common, the yere fine for renewing the lease of Malton	100	0	0
	Master & Fellowes gave out of the Commencement monyes	93	10	0
	And the profits of an Forsters Fellowship during the Vacancys	18	7	6
		813	1	6

MEN OF SCIENCE AND RELIGION

Above. Henry More (*left*), Fellow from about 1639 until 1687, and Ralph Cudworth, Master 1654–88, were two of the leading 'Cambridge Platonists'.

Below. William Paley (*left*), undergraduate and Fellow, 1759–75, went on to craft a new synthesis of science and religion, which Charles Darwin (*right*), who entered Christ's in 1828 as a prospective clergyman, would eventually blow apart.

Left. Sir John Seeley, undergraduate and Fellow 1852–69, the historian and propagandist of empire.

Right. John Peile, a Fellow from 1860 and Master 1887–1910, philologist, College historian and advocate of women's education.

Below. William Robertson Smith, Fellow 1885–94, an Orientalist and pioneer of social anthropology.

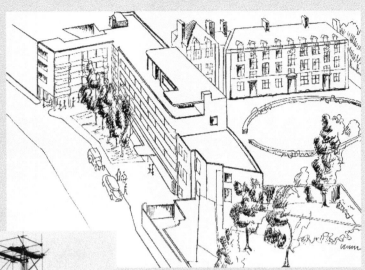

Above. The modernist design by Walter Gropius for one side of Third Court, rejected by the Fellows in March 1937. Eventually the Court was finished in more traditional stripped Georgian style by Edward Richardson.

Left. The Chancellor's Building of 1950 ('W' staircase), seen here under construction.

Right. On 21 October 1948 Queen Elizabeth, pictured with the Master, Charles Raven, visited the College to mark the 500th anniversary of the foundation of God's House.

Eminent Elizabethans

Above. Sir John Plumb (Master 1978–82), the distinguished historian.

Below, left. Lord Todd, OM (Master 1963–78), the Nobel Prize-winning chemist.

Below, right. The scientist and author Lord Snow (graduate student and Fellow from 1928 to 1950), who sought to bridge the 'two cultures'.

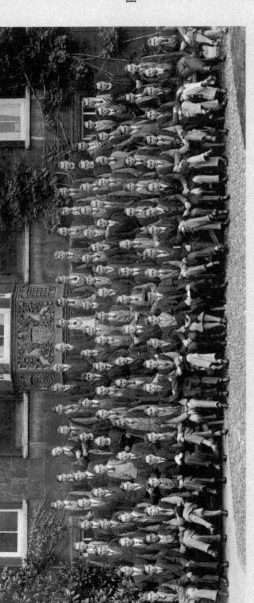

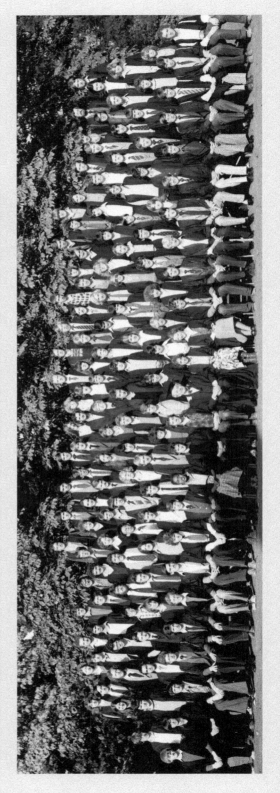

SNAPSHOTS OF A
HALF-CENTURY

Matriculation
photographs for October
1929, in front of the
Master's Lodge, and for
October 1979 – the first
year of women
undergraduates – taken
in the Fellows' Garden.

E. W. Hobson, Senior Wrangler and Fellow in 1878, who became Sadleirian Professor of Mathematics in 1910.

It must be remembered that, after a period of prosperity, from the early 1880s colleges were feeling the pinch from the fall of agricultural rents, though as an offset there was the rise in undergraduate numbers – Christ's undergraduates in residence more than doubled over the period to over two hundred. According to Peile, Fellows' dividends were reduced from a high of £300 to £260 in 1879–80, though this was only a forewarning of 'days yet more evil'. One response to increased numbers imposed, in the short term, an additional financial burden in the erection of the Stevenson Building, in what is now Third Court, in 1888–9. It is said by Peile to 'correspond' with the Fellows' Building of the 1640s.[31]

It is not altogether easy to measure the input of Christ's to the teaching of the new Triposes because the names of the Fellows are not habitually followed by subject affiliation and lecture lists do not give the lecturer's college. The university teaching increasingly provided by lecturers and demonstrators gives no indication of the input of teaching within the College. One useful indication of the contribution made by Christ's graduates (though not necessarily Fellows) to university teaching is provided by the lists of Tripos examiners, which do give College affiliation.[32] We find no Christ's names for the whole period in moral sciences or history, but often one, even two and exceptionally three in the natural sciences. Candidates for the Triposes tell the same story. In moral sciences, a small Tripos, Christ's had only nineteen candidates over the whole period, an average of 0.32 per annum. In history the number of candidates fluctuated between 3 and 6 per cent of the totals, which, if respectable at the higher end, suggests no special attraction. In the natural sciences, on the other hand, over several five-year periods the percentage went to above 15, while around 10 per cent, with one or two dips, seems to have been normal – a considerable over-representation in the University.[33]

Overall, Christ's was clearly strong in the natural sciences, though one cannot tell from these figures the respective popularity of the numerous options within the Tripos. This is easier to see at the senior level. A crop of Firsts in the Tripos in the 1870s and 1880s produced the University demonstrators, Fellows and in some cases professors who made up Christ's contribution to university science, and the emphasis seems heavily on botany and zoology. Noteworthy Fellows in these subjects were Sydney Howard Vines, who became a Fellow in 1876 and is described in the *Dictionary of National Biography* as the virtual founder of the new school of botany, whose equipment he subsidized out of his own pocket, before he accepted a Chair of Botany in Oxford in 1888; Harry Marshall Ward, Fellow 1883–9, who became Professor of Botany; Francis Darwin, third son of Charles, Fellow from 1888 and lecturer in Botany; and Arthur Shipley, a pupil of Vines, Fellow from 1887 and a well-known zoologist, who succeeded Peile as Master in 1910.

By contrast it is difficult to avoid the impression that the humanities were allowed to languish somewhat towards the end of the century. Peile may have seen the need to remedy this, which may account for his support, otherwise remarkable, for what now seems one of the stranger initiatives of the period. The need to provide teaching in new subjects had led to *ad hoc* combinations of colleges for teaching purposes, thus achieving economies of scale. By far the most ambitious initiative of this kind was a proposal emanating from Emmanuel College in 1878 for a complete merger of Christ's with Emmanuel. Despite

Peile's benevolence towards the idea, the Master, James Cartmell, was opposed to it and the proposal came to nothing. It
had been serious enough to lead to the appointment of a joint
committee, and the project was revived several times, though
again without success.[34]

Christ's most distinguished representative of the humanities
around the turn of the century, and also its first outstanding
Jew, was a protégé of Skeat, Israel Gollancz.[35] He was a
university lecturer in English from 1896 to 1906 before going on
to the Chair of English at King's College, London and an
eventual knighthood. He produced a string of impressive
publications on medieval literature and, while he was still at
Cambridge, became a founding Fellow and Secretary of the
British Academy. It seems that the establishment of the Academy owed a good deal to his initiative. If we are inclined to
suspect prejudice in his non-election to a fellowship it should be
borne in mind that several Christ's FRSs employed by the
University in this period were also not elected to fellowships.[36]
All the same it's a pity the College was not able or inclined to
confirm the heritage of Skeat and offer support to the new
Medieval and Modern Languages Tripos (1878).

Christ's credentials as a liberal and open society were strong.
Soon after it became possible for students of any faith, thanks to
the Graham Commission, to proceed to degrees, we find admissions for 1864 including Fazul Nasser, 'a Mahommedan' and
Charles Sassoon, 'a Jew'.[37] Thereafter religious identification
is omitted, which is a pity in the case of Jews, since it becomes
a matter of guesswork. There is, however, a steady sprinkling
of Indian names – the most distinguished of whom, Ananda
Mohan Bose, matriculated in 1870 and became Chairman of
the Indian National Congress in 1898. Peile, who must have

known him, writes of his great personal charm and describes him as 'a critic of English ideas about India; but never bitter or unreasonable'. His son was admitted in 1897 and Bose himself died in 1906.[38] Another example of Christ's openness during this period was the connection formed, apparently as a result of Peile's friendship with Dom Cuthbert Butler, with the newly established community of Catholic priests, St Edmund's House.[39] Christ's and Downing became the two colleges that accepted students from St Edmund's, thus opening the University to them until, much later, St Edmund's was given collegiate status. Incidentally the *College Magazine* offers a small sidelight on the new eclecticism. Around 1870 it seems that Christ's men were commonly referred to as 'Christians', a usage which by the early twentieth century had died out instead of perpetuating a now tactless ambiguity.[40]

Historians have become wary of congratulating the past for beginning to look like the present. This chapter has tacitly or perhaps more than tacitly acquiesced in the not violently contested view that the changes it has described were on the whole for the better. As a possible corrective one looks, naturally, for the mark of the academic curmudgeon, the College Cato the Elder, to whom all change is evil in nature, dangerous in tendency and catastrophic in consequences. He is seldom hard to find in any academic community, or reticent when found. But in this period he has remained elusive. It is natural to have hopes, for example, of Joseph Shaw, briefly Master in 1849, who found his exile from the Combination Room impossible to bear and returned to it joyfully by immediately resigning the Mastership. Peile's epitaph on him is that 'in his later years he was a vigilant guardian of the College grass. I can remember the excitement caused by the discovery of a daisy.'[41] It is easy to feel that one knows him, but Peile also tells us that he was a liberal in politics and a supporter of Graham. Gunson's quarrel with the Master, Cartmell, which led to his resignation of the tutorship in which he had served the College so well, was apparently over a matter of no public importance,[42] while few alumni of either institution will now be likely to see Cartmell's opposition to the proposed merger with Emmanuel as wanton obstruction of the path of necessary progress. The Fellows of Christ's, in a period of extraordinarily rapid and profound change, seem to have played a creditable part while keeping their collective nerve and their collegiality. In the age of university reform there was no blood on the Combination Room carpet.

NOTES

1. John Peile, *Christ's College* (London, 1900) pp. 279–80.
2. Biographical information in this chapter is from the *Dictionary of National Biography* (DNB) unless otherwise specified.
3. Sheldon Rothblatt, *The Revolution of the Dons: Cambridge and Society in Victorian England* (2nd ed., Cambridge, 1981), p. 206. On Christ's as a liberal and reforming college see also pp. 156, 211, 230.
4. Peile, *Christ's College*, p. 278.
5. For Peile's activity see Phyllis Deane, *The Life and Times of J. Neville Keynes: A Beacon in the Tempest* (Cheltenham, 2001), pp. 208, 210. Keynes was Secretary of the Faculties.
6. For the general history of the University in this period, including useful statistics, see Christopher N. L. Brooke, *A History of the University of Cambridge, vol. IV, 1870–1990* (Cambridge, 1993).
7. For 1829–30 see George T. Atchison and Geoffrey C. Brown, *The History of Christ's College Boat Club* (Cambridge, 1922), pp. 1–2. Young is quoted in Peter Searby, *The History of the University of Cambridge, vol. III, 1750–1870* (Cambridge, 1997), p. 662. On changes in collegiate life in this period see Rothblatt, *Revolution of the Dons*, chs 6–7.
8. On examinations and coaching see Rothblatt, *Revolution of the Dons*, pp. 68–9.

9. Peile, *Christ's College*, p. 283.

10. Lord Wrenbury, '59 Years Ago', *Christ's College Magazine* (henceforth *CCM*), 100 (1923), p. 237. See also *Autobiography of Sir Walter Besant* (London, 1902), p. 83, and John Peile, *Biographical Register of Christ's College, 1505–1905* (2 vols, Cambridge, 1913), vol. 2, for 1843 – the date of Gunson's admission.

11. Fellowship numbers from Brooke, *History of the University of Cambridge*, appendix I. For undergraduate numbers, see Christ's College Admission Books, Muniment Room, T1, 1–2. I am greatly indebted to Christopher D. Thompson for procuring these and other statistics for this chapter.

12. J. R. Seeley, 'Christ's College Thirty Years Ago', *CCM* 1 (1886), p. 4.

13. The circular plot in First Court was once surrounded by railings, over which Calverley is said to have hopped. Walter Wren, 'Reminiscences of my College Days', *CCM* 14 (1890), p. 179. For a later photograph see *CCM* 228 (2003), p. 49.

14. Besant, *Autobiography*, pp. 99–102. On Calverley, see p. 89.

15. W. W. Skeat, *A Student's Pastime* (Oxford, 1896), p. xvi.

16. The chief source for Seeley's life is Deborah Wormell, *Sir John Seeley and the Uses of History* (Cambridge, 1980). For Seeley and university reform see also Rothblatt, *Revolution of the Dons*, ch. 5. On Seeley's Broad Church politics see R. T. Shannon, 'John Robert Seeley and the Idea of a National Church in Britain', in Robert Robson, ed., *Ideas and Institutions of Victorian Britain: Essays in Honour of George Kitson Clark* (London, 1967). On Seeley and political science there is Stefan Collini, Donald Winch and John Burrow, *That Noble Science of Politics* (Cambridge, 1983), pp. 225–34.

17. '. . . he was always somewhat grave, even austere' – Besant, *Autobiography*, p. 86. R. Seymour Thompson spoke not only of his power as a lecturer but also, rather unusually, of his 'deep and subtle charm'. See 'J. R. Seeley as a Teacher', *CCM* 49 (1902), p. 79.

18. *CCM* 1 (1886), p. 4.

19. John R. Seeley, 'History and Politics', *Macmillan's Magazine* 40 (1879), 295–6.

20. 'Our Insular Ignorance', *The Nineteenth Century* xviii (1885), p. 868. Thomas Hughes, author of *Tom Brown's Schooldays*, was an associate of Kingsley.

21. Leslie Stephen, ed., *The Letters of John Richard Green* (London, 1901), p. 248.
22. Wormell, *Seeley*, p. 43.
23. Peter Slee, *Learning and a Liberal Education: The Study of Modern History in the Universities of Oxford, Cambridge and Manchester, 1800–1914* (Manchester, 1986), p. 62.
24. Shannon, in Robson, ed., *Ideas and Institutions*, p. 259.
25. Ibid., esp. pp. 260–7.
26. J. W. Burrow, 'Victorian Historians and the Royal Historical Society', *Transactions of the Royal Historical Society*, 5th series, 39 (1989), pp. 132–3.
27. Robert Alan Jones, 'Robertson Smith and James Frazer: Two Traditions' in George W. Stocking Jr., ed., *Functionalism Historicised: Essays in British Social Anthropology* in *History of Anthropology*, vol. 2 (1984). For an estimate of the influence of Robertson Smith in anthropology generally see George W. Stocking, Jr., *After Tylor: British Social Anthropology, 1881–1951* (London, 1996), pp. 63–83.
28. Emile Durkheim, *Elementary Forms of the Religious Life*, trans. Joseph Ward Swain (London, 1915), pp. 45, 89–90.
29. Personal recollection.
30. Stocking, *After Tylor*, pp. 100–16. See also A. Hingston Quiggin, *Haddon the Head-Hunter* (Cambridge, 1942).
31. Peile, *Christ's College*, pp. 284, 291.
32. These are conveniently consulted in J. R. Tanner, ed., *Historical Register of the University of Cambridge. Supplement to the Calendar to 1910* (Cambridge, 1917).
33. I am grateful to Christopher Thompson for the percentages of candidates.
34. Brooke, *History of the University*, pp. 86–7.
35. See F. G. Kenyon's obituary of Gollancz in *Proceedings of the British Academy*, 1930, p. 424.
36. For instance H. J. H. Fenton and W. J. Sell. See J. A. Venn, *Alumni Cantabridgienses* (6 vols, Cambridge, 1940) – alphabetically arranged.
37. See Peile, *Biographical Register*. This is arranged by date of admission – see 1864.
38. Peile, *Biographical Register*, 1870 and 1897.
39. Brooke, *History of the University*, pp. 299–303. This connection was responsible for the author of this chapter, in the early 1960s, 'teaching' Catholic priests St Thomas Aquinas, selections from whom were part

of the History of Political Thought syllabus for the Historical Tripos. The priests kept admirably straight faces.

40. 'College Life Fifty Years Ago', [attributed to Seymour Thompson], *CCM* 75 (1911), p. 209.
41. Peile, *Christ's College*, p. 279; also Peile, *Biographical Register*, vol. 2.
42. Peile, *Biographical Register*, vol. 2, 1843.

PART FIVE

THE NINETEENTH-CENTURY COLLEGE

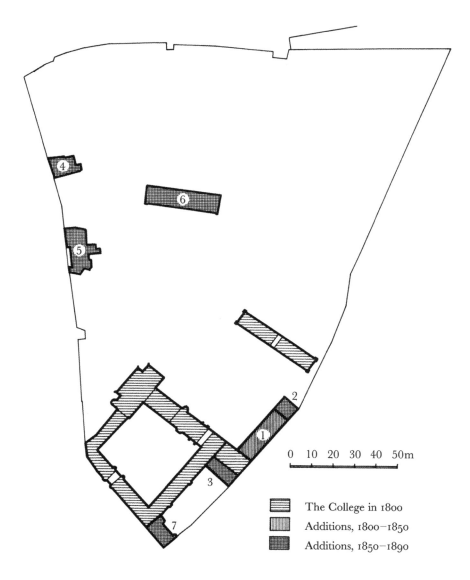

0 10 20 30 40 50m

The College in 1800
Additions, 1800–1850
Additions, 1850–1890

1 – Extension to Second Court (1825)   2 – Additional staircase (1867)

3 – Kitchen and buttery extension (1875)

4 and 5 – Houses on Hobson St. purchased in 1880s

6 – Stevenson Building (1889)   7 – Library extension (1896)

FELLOWS SUCH AS John Seeley and William Robertson Smith were men of ideas. Many of their students were more interested in the pleasures of the flesh. But all of them lived off the labour of others, for Christ's depended on a large array of workers simply to function day by day. For much of its history the College 'servants' are a vestigial presence but, thanks to the researches of Rachel Wroth,[1] we can enjoy a vivid glimpse of their roles in the nineteenth century.

Many of the senior staff rented College houses in the adjacent Christ's Lane. The porter was the only one to live within the walls, being responsible for College security round the clock. Until 1891 his lodge was actually a family home, occupied for most of the first half of the century by various members of the Moule and Nichols families, who were by way of being a Christ's dynasty. But the porter received only about half the stipend of the cook and – best paid of all – the butler. For more than a decade in the 1820s and 1830s, Christ's employed a French cook, Jean-Baptiste Boisellier, setting a fashion followed at Trinity and other colleges. There was no love lost between Boisellier and his under-cook or scullion, John Wisken, but the latter clearly derived solace from poetry. His doggerel verses, written about 1840, describe the scullion's day from six in the morning to ten at night, of which the most frenzied part was dinner in Hall at four in the afternoon.

> Wisken, bring me a glass of Beer
> Wisken, bring me some apple pie
> Wisken, bring me cel'ry and cheese
> Wisken, bring me water or I die.

As for his staff:

> The Waiters teetotallers are
> No! quite the reverse may be seen
> All glasses for the ale they inspect
> And swallow it down in the screen.

Wisken did not pretend he was a second Milton, but

> Although a Dirty Scull I don't see why
> I should not at the Muses have a shy
> What I do write the Public will not see
> I write to please myself – so all agree.

The butler ran his own business supplying members of the College with bread, butter, cheese and ale from the buttery. But the real justification for his stipend was that he looked after the College silver and wine and also drew up the termly bills for Fellows and students. 'He' is actually a misnomer, because, of the six butlers employed by the College from 1795 to 1900, four were female. One of them, Sarah Ann Nichols, held the post for half a century from 1851 to 1900. In the 1830s, Christ's also had a female barber and in the 1840s a female shoeblack – all extremely unusual in Cambridge at the time, though in many cases these women inherited the equipment and thus the job when their husbands died. To show that gender stereotypes were flexible on both sides, it should be noted that in 1825 William Bennett was appointed 'College Laundress'. It is unlikely he would have done the washing and ironing himself, however, probably sub-contracting it to a team of women and making his profit on their work.

The servants worked long hours in dirty conditions, but there was some relief such as the 'Servants' Treat' every August – a substantial feast – though who served the servants is not clear. From the 1850s there was an annual and keenly contested cricket match against the students, and in the 1890s began the tradition of a summer outing to the coast. Many servants worked for decades – Frederick Tarre died in 1822 at the age of ninety-six, apparently still College hairdresser. Although many aged in poverty, the College usually paid pensions to the very old and annual allowances to widows of servants who died in post. Yet long service could sometimes be the path to real riches, particularly for those running their own businesses such as the cook, butler and scullion. Bills were only rendered once a term and few undergraduates kept track of the beer they ordered in Hall or the Buttery. Likewise Fellows and students had only the vaguest idea of the wholesale cost of food bought for preparation in the kitchens. So those who kept the bills had plenty of opportunity for profit-making and simple over-charging. John Wisken died in 1873, after forty-four years service, leaving an estate of nearly £8,000.[2] But that was eclipsed by Richard Lenton, who died in 1870 after thirty-two years as College cook, having amassed £12,000 – at a time when average annual earnings in the United Kingdom were only about £50.[3]

Upstairs, downstairs – one begins to wonder who was really on top. But clearly domestic life at Christ's in the nineteenth century was full of surprises.

NOTES

1. See *Christ's College Magazine* 229 (2004) 56–9.
2. For background see Alice Raynes, 'John Wisken, Scullion of Christ's College', *Christ's College Magazine* 192 (1967), 33–6.
3. Contemporary comparisons are, of course, problematic but see the tables for UK earnings on the Economic History Services website at http://www.eh.net/hmit

The Two World Wars

THIS CHAPTER TELLS THE story of a traditional community under untraditional pressures.[1] Looking at the period 1914–50, it considers the question of collegiate continuity: how Christ's remained identifiably the same institution while experiencing the shocks of world events and the sweeping economic and social changes which made the first half of the twentieth century such a dramatic – even calamitous – period in national and international history. As always, tradition shaped attitudes. In March 1945, for example, as the Second World War drew to its thundering close, the editor of the *College Magazine* saw Christ's and the University community in a passive role: 'It is a commonplace that we are living at the end of an epoch and are watching from within the coming of the new.'[2] But 'the coming of the new' also involved active responses and change. That implicit symbiosis is the theme of this chapter.

The dramatic impact of outside events began in 1914–18 with the Great War, which destroyed the nineteenth-century balance of nations and empires, began a huge shift in the global authority of the country and its institutions, accelerated powerful dislocations of social structures and economic relationships, and introduced a relatively complacent population to the idea of violent death as an almost banal commonplace. Followed as the war was by twenty years of extreme economic volatility and distress for the world as well as Britain, and then by another global conflict with even larger consequences and greater horrors, these decades placed heavier demands on the College's continuity and attachment to tradition than any other period since the Civil War. Of course, many of these events had only indirect and remote consequences for collegiate life. But they could not be ignored, and ultimately transformed the realities to which the College had to adjust.

Those adjustments took a variety of forms. In spite of its large degree of legal and financial autonomy, Christ's had to accommodate itself to changes in government policy involving greater intervention and a substantial expansion of higher education. Further, economic and financial upheaval reshaped collegiate income and expenditure, and enforced heroic changes in outlook and behaviour – towards employees, towards policy, and towards the use of resources. There was a growing assertiveness of wage-earners (even College servants), women and students; and a substantial expansion in higher education and the emergence of a much more professional structure for its governance. The Second World War brought these trends to a heightened degree of intensity. And by the late 1940s Christ's was assuming a new character, albeit one that in many respects would have still been familiar to previous generations. The economic, physical and institutional bases for a growing college population had been established and strengthened; the student voice was heard if not always listened to; the acceptance of women, although not yet as first-class citizens, was at last on the (remote) horizon. And another major historical trend was reflected in Christ's as the College increasingly came to terms with the technology that, like total war, characterized the twentieth century: the internal combustion engine, radio, television, even (and almost last) modern plumbing.

Of course, whatever the general impact of such grand themes, for many (and they were undoubtedly the more fortunate), the twentieth century was in part experienced *not* as high drama, but as piecemeal adaptation. Nevertheless, persistent piecemeal adaptation ultimately produces radical change. And as it reacted to events on the larger canvas of national and international history, that was also Christ's experience.

*

During the interwar years, and indeed for some time afterwards, Christ's, like many other colleges, enjoyed a large degree of independence through its control of adequate resources and income flows. External pressures and opportunities, such as resulted from the Royal Commission of 1919–22 and the consequential legislation, or the emergence of public funding for universities, had only a marginal or indirect effect on the resources and core activities of the College. On the other hand, less explicit pressures – the evolution of academic professionalism and specialization, and closer attention to the business management of the College – gradually shifted the composition and policy of the institution. This was ultimately reflected in the growth in graduate student numbers, a more conscious search for new Fellows in particular fields, and a more entrepreneurial attitude to College affairs.

The trajectory of student numbers paralleled that of the national student population. Before 1914 Christ's had been a relatively small society by modern standards, with 176 students in Easter Term 1914. After a spectacular fall in the Great War, the number recovered to almost 300 throughout the interwar years. There was a similar collapse and revival in numbers across the Second World War. And in the Michaelmas Term of 1950 the student population was 410. Within these figures, however, undergraduate numbers in peacetime (after 1918) were fairly stable at about 250 to 300. The more dramatic changes came in the size of the graduate population, although this was mostly represented by BAs (twelve in 1920, thirty-one in 1921, and an average of ninety-five in 1948–50). This presumably resulted from the growth of diploma and one-year courses. Designated research students remained at about ten or less until the late 1940s, when their number rose to twenty-two in each of 1949 and 1950.

Unfortunately, the archives say too little about the thirty or so College servants to derive an adequate picture of their lives or roles in this period – except at one moment of particular tension which is considered later in this chapter.

Compared with both the size and the variations in the numbers of students, the Fellowship was small and relatively stable. In addition to the Master, it stood at twelve across the First World War, and rose gently to fifteen in 1923, with one or two more added by the 1930s. The number in post declined slightly in the early 1940s, before rising again with the return of peace. (Significantly, the number quadrupled in the next half-century – to seventy-four in the academic year 2002 to 2003.)

In practice, Christ's essential character was determined by the fact that it was a very compact society of senior academics, attracted or forced into close working relationships, meeting fairly frequently at High Table and Governing Body, and able to focus almost exclusively on their responsibilities as trustees and their rights as beneficiaries of the College's endowment and income. C. P. Snow's picture of College life in *The Light and the Dark* (1947) and *The Masters* (1951) may have been too self-conscious and stilted to be humanly persuasive, but its description of the almost claustrophobic activities and outlook of the Fellowship was far from fictional.

Much of this is confirmed by the minutes of the Governing Body and Council. In spite of their laconic style, they reflect the disproportionate amount of time that was devoted to such non-student matters as the determination of the composition of the Fellowship, the management of assets and rents and the monitoring and disposition of income, the oversight of the College and its fabric and services. The interwar community of Fellows must have led a comfortable, even luxurious, life; racked occasionally by rivalries or academic and hierarchical tensions, and more intermittently by echoes of larger physical or ideological conflict, but essentially calm by the standards of the world outside Cambridge in these turbulent decades. In the fictional Lewis Eliot's words on the eve of the Second World War, 'Wars might be near us, but Arthur Brown [a character modelled on the then Senior Tutor, Sidney Grose] took it for granted that the college government must be carried on'.[3]

Except at moments of great national perturbation, the outside world remained outside. This is confirmed by the daily records of a central aspect of the Fellowship's sociability – the presentation of bottles of post-prandial wine by individuals to mark ostensibly significant events. The occasions for such presentations were largely domestic: they rarely went beyond the marking of such occasions as the arrival or departure of Fellows, the honouring of visitors or elections to the Royal Society, or the commemoration of academic or, more often, sporting achievements by students. University happenings occasionally intruded and very few political events were acknowledged (an exception being Baldwin's acceptance of the premiership in 1923). Only as war approached (but not, curiously, at its outbreak) or when it ended did the wine books record events. For example, on VE Day, 8 May 1945, the 'custom of the Room' was broken, and the Fellowship stood, rather than sat, to give the loyal toast and honour the memory of three Fellows killed during the war. On 15 August, the Fellowship took wine to celebrate Japan's surrender and the three members of the College who had been closely associated with victory: a Field Marshal and an Admiral – Smuts and Mountbatten (the latter Commander-in-Chief in South East Asia) – and the former Master, Sir Charles Darwin, Director of the National Physical Laboratory, who was one of those centrally involved with the development of the atomic bomb.

Christ's at this time was a conservative (occasionally even a parochial) institution, suspicious of rapid growth. In 1944, for example, in the face of pressure for postwar expansion, the Governing Body recorded that it had no wish to increase the number of undergraduates above the prewar level of about 300 (pointedly indicating that that was twice the 1913–14 number). And in March 1945, even when C. P. Snow persuaded the Fellows to appoint a committee to consider a possible expansion to 450 undergraduates by 1950 (that is, 50 per cent above the level of the 1930s), the decision was taken grudgingly: the Governing Body insisted that the committee should take account of the costs of growth, the unwieldiness of a larger Fellowship, the rival claims of fellowships and scholarships on the budget, and the effect of an expansion on the life of the community. In the event, the symbolic figure of 450 was not reached until the 1960s. (In the academic year 2002 to 2003 it was some 520.)

Yet the parochialism should not be exaggerated. First,

because the College did adjust to pressures for institutional change; second, because the Fellows' caution was based on prudence; and third, because financial and institutional continuity were needed to underpin the vital academic purposes of the College.

The first of these considerations – external institutional pressure – was best exemplified in the 1919 Royal Commission on Oxford and Cambridge. The commission, which reported in 1922, was one in a long line of rather inconclusive attempts to reconcile national needs, reforming instincts and private interests and trusts. In the event its recommendations offered only modest threats to collegiate autonomy: greater financial rationalization and transparency, a more efficient approach to catering, the encouragement of research and the appointment of many more non-stipendiary Fellows, control of scholarship levels, economic rents for non-scholars, and greater security for university academic employees. Not all of these were accepted. But, although hardly radical, some changes *did* result for colleges: minor reform of financial procedures and the management of trust funds; a measure of more efficient management; greater stability and security of employment (and a pension scheme) for the university's academic employees; and a new emphasis on research activity and Research Fellows.

The second consideration – the need for caution because of the costs of growth at a time of violently fluctuating economic values – was relevant because funds had to be put aside in anticipation of building needs and possible expansion in the Fellowship. In those unreformed days all Fellows were paid a reasonable stipend in return for their commitment to the College. Apart from accommodation and subsistence facilities (for only some of which Fellows were charged), their material rewards came in the form of annual 'dividends'. These normally exceeded £250 and could rise to £450 depending on seniority and circumstances. By 1935 the average cost of a Fellowship in stipends and allowances was between £375 and £400.[4] At these levels, the material standing of Fellows was more than modest – certainly above that of male schoolteachers. And when we add in the proceeds of actual effort – that is, stipends from College offices and/or University appointments – they were probably in the same league as the higher professions of lawyers and doctors and dentists.[5]

Thirdly, there is an alternative institutional view to that of the Fellowship as an inward-looking society, devoted to its own comfortable management. The point here is that Christ's, like other colleges, was a community ultimately dedicated to education and the facilitation of research. And that dedication was realized not so much by any collective effort as by the maintenance of an economic and social environment within which its individual members, as individuals, could pursue those ends, undisturbed by unwieldy growth.

In fact, over the years Christ's obviously housed not only academic passengers, but active teachers and researchers; a handful of outstanding, even world-renowned, scholars; some distinguished participants in the crucial controversies and conflicts of the twentieth century; and a number of lively younger Fellows who went on to substantial achievement in academic life and war work. Three of those who came to national and international prominence in later years (Snow, Plumb and Todd) are considered by David Cannadine in the next chapter. Here, we may note another triumvirate, Sir Arthur Shipley, Sir Charles Darwin, and Canon Charles Raven.

Sir Arthur Shipley was elected a Fellow in 1887, Master in 1910, and Vice-Chancellor in 1917–19. He died in 1927. A dedicated and conservative member of the College, he was an active and versatile zoologist and 'a strenuous patron of science' who popularized the life sciences, and moonlighted as Cambridge correspondent for *The Times*. Before 1919 Shipley was very active in the myriad affairs of the University, but subsequently threw himself into the life of the College. He also travelled extensively – often on a consultative basis (for example, he chaired the governing body of the Imperial College of Tropical Medicine in Trinidad). But, unlike Darwin and Raven, his was a life of administration and of scholarship, largely devoted to his own field and to its professional confines.

Sir Charles Darwin, FRS (Fellow 1919–22, and Master 1936–8) carried the most familiar name: he was the grandson of the author of *On the Origin of Species* and a very distinguished theoretical physicist. He became Director of the National Physical Laboratory, wartime adviser on the atom bomb, and scientific adviser to the War Office. It was his election that provided the template for C. P. Snow's *The Masters*.

Canon Charles Raven was elected to a Fellowship in 1932 and (after an interval away from Cambridge) to the Regius Chair of Divinity and the Mastership of Christ's, which he held from 1939 to 1950. He was perhaps the best known and most interesting of all the Fellows who reached their maturity in the interwar years. A saturnine and forbidding figure, he was a widely respected writer not only on theology and natural history, but more famously on the compatibility of the divine and the secular – the possible marriage of faith, reason and science.[6] Thus, he fitted into a College tradition stretching back to Cudworth, More and Paley (see Roy Porter's chapter). He was also a notable pacifist – a characteristic which was naturally uncomfortable during the Second World War but which he sustained with dignity and respect. And Raven's concerns with wider social issues as well as the relationship between religion and science were also reflected in his hosting of wartime meetings of Archbishop Temple's informal Cloisterers' Group of Christian leaders, which met regularly at Christ's.

There was, then, a contrast between the introspective character of Christ's considered as a self-governing community, and the scope of outlook and action of its members considered as individuals. But it is worth emphasizing that this was part of the essence of the ideal model of a college, which (whatever its collective insularity) husbands resources to maintain a society within which individuals can choose between committing themselves, on the one hand, to local horizons and on the other to undertaking larger and more adventurous expeditions into the worlds of scholarship, culture and ideology.

But there is also another consideration here: however cosy Christ's may have been, it could not ignore the more insistent intrusions of the two twentieth-century World Wars and the swingeing economic disruptions that lay between them.

*

Modern historians often see the Great War against the background of Britain's prewar economic performance and social dislocations – and conclude that it was less of an abrupt watershed than was once believed. But this was not universally the case. Consider two respects in which the war had a quite specific impact. On the one hand, it injected the experience or perception of atrocious conditions and mass killing and maiming into lives that had no real experience or previous conception of such horrors. On the other, the acceleration of economic and social disruption obliged people and institutions to adjust inherited behaviour and economic relationships with unprecedented speed.

Such effects were not necessarily long-lasting or universally felt. But as long as they were felt they were the more magnified in the case of institutions, like Cambridge and Oxford Colleges, whose relatively tranquil ways and privileged and comfortable lives had known nothing like them. So it was at Christ's, where it ultimately became necessary to accept as everyday occurrences the existence of premature and violent death, institutional upheaval and extreme economic volatility.

Initially, as in so many other areas of national life, the war presented itself more as an adventure than a tragedy. War was declared on 4 August 1914. By Christmas nearly half the 175 students in residence in 1913–14 had volunteered, and just over a third (sixty-two) of them had obtained commissions, while six of the College's thirty or so servants were also under arms.[7] As student numbers fell, forty-four sets of rooms became vacant, and landladies were compensated for the loss of rents as their lodgers went to war and others moved into College. Meal charges were reduced (only to be increased in 1915), and quarterly dues were remitted for volunteers (whose rooms were – alas, so poignantly – kept vacant for an early return that was not to be). College grounds and boathouses were placed at the disposal of the armed forces; hospitality was extended to service officers on short courses; and senior officers were given membership of the Fellows' Common Room. The head porter volunteered and the College agreed to pay the consequential difference in his income (£43 per annum). Twelve Belgian student-refugees were allowed to use College facilities. Air-raid insurance was taken out.

But the almost festive sense of adventure and innocuously

eclectic change must have abated as mass armies clashed.[8] By Easter Term 1916 four Fellows had joined the services and the number of students had fallen to forty-eight – of whom a majority were foreigners, medical students or clergymen, and therefore effectively exempt from active service. The Great War was truly a young man's – even a boy's – war: in the whole of the University in 1916 the number of resident undergraduates was only 550, as against 600 senior members.[9] And it was not long before the war's tragic elements began to come to the fore – not merely among the academic members of the College, for in May 1915 the Governing Body noted the death in Flanders of E. Freeman, previously a member of the kitchen staff. His parents were offered a gift of two pounds. By the next year, the College's Roll of Honour of deaths among academic members had risen to twenty-five (it was to exceed one hundred by 1918). The war's shadow blanketed the College, and the *Magazine*'s editor wrote of 'an atmosphere of . . . patient waiting for a better time' and of the growing lists of 'those who will not return'.[10] Consciences were moved, as allowances were made to the wives of servants on military duty.

It is true that even at the worst of times the College adjusted to the need for normality in the midst of abnormal hostilities – and the increasingly grim record of war's more violent impact was clothed in civilized (if faintly patronizing) discourse: in June 1917 the Governing Body agreed to accept ten or fifteen wounded colonial soldiers during the Long Vacation 'to give them a taste of English university life'.

But there was no escaping the fact that the language of Death had become common currency and each issue of the *College Magazine* contained sombre additions to 'The Roll of Honour'. The first Christ's man to die on active duty in the war was George McVittie, who came up in 1914, albeit his death was caused by heart failure en route to India in March 1915. More dramatic was the fate of Leslie Standen, who matriculated in 1913 – killed by a stray bullet while digging a trench in Flanders in March 1916. Standen had been an outstanding sportsman at College. By contrast, Henry Kelleher, an Irishman who came up in 1910 to read law, had a weak heart and never graced the sportsfield. He derived great satisfaction from being able to serve on the field of battle, and bravely ventured into no-man's-land in April 1916 on an unarmed mission to determine the nationality of soldiers dressed in British uniforms – they turned out to be Germans. On his body was found an unfinished letter to his former tutor, Norman McLean. These three were young men but the war took its toll of older alumni. Maurice Black, from Edinburgh, an undergraduate in 1895–8 and then a regular officer in the Guards, was severely wounded in France in October 1914. Determined to avoid a desk job, he joined the Royal Flying Corps and was killed in a dogfight in 1917.[11]

Nor were Christ's men remote from the new technology of mass warfare of the twentieth century. Thus, William Livens, a civil engineer who matriculated in 1908, joined the Special Companies and devised an early flamethrower for use on the Somme in 1916. But its cost (it required a ton of fuel for a ten-second shot) meant that it was only fired ten times. He was also involved in the invention of 'The Livens Projector' which was cheaper to operate, though not very accurate, and was widely used during military engagements in 1917–18.[12]

Altogether, when the war memorial was unveiled in the Chapel in 1921, it contained 114 names (a memorial to College servants was also unveiled in the kitchens).[13] By that time, however, it may be assumed that, whatever the poignancy of the event, memories of the horrors of war were ceasing to be influential among those who had not fought. In any case, peace had brought new problems – mostly economic – and they, too, demanded untraditional solutions.

*

During the war retail prices doubled and national wages had grown by a little more than that. In the boom of 1919, national prices and wages rose by 15 per cent. But in 1920, as prices fell back, wages continued to rise to a level some 30 per cent above that of 1918. They then tumbled by 25 per cent in the next two years as a harsh slump followed an artificial boom.

Obviously, Christ's could not escape the resulting pressures, and in October 1919 – a year marked by great turbulence in industrial relations – the Governing Body took a remarkably 'progressive' step for the time: it appointed a consultative committee of three Fellows and three servants to discuss employment, living costs, and wages, and (in a coy but telling phrase) 'to monitor harmony' between the authorities and the College servants. Paternal radicalism now flourished: servants' wages were increased substantially in December 1919 and again in the spring of 1920; hesitant deliberations with trade unions were initiated; and new wage structures were actually discussed with the putative recipients, through the 'Servants' Council'. Nevertheless, wages followed prices down in 1922–3. Final power still lay with Governing Body, but it was now tempered by University-wide agreements and sensitivity to the realities of local industrial relations. In 1922 the College even introduced an employees' pension scheme, involving wage deductions of 3.5 per cent and an equal contribution by the College.

Like the country as a whole, in spite of the need to accept

extraordinary changes in monetary values and management policies, the College survived the huge swings in economic activity and price levels that ushered in the peace, and became somewhat less paternalistic in the process. Novelty was clearly in the air.

In a longer-term perspective, however, Christ's (except in the matter of student numbers) underwent only relatively modest changes in the quarter century after 1914 – although in some cases (for example, the University-wide and unofficial abandonment of compulsory chapel during the war)[14] dedicated traditionalists might not have agreed. The fact of the matter was that the College, like others, possessed resources and a social role that insulated it from the more drastic upheavals associated with the Great War and its aftermath, and enabled it to resist many adverse winds. But some bending was necessary – as with the doubling of student numbers between 1914 and 1919, in line with national trends.[15] As the *Cambridge Review* of January 1919 argued: 'The life of new Cambridge should differ but little from the old. There is not much to be altered. It must be more strenuous. It must be more serious . . . It must be more progressive.'[16] Indeed, 'more strenuous . . . more serious . . . more progressive' might serve as a motto for the College's history – or at least its aspirations – in the first half of the twentieth century.

The glimmerings of new attitudes were exemplified not only in growth, but also in an enhanced awareness of demands for change in the world of the two ancient universities and (more decisively) in responses to fundamental economic pressures.

I have already mentioned the limited effect on collegiate autonomy of the Royal Commission of 1919–22. For example, the Governing Body resisted such proposed changes in the Fellowship as the appointment of more non-stipendiary Fellows or the external control of room rents. Nevertheless, the College was persuaded into a greater emphasis on research, a progressive pensions scheme, and a more businesslike approach to catering.

At the same time, peer-group pressures enforced a more outgoing and cooperative attitude to other colleges. In November 1919, for example, Christ's had already agreed to regular intercollegiate meetings to discuss closing hours and naval-officer students (one of whom was the young Louis Mountbatten, an avid debater, who quickly moved on from the Milton Society to the Union). In April 1921 the Governing Body voted to support the Vice-Chancellor of Oxford in a curiously effete attempt to ban athletics competitions between Oxford and Cambridge Colleges – hardly a more strenuous, but certainly a more serious, step. And in the same year the College stewards (following a recommendation of the Royal Commission) met to arrange matters of mutual concern and to employ business consultants – moves financed by a levy of threepence per resident student. On the other hand, it is reported that when a new, and surely harmless, committee of tutorial representatives was set up, the Master, Sir Arthur Shipley, an atavistically reassuring voice from a previous generation, commented that Cambridge was gradually passing under the rule of a Soviet government.[17] Fraternal influences were also at work: in 1932 the College initiated an enduring link by authorizing a 'Treaty of Friendship' with Wadham College, Oxford – awarding dining and combination-room rights to the Fellows of Wadham, in spite of 'the very real difficulties' that beset Christ's in that nadir of the slump.

Introspection was, therefore, being slowly eroded, and economic pressures introduced a more insistent note. But that note was occasionally ambiguous. This was exemplified in the effects of the extensive changes in the structure and performance of the British economy throughout the interwar years. Stagnation threatened Britain's manufacturing core. Coal, iron and steel, heavy engineering, and textiles – admittedly not themselves prominent features of the Fenland economy – all declined; and unemployment stood at 12 per cent in the 1921 slump, about 8 per cent throughout the 1920s, and (after a peak of 17 per cent in 1932) remained above 10 per cent for most of the 1930s.[18] On the other hand, the College was part of the growing service economy, which benefited from structural changes. The point is that a large part of the College's income consisted of student fees and room rents and service charges. Even its 'external revenue' was dominated by rents for land and houses – which accounted for two-thirds of the total in 1919–20 and was still some half of the greater figure for 'external revenue' in 1936–37.

Apparently, then, as long as the College chose its property investments wisely and was not too charitable towards tenants and students, it was protected against penury. Unfortunately, owing to the antediluvian opacity of collegiate accounts, the specific consequences of all this for the College are not obvious, but some generalizations are possible.

First, the College's general income actually rose by 50 per cent during the long-run deflation between 1919 and 1920 and from 1936 to 1937.[19] Second, in policy terms, there was an increasing alertness to the need for more businesslike attitudes and 'economistic' internal management, which was reflected in the wording of the statutes. Those of 1915 specified that the College Council's role was 'to control the educational business of the College', whereas the new statutes of 1926 contained the injunction to manage the estates, income, expenditure and educational business of the College (apparently in that order). And in the same year, the Governing Body established two reserve funds (one for buildings and the other to underwrite fellowships), which were fed fairly generously over the next decade. By 1935 they stood at £34,000 and £38,000 respectively.[20]

The new attitudes were evident at lower levels as well. A much more systematic costing of and charges for meals and services (for Fellows as well as students) was introduced. In 1921 the kitchen manager's contract offered a 10 per cent commission on the first £1,000 of the profits of the kitchen and buttery. And in May 1939, with a still politically correct commercialism, the steward was authorized to join the tobacco traders' association, display advertisements for Players' cigarettes, and secure bonuses on sales for the College. On the other hand, in November 1923 the Governing Body (in an intriguing anticipation of the controversy about top-up fees) opposed the Royal Commission's suggestion that students pay economic rents, on the grounds that this would handicap and could even exclude poorer undergraduates.

In spite of all this, and partly as the average cost of a fellowship rose, prudence remained the watchword. In 1935, for example, the Senior Tutor, Sydney Grose, issued a profit warning to the Governing Body. Proposals to increase the Fellowship by one or two, he argued, should only be pursued if the reserve fund were increased. And (an even more telling indication of the times) he warned that market conditions made a continued decline in asset values very likely. As a result, he urged, it would be unwise to move even a modest proportion of the fellowships fund out of cash into investments (which, not unwisely after a period of deflation, then accounted for the very low proportion of one-sixth of the reserve).[21]

As suggested above, it may well be that Christ's even

benefited from structural change. Nevertheless, the College was a complex economic entity, being an investor, a consumer and an employer. As such, it had to come to terms with changes in profits, prices, wages and industrial relations, just as the Governing Body had occasionally to acknowledge the nature of social ills: as happened when it hired unemployed men to help in the development of the new Third Court in 1921. Yet there were no signs of corporate economic distress – a fact partly explained by the Governing Body's reluctance to assume commitments not matched by guaranteed sources of income. In 1923, for example, a benefaction from the American banker J. P. Morgan (a good friend of the Master's, Sir Arthur Shipley, and an honorary member of the College) enabled the College to proceed immediately to the creation of an additional fellowship. Yet it took seven unsentimental years before Sir Arthur Shipley's own testamentary bequest of £5,500 to found a fellowship (1927) was judged to have accumulated sufficiently to warrant its creation.

A more important consideration was that the College's dependence on sources of fixed income could be an advantage in a period of falling prices and weak wages. Thus, after the inflation of the Great War, the purchasing power of College income and Fellows' dividends rose as retail prices sagged by 40 per cent between 1919 and 1932, and increased only marginally until 1938 – a trend magnified by the increase in the College's total money income during this period.

In any event, by the mid-1930s the economy was experiencing a modest recovery and (as will be described later) the College's finances were sufficiently healthy for a major building programme to be contemplated. In December 1936, when the Governing Body detected a significant annual surplus in the collegiate accounts, it even charged the Council with the drawing up of a plan to spend it. Soon, however, the threat of another major war loomed, bringing with it very different preoccupations.

*

Christ's was forced to acknowledge few of the premonitory developments of the years before the outbreak of the Second World War. An exception was the offer of a modicum of hospitality to German refugees (just as the College had welcomed and supported refugee students from Belgium, Russia and Serbia during the Great War and immediately afterwards). More tellingly, the new character of the times was prefigured in the death of Ivor Hickman, a metallurgist who went down in 1936 and in September 1938, not yet twenty-five, was killed fighting in the International Brigade in Spain – one of the last of its members to die in battle.[22]

In the event, the Second World War itself was possibly a more intrusive event for Christ's than the First had been. The number of members killed was roughly the same: the 1939–45 War Memorial contains 117 names, as against the 114 of 1914–18. But it is very likely that by the 1940s the nature of total war and its consequences for civilian life, together with the ideological overtones of the conflict, meant that its experience was felt more keenly and continuously.

As in 1914–18, members of the College both joined the forces and (in the case of seven Fellows) went into various forms of non-combatant war service.[23] But in 1939 to 1945 the non-combatant contribution seems more critical, whether in the upper reaches of the Civil Service (C. P. Snow), or scientific warfare and policy (Sir Charles Darwin), or in the code-breaking community at Bletchley. This last recruited Jack Plumb, a

former research student and future Fellow, and Charles Allberry, the brilliant but neurotic Orientalist, who was the model
for C. P. Snow's Roy Calvert, and later volunteered for aircrew.
The Second World War was wrong, Allberry had written in
1940, but 'I should, and shall, fight when I have to – (because
no gentleman can refuse to fight really when it comes to the
point for his native land) . . . I feel myself to be . . . under
sentence of death'.[24] A poignant prophecy – Allberry was killed
during a bombing raid on Essen in 1943.

Within Cambridge, the disruptive impact of war was also
more tangible than it had been a quarter-century earlier. Com-
pensation was secured from a chastened Air Ministry, which
had despoiled the College playing fields without prior permission. College accommodation and hospitality were provided
for service officers throughout the conflict, and for 150 students
and 36 staff of the School of Oriental and African Studies
in the first year of the war.[25] In preparations for emergencies
the College accumulated food stocks, laid plans to shelter one
hundred people in the buttery cellars, and anticipated feeding
and providing bathing facilities for up to two hundred civilians.
Air-raid shelters were erected in the Garden, an observer's post
topped the seventeenth-century Fellows' Building, and senior
and junior members took their turns on the rosters for fire-
watching. Elaborate arrangements were made for collective
meals, including the ingenious creation of 'eating groups' which
pooled their points and rations.[26]

In 1946, the Master looked back at the war: 'the abiding
memory is of the extraordinary loyalty, friendliness and zest
with which everyone, seniors and juniors alike, carried on.
We were all overworked; sirens and black-out, ration cards
and queues, fire-watching and parades, a hectic present and an

uncertain future played havoc with our nerves; but the College maintained its quality, and in certain directions at least improved its status.'[27]

Of course, the war was not simply a matter of physical inconvenience and novel management tasks. The very nature of the University was changed as the practical aspects of education came to the fore. Cambridge, in the words of the *College Magazine*, was to be 'organized for direct national service' – snobbishly characterized by the editor as the 'threatened encroachment of the technical-college ethos'.[28] With an unappealing mix of pomposity and panic, the *Magazine* argued that wartime circumstances were transitory and warned of the danger of degrading the College to the level of 'a penny-in-the-slot training centre'.[29]

Yet the war (in College as for the nation) was also an occasion for rather deeper thoughts on society and the future. In 1943, for example, the *College Magazine* pointed out that there was much very active discussion of science and religion – no doubt influenced by the magisterial preoccupations of Charles Raven. A 'returning exile' found that debate was now not about the war but the 'future peace'. Despite 'plenty of service training', he found 'plenty of visionary discussion as well, and, despite the youthfulness, there is often a strange maturity to be detected in the questions asked'.[30]

*

'Maturity', of course, might also mean 'modernization'. It is appropriate, therefore, to ask how far Christ's experience in these years reshaped it into a community more obviously familiar to modern eyes.

Superficially, it can be argued that the College of the 1940s would have been very familiar to the generation of 1914–15 – more so, perhaps, than to the generation of 1974–5, let alone 2004–5. Yet, as we have seen, there had already been important changes – in academic governance, intercollegiate cooperation, financial management, industrial relations, and assumptions about size and accommodation. Beyond this, the outlook and activities of the Fellowship also reflected the themes and issues of modern academic life. This was in part the case with the growing importance of science among the Fellowship (culminating in the eager search for science Fellows in the 1940s and the election of the future Nobel Laureate, Alexander (later Lord) Todd in 1944). But it was also exemplified in the broader-based, even worldly, outlook of C. P. Snow (Fellow from 1930); and perhaps pre-eminently in the vigorous activities of Charles Raven.

Certainly, such 'modern' intellectual controversies as surround issues of war and peace, science and the humanities, religion and secularism could not have been alien to the High Table. In terms of the collegiate community, however, the more everyday manifestations of modernity are more telling: the acceptance of new technology, and the social incorporation (however hesitantly) of less privileged groups.

Technological progress was exemplified by a number of innovative, if halting, decisions. A public telephone was installed in 1921, when students (other than club secretaries) were to be charged 1.5 old pence per call. A so-called 'radio mast' to 'receive wireless messages' was erected on the Fellows' Building in May 1922. Electric lights were put up in Third Court in 1921 (although the 1933 experiment of two electric pendants in the Chapel was abandoned as a failure). In May 1935 the Governing Body decided to construct a garage for Fellows' cars behind the Stevenson Building, although it took eighteen months before an estimate (£65.5s for four car spaces) was obtained. And in April 1948, in a symbolic tuning in to *real* modernity, the College accepted the gift of two television sets.

Of course, technological devices do not exist in a social and cultural vacuum. Unfortunately, however, nothing is recorded about the context and social usage of these slivers of progress. On the other hand, there were some material innovations that reflect a little more explicitly on everyday aspects of social change. In 1938 it was decided to construct bathrooms *inside* the Fellows' Building (rather than challengingly nearby, as first envisaged) – and to charge Fellows for the luxury. Indeed, 1938 was something of a landmark year for sanitary engineering. In response to insistent demands from students, plans were accepted for a 'ladies' room' in College (hitherto an embarrassing lacuna). At the same time it was decided to construct a lavatory for kitchen staff (surely an even more disturbing omission) – although that was subsequently, and unhealthily, postponed. Later in the same year it was agreed to enlarge the student lavatories in Second Court. Two years later, as the war got under way, it was decided to install bathrooms and basins in the Stevenson Building (built in 1888–9). But in an unwitting disincentive to bathing, gas fires did not become universal in College rooms until 1947–8.

In themselves, these rather prosaic examples of improved plumbing are possibly of antiquarian concern. But they had some larger significance, for they were in part associated with the slow-growing but inexorable influence of two minority interest groups in twentieth-century higher education: students and women.

At the level of student politics, Christ's seems to have shared the general University attitudes – insofar as these can be gleaned from union debates and newspaper articles. Hostility to trade unions in the turbulent aftermath of the Great War elided into mild resentment at the General Strike of 1926, and enthusiasm for the opportunities it offered for 'a gigantic and well-timed rag', in the words of an article in the *College Magazine*. The 'haste to volunteer was less from lack of sympathy with the individual striker than anxiety not to be left out of the fun' or 'a wish to escape from the ordeal of the examination room, while even the most hardened socialism was apt to break down before the lure of realizing at last a latent but long-cherished desire to drive a real train'.[31] On the other hand, during the 1930s the broad hostility towards socialism of the previous decade rapidly gave way to more mixed feelings (one Christ's undergraduate wrote to *Varsity* in 1937 to protest at the 'noisy demonstrations' and heckling of lecturers in history and economics).[32] Pacifism and appeasement, although hardly majority views, found their advocates. Yet even here, as the threat of totalitarianism mounted in the 1930s, attitudes hardened towards a patriotic if not always an ideological firmness, and Union debates became increasingly critical of the government. In the summer of 1939, the *College Magazine* carried an article advocating conscription on the grounds that 'defence is not merely a professional occupation for those who like it, but a national duty to be borne by everyone'.[33]

But the typicality or significance of these views cannot be easily determined. More certain is that throughout this period, students rarely intruded into the administration and policy-making of the College, just as they are hardly prominent in Snow's novels. Nevertheless, some faint premonitions of a new situation could be detected in the late 1930s and during the war years.

In 1938, for example, the *College Magazine* published a student

article provocatively entitled 'Shall I send my son to Christ's?'
It voiced complaints about what were delicately described as
'awkward situations' arising from the absence of ladies' lavatory
facilities, as well as about the lack of a College nurse, cooking
facilities, hot water, and adequate furniture and carpets.[34] Such
pressures persuaded the Governing Body to approve plans to
install a ladies' room and improved bathing facilities in Second
Court, and to discuss the appointment of a College nurse
(although an appointment was not made until 1948), as well as
to begin the much-needed reform of the College's plumbing.

The war loosened student inhibitions even more, but after a
slightly more determined push at the door, it remained effectively closed for three decades. In the Michaelmas Term of 1939
Christ's was the first Cambridge college to form a Students'
Representative Council.[35] Symptomatically, the Council's first
act was to raise the matter of catering – that evergreen topic
of student dissatisfaction, but now flavoured by the advent of
rationing. The innocuous (and predictable) outcome was no
more than an interview with the Bursar; and the prospective
next moves towards a larger arena – collegiate membership of
the Undergraduate Council (a University-wide pressure group)
and contact with the National Union of Students – came to
nothing.

It may well have been that these developments lacked
spontaneity. Looking back to the war years, the Master, with an
overtone of worldly condescension, described the Students' Representative Council as 'a product of the sojourn in Cambridge
of the London School of Economics, and commonly supposed
to be a Soviet for the liquidation of dons. Its executive met on
Mondays; planned revolutions until 10 p.m.; and then adjourned
to my study to discuss how to proceed.'[36]

In fact, by 1941 the Council had disaffiliated from the University Undergraduate Council,[37] and its main job was seen as carrying forward ideas and proposals recorded in a formerly despised suggestions book. As the war drew to a close, student opinion found its outlet neither in political activism nor in the advocacy of structural reform, but in domestic business: a Junior Combination Committee was established in the Lent Term of 1945[38] and the student body settled down to the rather complacent insularity which for decades separated Oxbridge collegiate opinion from the larger movements of national student life.

Compared with trends in the position of students, the role of women in Cambridge was much more virulently controversial. At the University level, and as early as the First World War, the exclusion of women from full membership was already seen by many as scandalous. The scandal was compounded in 1921, when the vote admitting them to degrees but denying them full membership of the University led to triumphalist riots in the streets.

At Christ's, the atmosphere was no better than in most colleges. Admittedly, when Alfred Haddon FRS, the Reader in Ethnology, retired in 1925, women attended the dinner in his honour – reputedly the first time that females (presumably other than royalty and their ladies-in-waiting) had dined in a men's college hall in Cambridge.[39] But as we have seen, the installation of a lavatory for lady guests was slow in arriving, and when staff members of the School of Oriental and African Studies were given High Table rights in October 1939, those of the two women members of the school were restricted to lunch![40] Only in 1943 could women be seen regularly in Hall for the first time – as waitresses.[41] And in June 1948 the Governing Body ruled that if ladies attended private parties, a screen should be erected to protect the susceptibilities of High Table diners. But in October 1948 it did approve (with one dissenting vote) of a 'ladies dinner', with each Fellow allowed two guests.

*

Finally, around mid-century the College awoke to the need to match its physical as well as its institutional facilities to the substantial expansion in student numbers. Modernization (in the unlikely shape of the Third Court) had become an architectural issue.

The modern Third Court had begun to take shape in 1920–21, when the wall around the Master's orchard was taken down, electric lights erected, and a sunken lawn created and the ground levelled with the help of unemployed men.[42] In the late 1920s, the growth in numbers led to an expansion of Hall facilities, as the wall between the old combination room and the gallery was pierced. This allowed the entire College to dine in two sittings.[43] But the principal development of the College's facilities in these years came with the construction of buildings to complete the Third Court as we now see it.

Plans for such a large-scale development had been first seriously mooted in 1934. Reflecting the somewhat paradoxical position of a relatively wealthy College in a troubled national economy, the Council reported that the College's finances – notably the growth in the special reserve fund – made it feasible to build forty undergraduate sets at a cost of £32,000 (later increased to £40,000). But almost two years passed before it was agreed to locate a new building along the Hobson Street side of the Third Court. Surprisingly, the choice of architect settled adventurously on Walter Gropius, one of the founders of the Bauhaus and a leading representative of the Modern Movement.

A refugee from Hitler's Germany, he spent two years in the United Kingdom before moving on to America in 1937.

This was a courageous, and certainly a dramatic, decision for Christ's College. The proposed building had a number of practical advantages: abundant space and comfortable amenities for student sets, plenty of light, a potential income from shops to be developed on the ground floor, and the benefits of a landscaped area created by setting the building at an angle to Hobson Street. But this ultra-modern building proved too adventurous for the Governing Body's collective taste. On 2 March 1937 Gropius was invited into the Combination Room to explain his designs in person. After he left, a motion to appoint him as 'architect of the new building forthwith' was lost by thirteen votes to eight. An amendment proposing Sir Giles Gilbert Scott (who had already done Memorial Court at Clare and the new University Library) was then carried by fourteen to five. But the modernists were not finished. No approach was made to Scott and on 11 May the Governing Body, still bitterly divided, decided to 'postpone building for the present' and to disband the buildings committee.

Nothing further was done until the austere postwar years, when accommodation was needed not so much for any potential growth in the size of the student body, as to house more undergraduates within the College. In 1947 the Professor of Architecture at University College London, Edward Richardson, who was also an Honorary Fellow, was commissioned to design a new block. This became the Chancellor's Building, an altogether more traditional structure, along the side of the Fellows' Garden. It was opened in 1950, at a cost of £80,000, or about double the estimate for Gropius's building in the mid-1930s. Richardson was then commissioned to design a second and similar building on the other side of Third Court, near Hobson Street – known as the Memorial Building – thus finally enclosing the court on three sides with buildings and on the fourth side with the wall of the Master's Garden.

In later years there were those who deeply regretted the lost opportunity of having a Gropius building at Christ's. In an unusually critical article in the *College Magazine* of 1953 Richardson's neo-Georgian design was described as 'unsatisfying, and . . . uncomfortable, perhaps because it lacks conviction'. It was said to hanker after the past without assurance – whereas Gropius's design was praised as being unashamedly modern and a contribution to the enhancement of Hobson Street.[44] Naturally, there were vigorous defenders of the Richardson buildings – although one acknowledged that the absence of central heating was 'an incredible anachronism' and (not anticipating the insatiable need for car parking) regretted that the second building had left a 'squalid triangle of desert' behind it. Nevertheless the case for the defence rested on the still-to-be-proved assertion that Richardson's buildings 'are, and will be in a century, more satisfying than a monument of the transient phase which the Gropius design so typified'.[45]

With the opening of the first of Richardson's buildings in 1950 a chapter in the College's history was closed and another opened. Symbolic of this transition was that a recently elected Fellow, and future Master, the youthful Jack Plumb, took the lead in planning and overseeing the amenities of the new building.

This was more than a matter of symbolism. Christ's had come through the war without disastrous or even troubling disruption. On 16 April 1948 the entire College celebrated the quincentenary of the founding of God's House, having initiated a major building enterprise based upon a healthy financial position. And it is not perhaps too fanciful to see the replacement of the Gropius design as reflecting that mixture of traditionalism and cautious, securely based expansionism that had characterized the College as it came to terms, however haltingly, with economic, social and educational trends in the twentieth century.

Those trends surrounded the College – however remotely and indirectly – with violence and destruction, political and ideological upheaval, social uproar, human misery, and technical transformation. Hence, although the collegiate community, and many fortunate individuals, experienced the twentieth century in a relatively low key, there were other, and grimmer, stories. After all, individual men and women experience the grand themes of history in different ways. In any period of drastic change, some people (as was argued in the editorial of the *College Magazine* of 1945 quoted at the beginning of this chapter) 'shape the course of events' and move the world around them. Others suffer and are shocked into tragic despair or are killed. Others find their lives beneficially transformed. And yet others adjust their ways, without revolution, while 'watching from within the coming of the new'.[46] In the event, such a huge range of experience and reaction was exemplified, however unevenly, in the community and membership of Christ's College throughout these troubled decades.

NOTES

1. I have three debts of gratitude: to Rhiannon Thompson, who contributed so much, and so cheerfully, to the basic research while so preoccupied with her own doctorate; to Chris Moore-Bick, who

scoured the archives to fill some worrying gaps in my own knowledge; and to David Reynolds, for his firm but friendly editorial guidance.

2. *Christ's College Magazine* (henceforth *CCM*) 161 (1945), 85. Where dates are given with no further reference the source is the Governing Body minutes for that year.

3. C. P. Snow, *The Light and the Dark* (Thirsk, 2001, first published 1947), p. 267.

4. College Archives, paper dated 17 February 1935 and initialled S.C.G in folder 'Gropius and Royal Commission'.

5. Guy Routh, *Occupation and Pay in Great Britain, 1906–79* (London, 1980); see figures on pp. 63 and 70: e.g., averages 1935-7, solicitors £1,238, dentists £676, GPs £1,094, unweighted average of higher professions £741. Qualified male teachers earned £348 a year, female teachers £265 and veterinary inspectors £548.

6. See for instance *Evolution and the Christian Concept of God* (1936) and *Science, Religion and the Future* (1943).

7. *CCM* 86 (1914), 1–2, 3–15.

8. Conscription was imposed in January 1916.

9. *CCM* 90 (1916), 43–5.

10. Ibid.

11. *CCM* 87 (1915), 70–1 (McVittie); *CCM* 89 (1915), 10 (Kelleher); *CCM* 90 (1916), 55–6 (Standen); and *CCM* 91 (1916–17), 17–18 (Black).

12. Lawrence Haber, *The Poisonous Cloud: Chemical Warfare in the First World War* (Oxford, 1986), p. 120; see also Donald Richter, *Chemical Soldiers: British Gas Warfare in World War I* (Lawrence, Kansas, 1992).

13. Just over 2,000 university men were killed in the war, and 3,000 were wounded. T. E. B. Howarth, *Cambridge between Two Wars* (London, 1978), p. 16.

14. C. N. L. Brooke, *A History of the University of Cambridge*, vol. 4 (1993), p. 113.

15. 20,000 in 1900–1, 42,000 in 1924–5, 50,000 in 1938–9, and 82,000 in 1954–5. See A. H. Halsey (ed.), *Trends in British Society since 1900* (1972), p. 206.

16. Quoted in Howarth, *Cambridge between Two Wars*, p. 57.

17. Ibid, p. 61.

18. C. H. Feinstein, *Statistical Tables of National Income, Expenditure and Output of the U.K., 1855–1965* (Cambridge, 1976), T128.

19. That is from just under £22,000 in 1919–20 to just over £33,000 in

1936–7. College Archives: paper dated 17 Feb. 1935 and initialled S.C.G in folder 'Gropius and Royal Commission'; *The Reporter*, 24 Jan. 1938.

20. Paper of 17 Feb. 1935.
21. Ibid.
22. *CCM* 144 (1939), 47.
23. *CCM* 163 (1946), 5.
24. Patricia K. G. Lewis (ed.), *Charles Allberry (1911–43): A Portrait* (1984), p. 17.
25. The director of SOAS, Professor R. L. Turner, was a former Fellow of Christ's.
26. *CCM* 156 (1943), 38–40.
27. *CCM* 163 (1946), 6.
28. *CCM* 151 (1941), 117–18.
29. *CCM* 152 (1941), 1–2.
30. *CCM* 156 (1943), 40.
31. *CCM* 109 (1926), 280–1.
32. *Varsity Weekly*, 30 Oct. 1937.
33. *CCM* 145 (1939), 71–2.
34. *CCM* 141 (1938), 31–2.
35. *CCM* 147 (1940), 49–50.
36. *CCM* 163 (1946), 6.
37. *CCM* 151 (1941), 148–9.
38. *CCM* 161 (1945), 86.
39. *Dictionary of National Biography, 1931–40* (London, 1949), pp. 383–4.
40. *CCM* 163 (1946), 4.
41. *CCM* 156 (1943), 38.
42. The irises came later – they were planted in October 1946 as a gift from Mrs C. G. Seligman.
43. At the same time the Combination Room was moved to what had been the Master's Study, behind High Table.
44. *CCM* 177 (1953), 8–12.
45. *CCM* 178 (1954), 8–9. In the account in *CCM* 228 (2003), 100, Y block is said to proceede W (the Chancellor's Building) rather than the other way round.
46. *CCM* 161 (1945), 85.

PART SIX

THE COLLEGE BY 1953

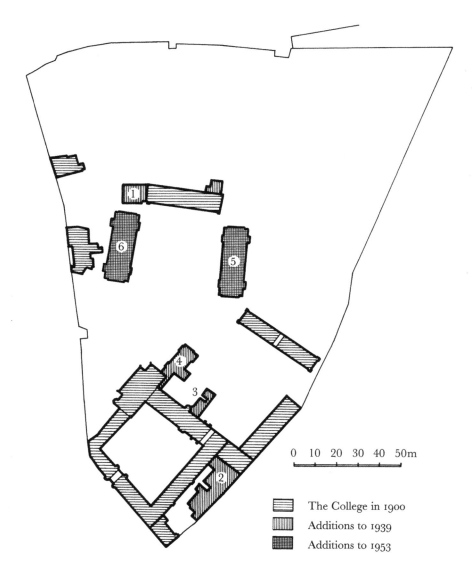

0 10 20 30 40 50m

The College in 1900

Additions to 1939

Additions to 1953

1 – Quatercentenary addition to Stevenson Building (1905)

2 – Bath House Court (1913)   3 – Extension to Fellows' Rooms (1928)

4 – Extension to Master's Lodge (1936)   5 – Chancellor's Building (1950)

6 – Memorial Building (1953)

WHEN QUEEN ELIZABETH visited Christ's on 21 October 1948, as part of the celebrations for the Quincentenary of God's House, the College was in transition from the war years. Rationing was still in force – including meat, petrol and clothing – and there was a large bulge of older students whose (formal) education had been deferred by the war. But the next two decades saw dramatic changes in university education throughout Britain, from which Christ's could not remain unaffected and for which the cautious progressivism described by Barry Supple was no longer appropriate.

In 1937 Britain had 21 universities; a quarter-century later the number had more than doubled – as had the student body, to well over 100,000. In the 1960s a new system of government grants replaced the piecemeal mix of state, county and university scholarships. The national expansion was replicated in Cambridge, with new colleges such as Churchill, Fitzwilliam and New Hall, and a proliferation of departmental buildings west of the River Cam, including the new Cavendish Laboratory along the Madingley Road and a Humanities and Social Science enclave off Sidgwick Avenue.

National Service was not abolished until 1958 and the last ex-conscripts came up in 1960. After two years of austerity, drill and regimentation, the restraints of College life seemed mild, or at least easily circumvented, to men of the Fifties. But the Sixties generation entered Cambridge without that background, and with a televisual awareness of the worldwide protest movements of the era. Early targets for Cambridge radicals were gate hours, guest rules and the wearing of gowns. Demands for student representation on college and university committees followed, and the Cambridge University Student Union (CUSU) was created in 1970. That February saw the notorious 'Garden House Riot' when a demonstration against the Greek junta got out of hand, resulting in serious injuries, substantial damage to the Garden House Hotel and six students being sent to prison.

Intellectually, Cambridge was also near the centre of national life in a way that had not been true since the Reformation. But now the dynamism came not from religion but from research, especially technocratic science and the humanities backlash. This was the era of Todd, Plumb and Snow – the most striking and influential triumvirate of the College's long history.

David Cannadine

The Era of Todd, Plumb and Snow

IN 1951, MACMILLAN published an unusual novel, set just before the Second World War, which was solely concerned with the fiercely fought election of the head of a Cambridge college – scarcely, one would have thought, a topic of general public interest or widespread contemporary concern.[1] With insight grounded in experience, the author depicted the claustrophobic atmosphere of 'closed politics' and factional manoeuvring, he described the 'knifing', 'infighting' and 'gang-warfare' of the Fellows, and he vividly evoked the thwarted ambitions, the disappointed hopes and the vengeful instincts that were such potent forces throughout the contest.[2] Only in a brief appendix did he rise above these parochial squabbles and bitter personal feelings to take a slightly broader view of things. The College, he noted, had been in existence for many centuries, and its buildings, officers and rituals were eloquent witness to its authentic antiquity. Yet in many ways, he insisted, such historic continuity was little more than a façade, behind which change had been constantly occurring, and especially during the last one hundred and fifty years. Like the novel which it framed and contextualized, this appendix was an insider's account of a very small world.[3] But the book became a bestseller (and later a successful stage play), it consolidated the author's reputation as a writer of 'relevant' and 'realistic' fiction, and it established a lasting and influential image of the College itself, which endured almost down to our own time. The novel was *The Masters*, the author was C. P. Snow and, although he disclaimed it in a too-much-protesting preface, the college was unmistakably Christ's – both in terms of its topography and also, more controversially, of its personnel.[4]

For more than a generation thereafter, *The Masters* was avidly read – by sixth-formers heading to a Cambridge (and even an Oxford) interview, by new Fellows of Christ's anxious to learn about their colleagues and the arcane post-prandial rituals of the combination room and, indeed, by anyone interested in academic life in the poison-ivory tower. Yet in many ways, Snow's picture of the College polarized around a Mastership election was misleadingly partial, with the Fellows so fixated on politics and personalities, and so addicted to drink (beginning with chablis at 11 a.m., and ending with whisky twelve hours later), that they had hardly the time (or the capacity) for teaching or research, let alone for any broader participation in public affairs. This was scarcely accurate in 1951, and it became even less so during the next decade. For by the 1960s, three College men were exceptionally well known in the greater world beyond Petty Cury: Snow himself, as a novelist, pundit and (briefly) government minister; Alex Todd, as a colossus of chemistry and statesman of science; and J. H. Plumb as a widely read historian and contemporary commentator. Together, they brought the College to public notice in a way that not even Field Marshal Jan Christian Smuts, Admiral Lord Louis Mountbatten and Sir Charles Darwin had quite done during the 1940s.[5] *That* illustrious trio had provided leadership and scholarship during the dark and difficult days of war; but they were rarely identified or linked together as Christ's men. By contrast, it fell to Snow, Todd and Plumb to provide leadership and scholarship in a no-less challenging era of peace, prosperity and anxiety, and the fact that they belonged to the same Cambridge college was often remarked upon. This, then, is an essay about the three men who were the public face of Christ's during one of the most highly profiled periods in its long history.

*

They were born within a few years of each other – Snow in 1905, Todd in 1907, and Plumb in 1911 – and as such, they belonged to what Noel Annan, following Maurice Bowra, called 'our age', by which he meant that generation of clever, well-educated Britons who grew up between the end of the First World War and the late 1940s, who thereafter joined what became known as 'the Establishment', and who wielded power and influence until the advent of Margaret Thatcher in 1979.[6] But in one significant way, this characterization is inappropriate. Most of the men about whom Annan wrote (and they *were* nearly all *men*) boasted metropolitan connections, came from upper-middle-class backgrounds, were educated at public school, and went on to Oxford, Cambridge or the LSE as undergraduates. By contrast, Snow, Todd and Plumb were very much outsiders: geographically (they were provincials), sociologically (their family circumstances were modest) and educationally (they were grammar school boys, who stayed at home for their first degrees). Todd was born in Glasgow, Snow and Plumb in Leicester. Todd's father was a clerk in a railway company, Snow's held a similar position in a shoe factory, and Plumb's worked on the shop floor in the same trade. All three attended their local grammar school: Todd went to Allan Glen's, and both Snow and Plumb to Alderman Newton's, where they were taught by an inspirational mentor, H. E. Howard.[7] Thereafter, Todd studied at Glasgow University, and Snow and Plumb enrolled at their local university college. They all obtained firsts. Snow reached Cambridge as a research student at Christ's in 1928; Todd went to Frankfurt for his first doctorate in 1929, and went on to Oxford in 1931; and Plumb followed Snow to Christ's in 1934.[8]

This account of their early careers might suggest that inter-war Britain was a more mobile society than it is sometimes fashionable to think, as these three young men of talent and ability made their way on their merits. But compared with most members of 'our age', theirs was scarcely a gilded path. They came up the hard way, and they were appropriately hungry for recognition and success. When Snow became a peer, he took as his motto *Aut Inveniam Viam Aut Faciam*, which translates as 'I will either find a way out or make one'. He had cherished these words as 'a brilliant boy from the Midlands', who was 'in relentless pursuit of fame', and as a description of youthful ambitions and aspirations, they apply with equal appropriateness to Todd and Plumb.[9] Not surprisingly, the themes of class and social mobility loom very large in Snow's later novels, especially in the case of Lewis Eliot, a thinly disguised version of himself, who is determined not to die unknown; and the conquest of provincial obscurity is a major subject in Plumb's life of Walpole, where the rustic, home-spun Norfolk squire transforms himself into a national figure and European statesman. And in Todd's case, such ambitions were given an additional edge (and also a helping hand?) when he married Alison Dale in 1937. For her father was Sir Henry Dale – a future Nobel Laureate and President of the Royal Society, a member of the British Order of Merit and holder of the German equivalent, Pour Le Merite. The young Alex Todd was determined to equal the achievements of his father-in-law – something which, eventually, he duly (and proudly) did.[10]

But this is to anticipate. From Oxford, where he worked on the structure of colouring matter in flowers, Todd moved on to Edinburgh, London and Pasadena, and in 1938 he was appointed Professor of Chemistry at Manchester University when only in his early thirties. Much of his work was on the structures of vitamins B1 and E, and he established a reputation as an outstanding leader of research, with a good eye for a big problem, and with a growing range of international academic connections. Snow took his PhD in 1930, and was elected a Fellow of Christ's in the same year. He revelled in being in Cambridge in the heroic age of Rutherford, he thought young scientists like Bernal and Blackett were progressive, meritocratic optimists, who could transform the world for the better, and he hoped that he, too, might make a big name for himself.[11] But his work was of uneven quality, it was never truly outstanding, and in 1932 he suffered a major setback, when his much-trumpeted claims to have synthesized vitamin A turned out to have been based on faulty calculations and misleading results.[12] By then, indeed, he had already turned to fiction, publishing three books in the first half of the decade; and in 1935 he conceived an ambitious novel cycle, entitled *Strangers and Brothers*, the first instalment of which appeared in 1940, based largely on the character of H. E. Howard. Plumb, meanwhile, began research under Professor George Macaulay Trevelyan into the social structure of the House of Commons during the late seventeenth century. But although he shared his mentor's belief that history must be a liberal, public enterprise, he was also much in awe of Lewis Namier's atomistic approach to the past, and this was reflected in his highly derivative dissertation. He obtained his PhD in 1936, but published scarcely anything from it, considered abandoning academic history altogether, and lived on the margins of University life until elected to the Ehrman Fellowship at King's in 1940.[13]

By the outbreak of the Second World War, Todd's career had already acquired an inexorable momentum which it would never lose: he was elected a Fellow of the Royal Society in 1942 (his father-in-law was then President), and he left Manchester to become Professor of Chemistry at Cambridge, and also a Fellow of Christ's, two years later. The University promised he could build a new laboratory once the war was over, and he brought his best students and colleagues with him, who would later form a dining club known as The Toddlers. He was already in demand in London, joining scientific committees in the Ministry of Supply, and he played an important part in aiding the recovery of German chemistry immediately after VE Day.[14] Snow's ailing academic career was brought to a merciful quietus in 1939, when he was seconded to Whitehall. He was put in charge of the recruitment of scientific personnel, initially for work on radar, subsequently on the atomic bomb, and he was awarded the CBE in 1943. At the end of the war, he became a Civil Service Commissioner (with responsibility for recruiting scientists), and in 1947 a Director of English Electric (ditto), and he finally resigned his College Fellowship in 1950. Plumb, meanwhile, went off to Bletchley Park to help break codes, and returned to Cambridge in 1946 when, at the advanced age of thirty-four, he was finally elected a Fellow of Christ's and given a temporary University lectureship. He was still unsure that history was his true métier, he had only published one scholarly article, and he was at the bottom of the academic ladder; Todd by contrast was already near the top, and could well expect to go higher.[15]

During the 1950s, Todd was able to build his massive, modern chemical laboratory in Lensfield Road, which was the largest in the country at the time, and which made him a university baron long before he became a life peer; and with a large (and increasingly international) research team he pushed forward his work on the structure and synthesis of nucleotides and nucleic acids. For twenty years, Todd was a toweringly powerful force in Cambridge science, both as a creative scholar and as an academic statesman, and his findings fed into those of Dorothy Hodgkin in Oxford, and Crick and Watson at the Cavendish.[16] One indication of his grandeur was the so-called 'Chemist's Prayer', composed at about this time:

> Lord give me leave to build a lab
> So large that when I've trod
> Its vasty naves and aisles, I'll think
> I'm in thy house – Oh Todd!

But there was also more substantive recognition, as Todd was knighted in 1954, and awarded the Nobel Prize for Chemistry three years later. By then, he was also well established in what would soon become known as the 'corridors of power' where, from 1952 to 1964, he chaired the Advisory Council on Scientific Policy, the most important committee lobbying for science in government. It brought Todd into contact with Whitehall mandarins and Westminster politicians at the very highest level, and had the Conservatives won the 1964 general election, he might have been appointed Minister for Science.[17]

In London, Snow's two postwar part-time jobs gave him

leisure to establish his reputation as a writer, and he rapidly produced the novels of his *Strangers and Brothers* sequence. In their form and structure, they consciously harked back to nineteenth-century realistic fiction, especially Trollope's, and like him, they often evoked 'privileged and secretive social groups unknown to outsiders'. But in their content, they were entirely contemporary, dealing with science, education and government, with the 'closed politics' of committees and personality clashes, and with the manipulation of power by men drawn from a wide variety of social backgrounds, whose inner lives were often troubled and unhappy.[18] Snow married another novelist, Pamela Hansford Johnson, in 1950; he was knighted in 1957, for his work as a Civil Service Commissioner; he was befriended by Harold Macmillan, who now became his publisher; and he was a member of the Labour Party's informal Science Advisory Group which, following the views of Blackett and Bernal, persuaded the leadership to accept the radical agenda that science and technology were the key to social progress and economic success.[19] By this time, Plumb's career was also beginning to acquire its own belated momentum, both inside Cambridge and beyond. He was a brilliant lecturer in the History Faculty; he was an unrivalled nurturer of young College talent, including Barry Supple, Rupert Hall, John Kenyon, Neil McKendrick and Eric Stokes; and he produced books on eighteenth-century England, and on Chatham and Walpole, which established his public reputation as a stylish and accessible writer. But he still felt intimidated by Namier's brooding (and increasingly hostile) presence, and it was only with his death in 1960 that Plumb finally found his own authentic voice.[20]

Throughout the ensuing decade, all three men enjoyed notable professional success, which both enabled and emboldened them to participate in some of the great public issues of the time. For Todd, recognition now came at flood tide: he was Master of the Salters' Company at the beginning of the decade; he was made a life peer in 1962 (would he, Plumb wondered to Snow, take the title Lord Christ? And would Lady Todd, he teased the new notable, insist on an expensive tiara?); he was elected unopposed to the Mastership of Christ's in the following year; he became the first Chancellor of Strathclyde University in Glasgow in 1965; and at the same time he received, as had his father-in-law, the Pour Le Merite from the German government.[21] But as usual with Todd, there was also power to accompany the pomp: he spoke well and influentially in the House of Lords, on Scottish and scientific affairs; he oversaw the construction of New Court at Christs's, designed by Sir Denys Lasdun; he chaired the Royal Commission on Medical Education from 1965 to 1968, which successfully urged the doubling of the number of students, and recommended major structural changes in clinical education; and he was also chairman of the Board of Governors of the United Cambridge Hospitals, where he presided over the construction of the new Addenbrooke's, designed by the same architects he had used for his chemistry laboratory.[22]

During this period, Snow's reputation as a writer was also at its peak: *Corridors of Power*, which rivalled *The Masters* in popularity, was published in 1964, and with two more novels, the *Strangers and Brothers* sequence was triumphantly concluded at the end of the decade. To his admirers, Snow now occupied a place in English life and letters that merited comparison with Arnold Bennett and H. G. Wells; he was feted and applauded on the lecture circuit in the United States and Soviet Russia; and (as with Todd) the honorary degrees flooded in. In the

Labour government of 1964, he was appointed Parliamentary Secretary to the new Ministry of Technology, and he, too, was given a peerage (Lord Snow of Leicester), to which he proudly attached his long-cherished Latin tag.[23] By this time, Plumb was also catching up. In the College, the flow of outstandingly gifted undergraduates continued, among them Simon Schama, Geoffrey Parker and Roy Porter. In the university, he was made a Reader in 1962, he was awarded a personal chair four years later, he was Chairman of the History Faculty Board from 1966 to 1968, and he was elected a Fellow of the British Academy. And he was also making a wider reputation: as a visiting professor at Columbia University in New York, as Fords Lecturer at Oxford, as historical adviser to Penguin Books, and as a reviewer and essayist in papers and periodicals on both sides of the Atlantic.[24]

But what, meanwhile, of their relations with their College – and with each other? The differences were more revealing than the similarities. Todd arrived at Christ's with his career and reputation already made; as Master he left the day-to-day running of the place to Gorley Putt (whom he appointed Senior Tutor) and Charles Phillips (whom he brought in as Bursar); and although he and Lady Todd were attentive to the undergraduates, he spent much of his time in his lab and in London.[25] By contrast, Snow's career took off only when he left Christ's, and he never regretted that decision. He deeply offended many of the Fellows by (as they saw it) caricaturing both the College and themselves in *The Light and The Dark*, *The Masters* and *The Affair*, and it was only after a long and hard-fought battle that he was finally elected an Honorary Fellow in 1966. But after his own fashion, he remained abidingly loyal to Cambridge and to Christ's, he never forgot (and increasingly romanticized) the great days of heroic science in the 1930s, and he dined in College each year on 13 December, St Lucy's Day, the anniversary of his initial election to the Fellowship.[26] In Plumb's case, the relationship was different again. His belated Fellowship had been the making of him, and as a resident bachelor don, who regularly dined and combined, and who was successively Steward, Director of Studies in History, Tutor and Vice-Master, he was closely involved in College life. But his acerbic tongue and militant agnosticism also made him many enemies (hence his failed bid to become Bursar), and he was not temperamentally suited to consensual collegiality. 'My effect on people', he once admitted, 'is very odd.' Yet although he received offers from other universities on both sides of the Atlantic, and encouraged his protégés to leave for the United States, he could never bring himself to sever his College ties.[27]

Their interpersonal relations were equally complex. In many ways, Todd and Plumb were life-long antagonists. This was partly a matter of their subjects: the arts versus the sciences. It was partly a matter of professional rivalry: Todd's career was a success from the start; Plumb was a late developer, and he never fully caught up. It was partly a matter of physique and personality: Plumb was very short, Todd was very tall; Plumb was a maddening amalgam of buoyancy and misery, insight and mischief, whereas Todd was dour, tough, olympian, and apparently untroubled by doubt: 'an intolerably conceited Scots scientist', according to Tony Benn (and many others).[28] It was partly a matter of style: Plumb loved the good things of life, and was socially ambitious; Todd was not interested in what he regarded as such trivia. It was partly a matter of substance: for all Plumb's claims to be a well-travelled man of the world, Todd's international connections were incomparably wider than

Plumb's, and he was also a brilliant linguist. And when Todd obtained the Mastership, which Plumb himself also coveted, his envy and enmity knew no bounds. 'Just how awful Todd is', Plumb wrote to Snow, 'appears slowly but inevitably. He hungers for the trappings of power like a sex-starved adolescent for girls.'[29] (In fact, this was a serious misjudgement, for Todd was always much more clear about the distinction between the substance and the semblance of power than Plumb.) But while the two of them often divided the College across the decades, Plumb grudgingly recognized Todd's undeniable 'grandeur', and believed he was 'a great admirer of my written work'; and as Master and Vice-Master, they successfully steered through Snow's belated Honorary Fellowship in 1966.[30]

By contrast, Plumb and Snow were lifelong friends and allies from their Leicester days, who saw themselves as self-made provincials battling against 'the stuffed, envious and self-righteous' phalanxes of metropolitan complacency and Establishment condescension. They were also staunch Labour supporters, who were uncritically admiring of Harold Wilson, and who saw the election victories of 1964 and 1966 as portending a new 'time of hope' for the nation – and for themselves. 'Your time is just coming,' Snow wrote to Plumb. 'One can smell it in the air.' 'I have a strong suspicion', Plumb agreed, 'that the tide is with us.'[31] This put them at odds with Todd: he was a deeply committed Tory (whose relations with Lord Salisbury and Lord Hailsham were particularly close), he did not share Snow's admiration for such left-wing savants as Bernal and Blackett, and he had no time for Snow as a scientist or novelist. But he respected Snow's commitment to the public advancement of science and technology, they worked together to help establish Churchill College in Cambridge for scientists and technologists, and in both Christ's and the Lords, their relations were courteous and cordial.[32] Indeed, Snow was one of the few people who got on with both Todd and Plumb, and this may well have encouraged him to try to bring their two cultures together (though neither of them fitted the stereotypes he would later create: Plumb was far from being a reactionary humanist, and Todd was no radical scientist). Here, then, was a complex, potent, enduring and evolving web of professional, collegial and personal connections, which also bound the three of them together (and occasionally differentiated them) as they participated in the public affairs of the 1960s. What were those public affairs? And what form did their participation in them take?

*

'The Sixties' have never been an easy decade to define or describe or date: perhaps they lasted from 1958 to 1974, or alternatively (and especially in Britain) only from 1964 to 1968.[33] But some of their most significant characteristics may be easily summarized. In Britain, thirteen years of Conservative rule ended in 1964, to be followed by six years of Labour, after which the Tories returned to power again. Under Macmillan and Douglas-Home, the Conservatives increasingly seemed an effete and fading Establishment incapable of dealing with the many challenges facing Britain, both at home and overseas. Harold Wilson, by contrast, claimed he would get the country moving again, by wresting control from the public-school amateurs and by putting power in the hands of managers, scientists and technologists, who would be produced in the new universities and technical colleges recommended by the Robbins Report in 1964. By modernizing Britain's outdated educational system, social structure and business attitudes, he hoped to increase

productivity and revive the nation's faltering economic peform-
ance; and in the post-Suez era of decolonization and imperial
retreat, he also sought to create a new, more forward-looking
role for Britain on the world stage. Meanwhile, the newly
emancipated colonies needed all the help the West (including
Britain) could provide – massive injections of capital to jump-
start their fledgling industrial economies; hospitals, irrigation
schemes, universities and nuclear power stations; and scientists,
planners, economists and doctors. This was partly to bring to
them the benefits of modern, developed civilization; but it was
also to ensure that they allied with the West, rather than the
Communist bloc.[34]

The state of education, the state of the nation, the state of
the third world: these were some of the issues that were bub-
bling up in the Macmillan years, and which Sir Charles Snow
sought to define and address in his Rede Lecture on 'The
Two Cultures', delivered in Cambridge in May 1959. As he saw
it, the British education system was deeply flawed, because of
the entrenched divisions between the arts and the sciences: two
'polar groups' living in a state of mutual ignorance and misunderstanding. And it was clear where the blame principally lay:
for the arts had signally failed to appreciate the significance or
momentum of science. Indeed, most humanists were reactionary, elitist and irresponsible, natural Luddites opposed to the
very idea of material self-betterment, whereas the scientists
tended to be progressive, meritocratic and internationalist: the
men 'with the future in their bones'.[35] If Britain was to move
forward, Snow insisted, then the scientists and technologists
must have more resources and more influence: jam today and
jam tomorrow. But there was also a global dimension. In many
parts of the non-Western world, Snow observed, there were too

many people with not enough to eat. Their best hope lay in an industrial and a technological revolution – for, as the British experience had shown, this was one means whereby the mass of the population might improve their standard of living. And the only professionals who could bring about such a narrowing of the gap between the rich and the poor were the trained experts, the scientists and the technologists. At home and overseas, they were both the new men – and the necessary men – the only people who could bring what he termed 'social hope' to the majority of mankind.[36]

In drawing attention to the great divide between the arts and the sciences in contemporary Britain, Snow was endowing a debate which dated back to Huxley and Arnold with a contemporary significance that was both national and international – emphasizing the deficiencies of the British education system compared with the United States and the Soviet Union, urging the need for the nation to modernize if it was to avoid relegation to the margins of global affairs, and insisting that the West must confront and help solve the pressing problems of the third world.[37] As a piece of panoramic punditry, it was a tour de force of synthesis, simplification and speculation, and it established Snow's reputation as a public commentator with important things to say. Thus encouraged and emboldened, and having recently resigned his two part-time jobs, he took to the international lecture circuit to expound and expand his views. As Lord Rector of Aberdeen University, he told the undergraduates that the proper application of science and technology meant the world's poor did not have to be poor, and that global poverty could be eradicated in two generations. As Godkin Lecturer at Harvard, he argued that governments needed responsible scientific advisers, with foresight and a sense of future directions: men like Sir Henry Tizard rather than Lord Cherwell. And in a speech to the American Association for the Advancement of Science, he insisted that scientists were 'the most important occupational group in the world today' who, notwithstanding their creation of the atomic bomb, still held out the best hopes for improving and transforming the future of mankind.[38]

During the 1960s, Snow also refined, modified and embellished his original views on 'the two cultures', though in its essentials, his argument remained unaltered.[39] As higher education expanded, and as new subjects came to prominence on campuses in Britain and America, he came to believe that a third culture was developing, situated midway between the traditional arts and the hard sciences, which combined the insights of a revived humanism with a more rigorously scientific methodology. As Snow came to appreciate them, these fledgling social sciences – demography, sociology, economics, political science, psychology and social history – offered a new, exciting and relevant way of understanding the present. But of all these subjects, it was the new social history which most interested him. Plumb's influence may be readily discerned here, and he was also much impressed by the work of such scholars as Peter Laslett and Harold Perkin.[40] It seemed to Snow that they were approaching the past in a more imaginative and wide-ranging way than high-political obsessives like Lewis Namier; and their work also reinforced his own conviction that 'traditional' life was miserable, that 'no one in his senses would choose to have been born in a previous age unless he could be certain that he would have been born into a prosperous family', and that the only escape from such primitive deprivation was by going through an industrial revolution. In a world increasingly polarized between 'the rich and the poor' (the alternative title, he now revealed, for the original lecture), only industry and technology and science held out the hope of bridging the gap.[41]

Here, in the Sixties, was Snow in full blizzard as a public man: drawing on his own varied experiences, interpreting the arts and the sciences to each other, offering sage-like advice to young and old alike, and setting Britain's domestic problems in a broader global context. 'You have really broken through at the world level,' Plumb told him: Snow had become 'a voice of authority ... in tune with all that is restless, intellectual, creative'.[42] In Britain, Snow's words were invoked in support of many progressive Sixties causes: the inauguration of A-Level courses in General Studies, the reform of the Oxford and Cambridge undergraduate curriculum, the setting up of inter-disciplinary degrees at the new universities, and the creation of a Ministry of Technology and a Ministry of Overseas Development.[43] Both of these new departments were duly established by Harold Wilson when he won the general election in 1964, and Snow was a natural choice for a post in the Ministry of Technology – inhabiting the corridors of power in fact at just the same time that he was also evoking them in fiction. His maiden speech in the Lords urged the need for industry and academe and government to work together, and insisted that it was only by the application of science and technology that national decline could be halted. He returned to these subjects on many occasions, especially when welcoming the Robbins Report, which he acclaimed as 'one of the great state documents of our time', and which recommended a massive expansion in higher education, so as to produce more qualified scientists and technologists.[44] Indeed, from Snow's perspective, the Ministry of Technology was 'The Two Cultures' in action, and for a time a similar agenda was embraced by Plumb and Todd.

For Plumb, the 1960s would be his most important decade as an historian: his creative energy and intellectual curiosity were at their peak, and he was much involved in public discussion about the place (and point) of the past in the modernizing present. The death of Namier had lifted a weight from his scholarly shoulders, freeing Plumb to take a much more critical view of Namier's myopic methodology, his political conservatism, his love of tradition, and his veneration for Edmund Burke. Plumb had no time for any of this 'rubbish', and Wilson's electoral victories of 1964 and 1966 were like 1906 or 1945 all over again, an optimistic moment, when the defeat of the forces of obscurantism and conservatism seemed at hand.[45] But here was both a challenge and an opportunity, for history in general and for Plumb in particular: what purpose could the past serve in the brave new secular, radical, scientific, modernizing world that was now coming into being? It was a pertinent question, and Plumb had many reasons for wishing to answer it convincingly. As a student of Trevelyan's, he believed that history must reach a public audience and fulfil a public purpose, and thus be sensitive to the mood of the times. As a friend of Snow's, he was much influenced by his depiction of 'The Two Cultures', and he was anxious to make a case for history having more in common with the progressive sciences than the reactionary arts. As a supporter of Harold Wilson, he was eager to show that the study of the past could be mobilized in support of a modernizing political enterprise. And as someone who had vainly coveted the Regius Professorship in 1963, and hoped for it again when it became vacant on Herbert Butterfield's retirement in 1967, he was also determined to establish his position as the most publicly (and politically) engaged historian of his day.[46]

Plumb set about realizing these objectives in three influential and interconnected works. The first was *Crisis in the Humanities* (1964), which he edited and introduced, and which asked how arts subjects might (and must) 'adjust to the educational and social needs of the modern world'. In his opening manifesto, Plumb took off from Snow's hostile characterization of literary intellectuals as reactionary, irresponsible and self-absorbed. Dominated as they were by such people, it was small wonder the humanities were in crisis. 'They must', Plumb insisted, 'either change the image that they present, adapt themselves to the needs of a society dominated by science and technology, or retreat into social triviality . . . Old, complex, tradition haunted societies find change as difficult to make as rheumatoid arthritics to move.' He concluded, in words that Snow himself could have written: 'What is needed is less reverence for tradition, and more humility towards the educational systems of those two great countries – America and Russia – which have tried to adjust their teaching to the urban industrial world of the twentieth century.'[47] As for history itself, on which Plumb wrote a substantive chapter, the challenge was clear. For many academics, it was merely an intellectual pastime, obsessed with scholarly technique. Yet the real justification of history was its broader, public purpose: to record, explain and celebrate progress, both material and intellectual, especially with reference to 'industry, technology, science'. If historians accepted their obligation to describe and explain the past in this way, they would give contemporaries a greater understanding of the present and also an increased control over the future, and their rejuvenated discipline would thus fulfil its prime social function 'in government, in administration, in all the manifold affairs of men'.[48]

Having sketched out a revived and relevant future for the humanities in the Sixties era of white-hot Wilsonian technology, Plumb provided a specific example of how this could be done in *The Growth of Political Stability in England, 1675–1725* (1967), derived from the Ford lectures he had given in Oxford.[49] From one perspective, this was his best and most influential work of history, which sought to define and solve a big and serious problem: how did the revolutionary England of the seventeenth century become the stable England of the eighteenth century? But it was also a tract for the times, for its broader concern was to explore the complex relations between inertia and change in the past, and to tease out some implications for the present. Like many Sixties historians, Plumb explained change with reference to long-term social and economic forces, topped off by political action – usually leading to revolution, but this time yielding precisely the opposite outcome. Either way, this was how things happened. But the Tory Party had never wanted to make things happen. Their Burkean veneration for tradition, custom and slow, evolutionary development misunderstood and misrepresented the process of historical change. And so the culturally xenophobic, religiously bigoted, economically backward and politically maladroit party of Bolingbroke took flight from the present into the past – thus anticipating their successors in the 1960s. Nor, in the long run, were the Whigs much better. For in establishing stability, they brought into being a political culture and structure which for the next two centuries 'failed to adjust its institutions and its social system to the needs of an industrial society'. Hence, of course, the nation's current difficulties. And the implication could scarcely have been plainer: it was high time that these long-overdue adjustments and reforms were made.[50]

The Growth of Political Stability was an audacious way to link Queen Anne's England with Harold Wilson's Britain, by solving a substantive historical problem which simultaneously validated and reinforced a modernizing and contemporary political agenda. As such, it demonstrated the renewed relevance of history – a subject on which Plumb offered more general reflections in *The Death of the Past* (1969), based on the Saposnekow Lectures he delivered in New York, early in 1968.[51] His aim was to outline the place and purpose of history in a world where tradition and obscurantism were in retreat, where secular progress was in the ascendant, and where historians must engage with 'the new scientists and technologists, the men who man or run the power stations and computer services'. For Plumb, 'the past' had been misused in earlier centuries – by religion, by genealogy, by kingly cults, by ancestor worship, by myth and legend – to sanctify elite dominance and authoritarian regimes. Such 'doom-laden', 'ghost-haunted', 'backward-looking' attitudes had resulted in 'bigotry, national vanity and class domination'. But the growth of scholarly, scientific history, combined with the transforming impact of the industrial and technological revolutions, meant a new and better world had recently come into being: urban, democratic and meritocratic, which rejected the old 'past' of custom, precedent, faith and unreason. Accordingly, the purpose of history was to speed this discredited 'past' on its way to oblivion, and to give humanity confidence in its progress and possibilities: in short to give people 'social hope' (Snow's phrase again) in a 'forward-looking, scientifically-orientated' world. The past was dead, but history was alive; the past had been for the few, but history was now for the many.[52]

In these three works, Plumb's indebtedness to Snow was obvious, and their involvement in the contemporary issues of the 1960s was very much a joint enterprise – a serious attempt to secure appropriate recognition for both the arts and the sciences in Harold Wilson's Britain (along with, no doubt, appropriate recognition for themselves). At first glance, their highly profiled activities seem far removed from Todd's more cloistered world of the lab and the Lords. Unlike Snow and Plumb, he sought to keep out of the newspapers and had no ambitions to be what we would now call a public intellectual. Yet like Snow (and Plumb) Todd believed passionately that science and technology were the core cultures, crucial for human progress and fulfilment, which governments neglected at their peril, and during the 1960s he was a formidable force in their support, especially in the Lords. In his maiden speech, he drew attention to the decline of the Scottish economy, largely because the traditional industries had been indifferent to scientific research and technological progress. Time and again, he urged the need for more government funding of scientific research, for closer relations between industry and the universities, for better trained technologists and technicians, and for expert help to be sent to the developing countries. Like Plumb, he worried about the gap between 'the fantastic rate of social and technological progress during this century', and 'the very slow rate of change in our social attitudes and . . . our methods of government', and on several occasions, he was warmly congratulated by Lord Snow, who took pride in pointing out their shared connection with the same Cambridge college.[53]

Todd's speeches in the upper house were vigorous and trenchant, and his deeds matched his words.[54] As a director of Fisons Pharmaceuticals and a trustee of the Nuffield Foundation, he knew more than most university scientists about the limitations and possibilities of collaboration between industry and academe. As one of the founding trustees of Churchill College, Cambridge, he supported the idea of an educational institution exclusively devoted to science and technology, and he was responsible for its appropriately vigorous motto 'Forward'. As the first Chancellor of Strathclyde University, he promoted collaboration with local business, which helped to make it one of Europe's leading centres of education in science and technology, 'where people are not inhibited by the weight of tradition', and he took pride in describing (and commending) these developments in the House of Lords.[55] As chairman of the Royal Commission on Medical Education, he advocated the reorganization and broadening of the undergraduate curriculum, the rationalization of medical schools in London, the founding of three new clinical schools in the regions, and the updating of the popular image of general practice. And through his chairmanship of the Advisory Council on Scientific Policy, and his membership of the Trend Committee of Inquiry into the Organization of the Civil Service, he continually urged the need for long-term stability in the national funding of scientific research, and for a greater interconnection between scientific advice and government policy-making.[56]

At the very end of the 1960s, Todd stood back from these day-by-day activities, and offered a broader survey of contemporary science and society in his presidential address to the British Association for the Advancement of Science. It was subsequently published in *The Times*, where it was widely discussed, and it was clearly indebted both to Snow's 'Two Cultures' and to Plumb's *Death of the Past*. Like Snow, Todd regarded science as 'a cultural pursuit', the purpose of which was 'to enlarge our understanding of the world in which we live'; and like Plumb, he lamented the growing gap between 'fantastically rapid technical advance' and 'relatively slow social progress'. Traditional society, he insisted, had been characterized by an 'age-old pattern' of customary social, religious and political arrangements. Only with the industrial and scientific revolutions had the class barriers and widespread impoverishment of the old society been dissolved, and had technology come to transform and enhance twentieth-century life. But many unsolved problems remained. Abroad, there was a widening gap between the rich and the poor nations, with population growth threatening to get out of control, and at home, there was a scientifically ignorant democracy, which was a contradiction in terms. Not until social and educational change caught up with technological change, and helped inform it, would a 'scientifically-conscious democracy' be brought into being.[57] Self-evidently, these were Todd's own opinions, and he articulated them with his usual authority and conviction. But as a Sixties synthesis of his own views with those of Snow and Plumb, this address could scarcely have been bettered.

*

Here, then, were three clever, distinguished, ambitious College men, trying to make sense of the Sixties, and deeply involved in public debates about how to do that. They certainly sensed that they were engaged in a common enterprise, but their varied areas of interest and expertise, combined with the complex chemistry of their personal and College relations, meant that their views were never monolithic. Although he was a great public supporter of Snow during the 1960s, Plumb's initial reaction to the 'Two Cultures' lecture had been more guarded. There had, he insisted, always been such a gap between the sciences and the humanities; most scientists showed little interest in the humanities or the imaginative life (was this a dig at Todd?); and as he saw it, the crucial division in contemporary society was between the old literary class which was now on the way down, and the 'emerging classes of industrial society' which were on the way up.[58] For his part, Todd was too much of a Tory to be fully at ease with the Labour government's policies: he welcomed their commitment to education and modernization, but he thought their decision to divide science and technology between two separate ministries was idiotic, and he did not share the widespread enthusiasm for the Robbins Report. What was most urgently needed, Todd insisted, was not more university educated scientists and technologists, but more technicians.[59] Nor was he interested in joining Plumb and Snow in their crusade against reactionary literary intellectuals. Perhaps because he was Scottish, or perhaps because he was well married, or perhaps because he was largely indifferent to the arts, Todd never shared their concerns (and hang-ups) about class and the metropolitan intelligentsia.

In the light of their characters, their careers and their connections, these differences of emphasis and opinion should scarcely come as a surprise. But they were less important, and publicly less visible, than their shared assumptions, which enabled their opponents, on both the right and the left, to lump the three of them together as quintessential (and misguided) Sixties modernizers. And of no critic was this truer than F. R. Leavis. Initially, he engaged solely with Snow, belatedly denouncing the

'Two Cultures' lecture in 1962, in one of the most celebrated and vitriolic attacks ever mounted by one Cambridge figure on another, and which is still cherished to this day by connoisseurs of academic terrorism. Far from being a master mind or a great sage, wisely and compassionately pronouncing on the problems of contemporary civilization, Leavis insisted that Snow was 'portentously ignorant' of history and literature, and that he was intellectually as undistinguished as it was possible for any man to be. What claims did he have to be so knowing, so all-seeing, so worldly-wise? Who was he, a failed physicist and a hopeless novelist, to presume to act as a bridge between the sciences and the humanities? What did Snow know of high culture or creative thought or civilization? On what grounds could he possibly claim that scientists had 'the future in their bones'? Instead of offering serious insights into the human condition, Snow rode 'on an advancing swell of clichés', of which the idea of 'social hope' was the most absurd. The prospect that Britain's tomorrow would resemble America's today filled Leavis with gloom and alarm, and he scorned the view that industrialization and material improvement should be humanity's ultimate goal. 'Who will assert', Leavis concluded, 'that the average member of modern society is more fully human, or more alive, than a Bushman [or] an Indian peasant?'[60]

The general furore that Leavis's attack provoked has been described elsewhere; but two local responses merit attention.[61] The first was by Canon Charles Raven, who had been Master of Christ's from 1939 to 1950. Relations between Raven and Snow had never been friendly since Snow had turned against Raven at the Mastership election of 1936, and Snow's depiction of him as Dr Paul Jago in his Cambridge novels did scant justice to his wide-ranging and significant scholarship, which in some ways anticipated his own efforts to bring the 'two cultures' together. In a letter to the *Spectator*, Raven insisted that the 'Two Cultures' lecture showed 'no appreciation of the true nature of its subject', and he poured scorn on Snow's picture of College life in which intrigue and wire-pulling and drinking were the dominant activities. The Fellows, he countered, were committed to education, learning, religion and research. 'Without some such obligation', he concluded, 'there can be no true culture. Sir Charles offers us only careerism. That is the case against him.'[62] (Not surprisingly, Snow had to wait until after Raven's death in 1964 for his Honorary Fellowship.) Plumb, by contrast, and urged on by Snow himself, leaped to his friend's defence, denouncing Leavis, also in the *Spectator*, for his 'senseless dia-tribe', full of 'folly' and 'arrogance' and 'sheer blind ignorance'. It was well known among historians, Plumb insisted, that the Industrial Revolution had improved the lot of humanity, and there was no 'hidden virtue in ignorance, superstition, dirt, poverty, disease and early death'. He renewed his attack in *Crisis in the Humanities* and in *The Death of the Past*, noting that hatred of industrialism 'runs like dry rot through literary criticism', and insisting that Leavis lived in 'a never-never land of the past', where he subscribed to a 'picture of nineteenth-century England' that was 'totally unrealistic'.[63]

But Leavis hadn't finished yet. In a subsequent lecture, entitled 'Pluralism, Compassion and Social Hope', he attacked the 'elite of the progressive intelligentsia', of whom Snow, Plumb and Todd were his three prime examples. Once again, he ridiculed Snow, and the idea of 'social hope'. Once again, he denounced Plumb's view of the Industrial Revolution. But his sharpest criticisms were directed at Todd's presidential address to the British Association, which he dismissed as a 'ludicrously inadequate' display of 'spiritual philistinism' and 'emotional inhumanity'. Todd's insistence that science was a 'cultural pursuit' akin to the arts merely showed that he knew nothing of culture; his claim that science increased our understanding of the world was utterly wrong; and the very idea of a 'scientifically-conscious democracy' were an abomination. The most urgent tasks, Leavis concluded, were 'the maintenance of cultural continuity by a body of the educated', and the nurturing of high university endeavour as 'a creative centre of civilization', activities to which the 'non-thoughts' of Todd, Plumb and Snow contributed nothing.[64] Here, indeed, were some strange cross-currents at the end of the decade. In opposing new universities and 'relevant' history, Leavis found himself on the same side as the belligerently conservative G. R. Elton, who repeatedly denounced Sixties fashionableness, who was viscerally hostile to the new and expanding social sciences, and who scorned Plumb's view of history as progress. But in insisting that the Industrial Revolution had done harm rather than good, Leavis was also rehearsing arguments advanced from the left by Eric Hobsbawm and E. P. Thompson, the two chief pessimists in the 'standard of living' controversy which was then furiously raging. Thus did the elitist right and the socialist left make common cause against the modernizing Sixties *Zeitgeist*.[65]

But by then, indeed, that *Zeitgeist* was largely over. By late 1968, the early hopes and mid-decade euphoria had largely collapsed, as the Johnson administration in America and the Wilson government in Britain both ran into unprecedented difficulties: Vietnam in one case, and devaluation in the other. Snow's fiction had always been shot through with a sense of failure and foreboding, and in a lecture delivered at Fulton, Missouri, entitled 'The State of Siege', he declared that he had been 'nearer to despair in this year, 1968, than ever in my life'. The West was in turmoil; the global problems of poverty and population had not been solved; and by 2000 there would either be a nuclear war or a catastrophic famine. Yet his attempts to alert the world to its impending doom had been a 'total failure', and with the publication of his collected pronouncements in 1971, he effectively retired as a public sage.[66] By the early 1970s, Plumb was becoming equally pessimistic, lamenting the 'threats to social order and stability' presented by campus riots, urban terrorism, soaring inflation, drug abuse and political corruption, and fearing that the future for liberalism on both sides of the Atlantic was very bleak in the era of Heath and Nixon.[67] For his part, Todd had never shared the euphoric, left-wing expectations of Snow and Plumb, and as Master of Christ's he had to endure his share of student unrest in the College between 1969 and 1972. But he was less gloomy than Snow or Plumb, and he remained convinced that global poverty could be eradicated, by increasing food supply and limiting population growth, and by providing more technicians and trained manpower in the third world.[68]

Perhaps, too, Todd was less pessimistic because in his long prime he carried more weight: for *pace* Plumb (and also Snow), he very much knew where the substance of power lay. As both a scientist and a panjandrum, he was a massively influential figure in Cambridge University, far beyond the confines of the College, in a way that Plumb never was: dominating science, chairing policy committees, putting up buildings, founding new colleges. And in Whitehall and Westminster he was for three decades a far more formidable force than Snow briefly became as a minister. For all his claims to knowingness and worldly wisdom, Snow was never taken seriously in the corridors of power, and he attracted far more attention as a pundit in Russia and America (where he received most of his honorary degrees) than he did in England.[69] As for Plumb: he failed to persuade his colleagues that history had a prime public purpose to proclaim progress, he carried little weight in the councils of the nation, and (unlike Todd) he too easily assumed that social celebrity would translate into political influence. One of the reasons he cultivated Princess Margaret so assiduously was because he believed (as he informed Sir Roy Strong) 'the way to the "Headmistress" is through her sister'. 'Whatever is he after?' Strong perceptively mused. 'Endless buying of other people's silver and porcelain, and endless lunches and dinners, and Princess Margaret for the weekend won't get him anywhere.'[70] It was a shrewd observation and, unsurprisingly, Todd agreed. 'He thinks he's someone', Todd would later opine of Plumb, 'because he claims to know Princess Margaret' – a remark which reveals much about all three of them.

But as usual, there were also deeper forces at work. During the course of Todd's career, and especially after the Second World War, science *did* become an integral part of national government, and he himself was both a significant contributor to this development and also a prime beneficiary of it. The scientists still complained that they had insufficient influence and inadequate resources, but in the age of Todd and Blackett and Mott they had far more than they had ever dreamed of in the age of Rutherford or Thomson or Rayleigh. To be sure, such proconsular humanists as Noel Annan, Alan Bullock, Isaiah Berlin and Owen Chadwick had some entrée to Westminster and Whitehall; but they exerted no comparable leverage with politicians or civil servants, and the public impact which historians made through their writings did not compare with the power that came from running a large science department and enjoying privileged access to ministers and mandarins. Even if Plumb had realized his ambitions to be Regius Professor in Cambridge, President of the British Academy, and a member of the House of Lords, he would never have wielded the sort of influence that Todd did; and while Harold Wilson might have done well to create the post of Chief Historical Adviser, with Plumb as a plausible candidate, there was never the remotest prospect that this would happen. In that sense, there were truly two cultures in the Britain of the 1960s, but only one of them was a significant force in government.[71]

The rest of this story may be easily told. When the decade ended, Todd, Snow and Plumb still had many years before them; but they never played so prominent, or so agreed, a part in public affairs again. Snow's ministerial career was brief and inglorious, for he had resigned from the Wilson government in the spring of 1966, after only eighteen months in office. The Ministry of Technology was (as Todd had insisted) misconceived; Frank Cousins was neither a sympathetic nor successful minister; and after a brief period of energy and enlargement under Tony Benn, the whole enterprise was closed down by Edward Heath.[72] On the completion of his *Strangers and Brothers* series, Snow hoped for the Order of Merit, the Nobel Prize for Literature, the chancellorship of a 'new' university, or (at least) election to a Fellowship of the Royal Society. None of these honours came his way, although a lecture was founded in his name at Christ's, and he did become Visitor (effectively Chancellor) of Hatfield Polytechnic.[73] He produced three more novels, which were sombre in tone and did not sell, concerned with student unrest, with old age and national decline, and with the thin veneer that separated civilization from barbarism. He published a study of the great realistic novelists of the nineteenth century, lamenting that his own time was too pessimistic for such confident and creative fiction. And he completed *The Physicists*, once more harking back to the halcyon days of Cambridge science as he remembered and romanticized it in the Thirties.[74] But the Seventies were an unhappy decade for him, and (as he wrote of Trollope) there was 'a strong impression that his reputation was slipping precipitately' in his last years. He died in 1980, a few months before what would have been the fiftieth anniversary of his election to the Christ's Fellowship. 'It seemed', Plumb wrote to Snow's widow, Pamela Hansford Johnson, 'the first step in the long road to success, and it certainly linked Charles with Christ's for his lifetime.' And not only for his lifetime, as his ashes were eventually placed in an urn in the Fellows' Garden.[75]

While Snow's career faded during the 1970s, Todd's continued on its inexorable upward trajectory, as he garnered an array of glittering prizes and high-sounding offices that surpassed his father-in-law Sir Henry Dale. He resigned as Professor of Chemistry in 1970, but continued as Master of Christ's until 1978. By then, he had also served as a founding trustee of Robinson College, and as chairman of Cambridge University Press, where he successfully brought in Geoffrey Cass to revive a publishing enterprise that was close to collapse. He refused to be Vice-Chancellor of the University, in part because he regarded it as a non-job, in part because he thought it might prevent him being President of the Royal Society. In 1975, he finally achieved this ambition, and he used his presidential addresses to redefine the Society's purpose (he thought it had been too politically partisan under his predecessor Lord Blackett), and to warn that British industry and academe were good at invention and discovery, but bad at development and exploit-ation.[76] The Order of Merit duly came his way in 1977 and the Order of the Rising Sun of Japan in the following year. On his retirement from the Mastership, he became chairman of the Nuffield Foundation, the House of Lords Select Committee on Science and Technology, and the Croucher Foundation of Hong Kong. Beyond any doubt, his career had been 'rich in distinctions of the highest order', and on his death in 1997 he was saluted as the greatest Scottish scientist since Lord Kelvin. His will was proved at £1.7 million, and he left the College his medals and decorations, a portrait of himself, and the silver dish he had been given as Visitor of Hatfield Polytechnic, where he had succeeded Snow in 1978.[77]

As the junior member of the trio, Plumb outlived both his old Leicester friend and his great College rival, but not especially happily. In 1967, his ambitions to be Regius Professor were abruptly ended when Harold Wilson appointed Owen Chad-wick, and from this blow Plumb never recovered. To Snow's surprise, he all but gave up writing scholarly history and resigned his chair in 1974.[78] Abandoning his earlier radical beliefs, he became a staunch devotee of the monarchy, for whom he wrote *Royal Heritage* in 1977. In the following year, he succeeded Todd as Master, though Todd, Putt and Phillips had tried hard to prevent this outcome. 'I don't believe anyone else', Snow told him, with a magnificent combination of tactfulness and truthful-ness, 'who had expressed his temperament so freely could have made it.'[79] Plumb entertained lavishly in the Lodge, but he was given only a knighthood on his retirement in 1982, instead of the peerage he so ardently craved.[80] By then, he had aban-doned the Labour Party, and become an impassioned admirer of Margaret Thatcher. As a self-made provincial, who resented metropolitan condescension, this was not an entirely implausible reinvention. But it never convinced his right-wing critics, who always held his Sixties opinions against him.[81] He continued to believe that 'history must serve a social purpose', teaching wisdom about both the past and the present, and he promoted a new generation of protégés, among them Joachim Whaley, Linda Colley and Niall Ferguson; but his last years were clouded by ill-health, his ninetieth birthday brought him little pleasure, and he died soon after, in October 2001. Yet in his own maddening and cross-grained fashion, he had remained abidingly loyal to (and dependent on) the College in ways that far surpassed Todd or Snow. He had given it more than £500,000 in his lifetime, he had raised more than £1.5 million from his friends, and he had established the Glenfield Trust, with funds of more than £1 million, of which the College was to be the prime beneficiary.[82]

By then, Christ's was a very different place from that which Snow, Plumb and Todd had originally joined, and about which Snow had written. The postwar expansion in higher education meant it had grown, in terms of undergraduates, graduates and fellows, and also in terms of its physical scale and appearance: especially the construction of New Court during Todd's Mastership, and the purchase of County Hall in Plumb's Mastership, duly renamed the Todd Building.[83] And the arrival of women in 1979 fundamentally changed the all-male ethos which Snow had evoked so vividly (and so unselfconsciously). From the late 1940s to the early 1970s, the funding of higher education generally kept pace with its expansion, but thereafter the financial and political environment became much bleaker. In the 1970s, a succession of economic crises resulted in massive cuts in the education budget, and in the 1980s, the Thatcher government assailed universities with unprecedented ferocity, cutting their funding still further, imposing new regulations and restrictions, and unleashing the forces of populist philistinism against the life of the mind and those who lived it. By then, the picture of academics which Snow had given in the appendix to *The Masters* was scarcely recognizable. Then, Snow noted, the Fellows had been confident that society valued what they did and what they stood for; they lived free, comfortable, tolerant, assured lives; and the Master had to find additional things to do to fill up his spare time. Of course, the old buildings survive, the College offices continue, the stately rituals endure. But anyone who reads *The Masters* believing it describes Christ's and its Fellows in the year of its 500th anniversary would be very much mistaken.[84]

*

Yet Snow was surely correct in stressing, as he had done in his appendix to *The Masters*, the constantly shifting balance in the College across the centuries between continuity and change. And one consistent way of seeing a small, enclosed, self-governing community such as Christ's is as a place and as a base from which certain individuals mount more adventurous forays and ambitious expeditions into the greater worlds of scholarship and public affairs that lie beyond the confines of the College. These were roles that Todd, Snow and Plumb eagerly embraced and enthusiastically welcomed, and never to more emphatic effect, or with greater unanimity of purpose, than during the 1960s. Most Christ's undergraduates probably knew little of what they were doing in this broader realm, and many Christ's Fellows may have been similarly ignorant. Yet all three of them were deeply concerned about the state of knowledge, the state of the nation, and the state of the wider world during that (by turns) optimistic, challenging and disillusioned decade. To be sure, much has changed since the 1960s, but the debate on the 'two cultures' still periodically re-ignites, and the issues addressed by Todd, Plumb and Snow remain as urgent in our day as they had become in theirs: the arts and (or versus?) the sciences; the condition of higher education; the gap between the rich nations and the poor; the state of the world.[85] It is easy to expose the limits of their vision and the time-bound nature of their analysis and their prescription. But are we, now, doing that much better? And will posterity in its turn be any more indulgent to us?

In any case, whatever may be said for and against them, Todd, Plumb and Snow were indeed three extraordinary figures, and their lengthy association with one medium-sized college was no less extraordinary, endowing Christ's with a collective culture and a public identity which were unique in the Cambridge of their day. For truly they were (to borrow the title of another of Snow's books) *A Variety of Men*, by turns remarkable, inimitable and unforgettable, of whom it may very properly be said that their like will never be seen again. Here, then, by way of closure, is one final vignette, which not only brings this account as up to date as it is decently possible to do, but which also shows how Snow's novels continued to haunt the College long after they had ceased to describe or (depending on your point of view) caricature the place. In 1981, with Plumb's impending retirement from the Mastership, a bitter battle ensued to choose his successor.[86] The principal contenders were Sir Hans Kornberg, who was Professor of Biochemistry, and a Fellow of the College, and Sir Oliver Wright, who had recently retired as British Ambassador to Germany, and was an Honorary Fellow. Kornberg was Todd's candidate, while Wright was pushed equally hard by Plumb. In the end, Wright was elected. But in the aftermath of the Falklands War, he was called unexpectedly out of diplomatic retirement, and asked by Margaret Thatcher to take charge of the British Embassy in Washington. Putting country before college, he resigned the Mastership before ever even taking it up, and after another spasm of acrimonious disagreement, Kornberg was elected in his stead. During these increasingly febrile contests, which spilled out into the local and national press, *The Masters* was much in the minds of Fellows and journalists, as nature not only imitated art, but emphatically surpassed it. Could Snow, they wondered, have made *this* up? And if he had done so, would anyone have believed him? The answer to both questions was undoubtedly no.[87]

NOTES

Abbreviations

ART	Alexander Robertus Todd
CCA	Christ's College Archives
CCM	*Christ's College Magazine*
CPS	Charles Percy Snow
FWB	Fellows' Wine Book, Christ's College
HHL	*Hansard*, House of Lords
JHP	John Harold Plumb
Plumb MSS	Cambridge Univeristy Library
Snow MSS	Harry Ransom Humanities Center, University of Texas, Austin
TLS	*Times Literary Supplement*
Todd MSS	Churchill College, Cambridge

1. I am most grateful to Prof. Linda Colley, Ms Samantha Jordan, Ms Nomi Levy, Prof. David Reynolds, Sir Roy Strong, and Sir Keith Thomas for their help and for their comments on earlier drafts of this essay.

2. CPS, *Public Affairs* (London, 1971), pp. 130–7; *HHL*, 2 Dec. 1964, col. 1120; Noel Annan, *The Dons: Mentors, Eccentrics and Geniuses* (London, 1999), p. 104. CPS's account was based on the Christ's election of 1936, when the candidates were Sir Charles Darwin and Canon Charles Raven. CPS changed his vote from Raven to Darwin, thereby helping ensure the latter's victory, and provoking the former's enmity. In *The Masters* (London, 1951), Charles Percy Chrystal likewise changes his vote from Jago to Crawford, and with the same result. Incidentally, Charles and Percy were also CPS's given names, and snow is itself a form of crystal.

3. CPS, *The Masters*, Appendix.

4. CPS, *The Masters*, 'Author's Note'. For a list of the characters in CPS's novels, and their real-life originals, see P. Snow, *Stranger and Brother: A Portrait of C. P. Snow* (London, 1982), Appendix.

5. FWB, VJ Day entry for 15 Aug. 1945, specifically thanks these three College figures.

6. P. Hennessy, *Whitehall* (London, 1990), pp. 540–6; N. Annan, *Our Age: English Intellectuals between the Wars* (New York, 1990), pp. 3–18; D. Cannadine, *History in Our Time* (London, 1998), pp. 165–73.

7. J. Halperin, *C. P. Snow: An Oral Biography* (Brighton, 1983), pp. 15–16, 38. Howard appears as George Passant in CPS's *Strangers and Brothers* novels.

8. J. B. Morrell, 'The Non-Medical Sciences, 1914–1939', in B. Harrison, ed., *The History of the University of Oxford, vol. viii, The Twentieth Century* (Oxford, 1994), p. 159. For JHP's efforts to get to Christ's, see Plumb MSS: CPS to JHP, 2, 10 July 1934; S. W. Grose to JHP, 18 Feb. 1956.

9. Halperin, *Snow*, p. 24; A. Kazin, *Contemporaries* (London, 1963), pp. 171–7; P. Snow, *Stranger and Brother*, pp. 161–2; idem, *Time of Renewal: Clusters of Characters, C. P. Snow and Coups* (London, 1998), pp. 87–8; S. G. Putt, 'Techniques and Culture: Three Cambridge Portraits', *Essays and Studies* xiv (1961), p. 19; idem, *The Wings of a Man's Life* (London, 1990), p. 94.

10. JHP, 'The Walpoles: Father and Son', in idem, ed., *Studies in Social History: A Tribute to G. M. Trevelyan* (London, 1955), pp. 179–207; ART, *A Time to Remember: The Autobiography of a Chemist* (Cambridge, 1983), p. 192; W. Feldberg, 'Sir Henry Hallet Dale (1875–1968)', *Dictionary of National Biography, 1961–70* (Oxford, 1981), pp. 262–4.

11. C. N. L. Brooke, *A History of the University of Cambridge, vol. IV, 1870–1990* (Cambridge, 1993), pp. 185–91; CPS, *Variety of Men*

(London, 1967), pp. 1–2, 9–11; idem, *HHL*, 28 Feb. 1968, col. 858; idem, 'J. D. Bernal: A Personal Portrait', in M. Goldsmith and A. Mackay, eds, *The Science of Science: Society in the Technological Age* (London, 1964), pp. 19–29; idem, *HHL*, 4 March 1970, col. 405; Snow MSS 58.18, CPS to Blackett, 22 May 1968. CPS's admission to his College Fellowship is recorded in FWB, 14 Dec. 1930.

12. J. C. D. Brand, 'The Scientific Papers of C. P. Snow', *History of Science* xxvi (1988), 111–27; cf. N. Bezel, 'Autobiography and the "Two Cultures" in the Novels of C. P. Snow', *Annals of Science* xxxii (1975), 555–71.

13. JHP, 'Elections to the House of Commons in the Reign of William III' (University of Cambridge, Ph.D. thesis, 1936); *The Collected Essays of J. H. Plumb* (Hemel Hempstead, 1988), vol. I, pp. 8–9, 29–44; Plumb MSS: JHP to CPS, 25 June and 1 July 1936, 30 March 1937.

14. Todd MSS: 4/12, Research Reports submitted by Prof. Todd to the Ministry of Supply (1939–44); Box 44, The Toddlers Club, reunions and correspondence, 1972–1990; Brooke, *Cambridge, 1870–1990*, pp. 264–5; Sir James Baddiley, 'A Chemical Group Migration: Professor Todd's Move from Manchester to Cambridge Fifty Years Ago', *CCM* 219 (1994), pp. 13–18. ART's admission to his College Fellowship is recorded in FWB, 2 Oct. 1944.

15. Snow MSS 166.1: JHP to CPS, 24 Aug. 1945, 26 Feb. 1946. JHP's admission to his College Fellowship is recorded in FWB, 28 May 1946.

16. Todd MSS: Box 47, CPS to ART, 10 June 1954; 8/6, ART, 'Planning for the Development of Natural Sciences in Cambridge'; Brooke, *Cambridge, 1870–1990*, pp. 199–201; *CCM* 183 (1958), p. 12; ART, *Time to Remember*, pp. 88–9, 93, 129; J. D. Watson, *The Double Helix: A Personal Account of the Discovery of the Structure of DNA* (London, 1968), pp. 205–14; G. Ferry, *Dorothy Hodgkin: A Life* (London, 1999), pp. 250, 255, 261–4, 287.

17. The 'Chemist's Prayer' is quoted in *The Times*, 21 Jan. 1997, p. 23. For the Advisory Council on Scientific Policy, see: J. G. Crowther, *Science in Modern Society* (London, 1967), pp. 50ff.

18. CPS, 'Science, Politics and the Novelist', *The Kenyon Review* xxiii (1961), 1–17; idem, *Trollope* (London, 1975), pp. 109–10; G. Watson, 'The Future in Your Bones: C. P. Snow (1905–1980)', *Hudson Review* liv (2000), 595–602.

19. A. Horne, *Macmillan, vol. I, 1894–1956* (London, 1988), pp. 63, 81, 295, 402; B. Pimlott, *Harold Wilson* (London, 1992), p. 274; Snow MSS 197.3: ART to CPS, 2 Jan. 1957; CPS to ART, 9 Jan. 1957.

20. JHP, *Essays* i, pp. 45–108; Snow MSS, 166.6: JHP to CPS, 19, 28 April 1956, 27 Nov. 1956, 10 July 1957; Plumb MSS: CPS to JHP, 5 Feb. 1953, 1 Jan. 1956, 26 Jan. 1959.

21. Snow MSS 166.9, JHP to CPS, 10 April 1962; Todd MSS Box 48, JHP to ART, 29 March 1962. For ART's views on becoming Master, see 'Lord Todd, an interview with David Hammerton-Eddy', *CCM* 188 (1963), pp. 5–8. Todd MSS 9/23 contains correspondence of March–April 1963 relating to this interview.

22. Todd MSS: 9/1, correspondence re building of Addenbrooke's Hospital, 1964–71; Box 94, ART to S. E. T. Cusdin, 17 May 1954; Cusdin to ART, 29 May 1974.

23. Snow, *Stranger and Brother*, pp. 122–4, 130; A. Horne, *Macmillan, vol. II, 1957–1986* (London, 1989), pp. 590–1; Snow MSS, 166.11: JHP to CPS, 19 Oct. 1964.

24. JHP, *Essays*, ii, pp. 8–11, 46–50, 129–31; Snow MSS, 166.11, JHP to CPS, 25 Nov. 1963.

25. S. Gorley Putt, *The Wings of a Man's Life* (London, 1990), pp. 283–9, 319–21; ART, *Time to Remember*, pp. 168–9; Todd MSS: 9/24, Plans for Christ's College office administration, 1963; Box 16, ART, Tribute to Charles Phillips [undated, 1983], reprinted in *CCM* 209 (1984), 31–4.

26. Halpern, *Snow*, pp. 29, 145–50; Putt, *Wings*, pp. 68–82; Snow, *Stranger and Brother*, pp. 86–7; Snow MSS 197.4: CPS to ART, 2 Dec. 1969, 26 Nov. 1970; 166.17: CPS to JHP, 20 Sept. 1979.

27. Annan, *The Dons*, p. 104; JHP, *Essays* ii, p. 8; Snow MSS: 166.1, JHP to CPS 29 Aug. 1945; 166.2, JHP to CPS, 19 June 1948; 166.5, JHP to CPS, 27 Jan. 1955; Plumb MSS, CPS to JHP, 26 Jan. 1955.

28. T. Benn, *Office Without Power: Diaries, 1968–72* (London, 1988), p. 148.

29. Snow MSS 166.9, JHP to CPS, 7 Dec. 1962.

30. Snow MSS: 166.5, JHP to CPS, 1 June 1951; 166.11, ART to CPS, 29 Jan. 1966, CPS to ART, 1 Feb. 1966; 166.11, JHP to CPS, 26 Jan. 1966.

31. Plumb MSS, CPS to JHP, 26 Jan. 1955; Snow MSS: 166.7, CPS to JHP, 11 May 1960; 166.10, JHP to CPS, 11 Sept. 1963; 210.17, CPS to Harold Wilson, 16 Oct. 1964; 166.11, JHP to CPS, 11 Nov. 1964.

32. Todd MSS: 5/10, Salisbury to ART, 24 Oct. 1956, Hailsham to ART, 15 July 1964; Box 47, Salisbury to ART, 11 June 1954; Box 48,

Hailsham to ART, 30 March 1962; Salisbury to ART, 16 April 1962; Plumb MSS, CPS to JHP, 21 Sept., 1959; Halperin, *Snow*, pp. 18, 54, 60, 73, 67, 90–1; Brooke, *Cambridge, 1870–1990*, p. 568; ART, *HHL* 23 Feb. 1972, cols 509–10; ART, *Time to Remember*, pp. 194–5. But CPS's brother thought relations between CPS and ART were never close: Snow, *Time of Renewal*, pp. 176–7.

33. A. Marwick, *The Sixties: Cultural Revolution in Britain, France, Italy and the United States, c.1958–c.1974* (Oxford, 1998), pp. 3–22.

34. Pimlott, *Wilson*, pp. 300–1; A. O. Hirschman, 'The Rise and Fall of Development Economics', in his *Essays in Trespassing: Economics to Politics and Beyond* (Cambridge, 1981), pp. 7–13.

35. Notwithstanding these stereotypes, it should be mentioned that in *The Masters*, CPS's alter ego, Lewis Eliot, votes for the reactionary humanist (Jago) rather than the radical scientist (Crawford).

36. CPS, *The Two Cultures*, ed. Stefan Collini (Cambridge, 1998), esp. pp. 3–11, 44, 48. See also CPS: 'The Two Cultures', *New Statesman*, 6 Oct. 1956, pp. 413–14.

37. It is not clear that CPS had read Arnold: G. Himmelfarb, 'Social Darwinism and the "Two Cultures" ', *CCM* 206 (1981), p. 10.

38. CPS, 'On Magnanimity', *Harpers Magazine*, July 1962, pp. 37–41; idem, *Public Affairs*, pp. 99–150, 187–8.

39. CPS, 'The "Two-Cultures" Controversy: Afterthoughts', *Encounter*, February 1960, pp. 64–8; idem, 'The Two Cultures: A Second Look', *TLS*, 25 Oct. 1963, (subsequently reprinted in Collini, ed., *The Two Cultures*); idem, 'The Case of Leavis and the Serious Case', *TLS*, 9 July 1970, pp. 737–40 (subsequently reprinted in CPS, *Public Affairs*, pp. 81–98).

40. Collini, ed., *Two Cultures*, pp. 70, 79, 82–4; P. Laslett, *The World We Have Lost* (London, 1965); H. J. Perkin, *The Origins of Modern English Society, 1780–1880* (London, 1969).

41. For JHP's help to CPS on the standard of living and the industrial revolution, see: Snow MSS: 166.9: CPS to JHP, 24 May 1962; JHP to CPS, 1 July 1962, 7 December 1962; 166.10: CPS to JHP, 3 Sept. 1963, thanks JHP for the quotation 'no one in his senses would choose to have been born in a previous age, unless he could be certain that he would have been born into a prosperous family, that he would have enjoyed extremely good health, and that he could have accepted stoically the death of the majority of his children', which JHP wrote

explicitly for CPS, and which he used: see Collini, ed., *Two Cultures*, p. 82.

42. Snow MSS, 166.7, JHP to CPS, 29 Dec. 1959; Plumb MSS, typescript article on CPS, undated [*c.*1962].

43. Snow MSS, 56.16, Blackett to CPS, 11 Feb. 1965, enclosing 'The Case for a Ministry of Technology', September 1964, sent to Harold Wilson; J. Harris, 'The Arts and Social Sciences, 1939–1970', in B. Harrison, *Oxford: Twentieth Century*, pp. 219, 224; J. Roche, 'The Non-Medical Sciences, 1939–1970', in ibid, p. 287.

44. Snow, *Stranger and Brother*, p. 127; CPS in *HHL*, 18 Nov. 1964, cols. 590–8; 2 Dec. 1964, cols. 1117–25; 1 Dec. 1965, cols. 1293–1305.

45. JHP, *Essays* i, pp. 24–8, 108–12, 190; idem, *Essays* ii, p. 131. For an indication of JHP's anti-establishment radicalism at this time, note his denunciation of old, faded, elite history, which appealed only to 'those who had nannies, prep-schools, dorms, possess colonels and bishops for cousins, and now take tea once a year on the dead and lonely lawns of the Palace', in 'Hall of Fame', *The Spectator*, 16 March 1962.

46. JHP, *Essays* ii, p. 186; Plumb MSS, CPS to JHP, 6 March 1963, 30 April 1963, 23 Oct. 1963, 27 January 1967; Snow MSS: 166.10, JHP to CPS, 12 April 1963; 166.12, JHP to CPS, 31 Jan. 1967.

47. JHP, 'Introduction', in idem (ed.), *Crisis in the Humanities* (Harmondsworth, 1964), pp. 7–10.

48. JHP, 'The Historian's Dilemma', in *Crisis in the Humanities*, pp. 24–44.

49. For a more detailed discussion of this book, see D. Cannadine, 'Historians in the "Liberal Hour": Lawrence Stone and J. H. Plumb Re-visited', *Historical Research* lxxv (2002), 316–54, esp. pp. 331–9.

50. JHP, *Essays* i, pp. 113–49, for further extensions (and contemporary implications) of this argument, esp. p. 149: 'Conservative forces continued to dominate English life in spite of universal suffrage. Not until 1945 did Britain have a really radical government.'

51. For other sketches and elaborations of the same argument, see JHP, *Essays* i, pp. 288–300, 358–62.

52. JHP, *The Death of the Past* (London, 1969), pp. 14–17, 24–5, 42, 56–7, 65, 104–7, 142–5.

53. For ART's speeches, see *HHL*: 23 Jan. 1963, cols. 46–52; 11 Feb. 1963, cols. 857–61; 27 Feb. 1963, cols. 125–33; 11 March 1964, cols. 436–48; 2 Dec. 1964, cols. 1097–1109; 3 Nov. 1965, cols. 829–35; 27 Jan. 1966, cols. 174–83; 14 June 1967, cols. 958–64; 25 June 1969, cols. 213–17.

The quotation in this sentence is from *HHL*, 15 Jan. 1964, col. 670. For ART, CPS and the College, see *HHL*: 2 Dec. 1964, col. 1117; 20 Dec. 1966, col. 1997; 4 March 1970, col. 408.

54. The original texts of ART's speeches in the Lords for 1963–70 are in Todd MSS 10/2.

55. Brooke, *Cambridge, 1870–1990*, pp. 568–69; ART, *HHL*, 25 June 1969, cols. 215–16; idem, *Time to Remember*, pp. 144–7, 174.

56. Todd MSS 2/23, Sir Burke Trend to ART, 30 Sept. 1963; ART to Trend, 8 Oct. 1963; ART, *Time to Remember*, pp. 162–3, 180–1; idem, *HHL*, 14 June 1967, cols. 960–1; Crowther, *Science in Modern Society*, pp. 76–83.

57. *The Times*, 3 Sept. 1970, reprinted in ART, *Time to Remember*, pp. 205–14.

58. JHP, 'A Unified Culture', *Encounter*, Aug. 1959, pp. 68–70.

59. ART, *Time to Remember*, pp. 163, 175–7, 211–14; Todd MSS 2/16, ART and S. Zuckerman, 'Minutes of Evidence Taken before the Committee on Higher Education', 27 Oct. 1961, 30 Oct. 1962; ART, *HHL*: 11 Dec. 1963, cols. 1278–84; 2 Dec. 1964, cols. 1108–9; 1 Dec. 1965, cols. 1322–7; 14 June 1967, cols. 959–62; 19 March 1969, col. 949.

60. F. R. Leavis, 'The Significance of C. P. Snow', *The Spectator*, 9 March 1962, pp. 297–303, reprinted in idem, *Nor Shall My Sword: Discourses on Pluralism, Compassion and Social Hope* (London, 1972), pp. 41–64.

61. S. Gorley Putt, 'The Snow-Leavis Rumpus', *The Antioch Review* xxiii (1963), 299–312; idem, *Wings*, pp. 259–75; R. Adams, 'Pomp and Circumstance: C. P. Snow', *Atlantic Monthly*, Nov. 1964, 95–8; L. Trilling, 'The Leavis-Snow Controversy', in idem, *Beyond Culture: Essays on Literature and Learning* (London, 1966), pp. 145–78; M. Green, 'Lionel Trilling and the Two Cultures', *Essays in Criticism* xiii (1963), 375–85. Collini, ed., *Two Cultures*, 'Introduction', pp. xxix–xliii.

62. Brooke, *Cambridge, 1870–1990*, pp. 147–50; Snow, *Stranger and Brother*, p. 41; C. E. Raven in *The Spectator*, 6 April 1962. JHP also disliked Raven: Snow MSS, 166.2, JHP to CPS, 15 January 1948: 'Raven doesn't matter. He's a cheap and vulgar character, and I'll get him and hurt him sooner or later.'

63. Plumb MSS, CPS to JHP, 7 March 1962; JHP in *The Spectator*, 30 March 1962; idem, 'The Historian's Dilemma', p. 42, and *Death of the Past*, p. 49, n. 1.

64. F. R. Leavis, 'Pluralism, Compassion and Social Hope', in *Nor Shall My Sword*, pp. 164–93.

65. Plumb MSS, CPS to JHP, 24 Nov. 1963; G. R. Elton, *The Practice of History* (Sydney, 1967), esp. pp. 41–50 for hostility to JHP (and E. H. Carr) as whigs who believed in progress; A. J. Taylor, ed., *The Standard of Living in Britain in the Industrial Revolution* (London, 1975), reprints most of the articles from the most famous (and most acrimonious) phase of the controversy.

66. Plumb MSS, CPS to JHP, 29 Nov. 1967; Snow MSS, 166.13, CPS to JHP 9 Feb. 1968; CPS, *Public Affairs*, pp. 8, 199–221, 223; idem, *HHL*, 6 July 1966, cols. 1133–40; 28 Feb. 1968, col. 862; 18 June 1968, col. 545; 4 March 1970, cols. 406–8; 10 Feb. 1971, cols. 145–54, 222–4; 27 March 1974, cols. 668–72.

67. JHP, *Essays* i, pp. 309–47, and *Essays* ii, pp. 169–254.

68. Putt, *Wings*, pp. 290, 294–8, 304–11; ART, *HHL*, 4 March 1970, cols. 408–13.

69. Annan, *The Dons*, pp. 2, 270; P. Ziegler, *Wilson: The Authorized Life of Lord Wilson of Rievaulx* (London, 1993), p. 176; Putt, *Wings*, pp. 93–4; Cannadine, *History in Our Time*, pp. 233–42. See in particular the exchange between CPS and Lord Eccles, where CPS failed to explain why, as a member of a government in favour of comprehensive schools, he had nevertheless sent his son to Eton: *HHL*, 10 Feb. 1965, col. 161.

70. G. Leff, review of JHP, *Death of the Past*, in *History* lvi (1971), 326–7; R. Strong, *The Roy Strong Diaries, 1967–87* (London, 1997), p. 283, with additions not included in this published version. I am grateful to Sir Roy Strong for permission to print them here.

71. F. M. Turner, 'Public Science in Britain, 1880–1919', in his *Contesting Cultural Authority: Essays in Victorian Intellectual Life* (Cambridge, 1993), pp. 201–2, 226–8. See also P. Gummett, *Scientists in Whitehall* (Manchester, 1980), pp. 32–5, 42–4, 170–3; H. Rose and S. Rose, *Science and Society* (London, 1969), p. 78. The argument advanced here also bears out the thesis advanced in K. V. Thomas, 'The Life of Learning', *Proceedings of the British Academy* cxvii (2002), 201–35.

72. Pimlott, *Wilson*, p. 328; R. Jenkins, *A Life at the Centre* (London, 1991), p. 178; R. Crossman, *The Diaries of a Cabinet Minister, vol. i* (London, 1975), pp. 36, 42, 117; *vol. ii*, (London, 1976), p. 378; Crowther, *Science in Modern Society*, pp. 88–96.

73. Plumb MSS, CPS to JHP, 30 Oct. 1970; Snow MSS: 197.4, ART to CPS, 5 March 1975; 166.17, JHP to CPS, 31 Oct. 1979; Snow, *Stranger and Brother*, p. 173; idem, *Time of Renewal*, p. 171; *CCM* 225 (2000), p. 14.

74. Plumb MSS, CPS to JHP, 9 Jan. 1980; CPS, *The Realists* (London, 1978), p. 254; idem, *The Physicists* (London, 1981), pp. 17, 35–9, 68, 138, 166; S. Ramanthan, *The Novels of C. P. Snow* (London, 1978), p. 67. See also J. Atkins, *Six Novelists Look at Society* (London, 1977), pp. 200–45.

75. Plumb MSS: JHP to Lady Snow, 16 July 1980; JHP to Philip Snow, 1 Aug. 1980; JHP to Donald Dickinson, 18 June 1985; Halperin, *Snow*, pp. 228, 233–6; CPS, *Trollope*, p. 107; Snow, *Time of Renewal*, pp. 222, 229. CPS's death was recorded in FWB, 2 July 1980.

76. Todd MSS: Box 16, ART to Owen Chadwick [Vice Chancellor], 30 Oct. 1970; Chadwick to ART, 31 Oct. 1970, 25 Sept. 1971; Box 96, ART, 'CUP – Reorganised and Rescued from Disaster, 1971–2' [Jan. 1973]; L. R. Lewitter, 'A Tribute to Lord Todd's Mastership', *CCM* 204 (1979), 8–9; ART, *Time to Remember*, pp. 215–57; idem, 'The Role of the National Academy', *CCM* 205 (1980), 7–9.

77. When ART agreed to follow CPS at Hatfield, he opined that 'a few less new universities, and a few more good polytechnics would do this country a deal of good': Todd MSS Box 108, ART to CPS, 3 July 1978. ART presented half a bottle of port to celebrate Thatcher's victory (FWB, 6 May 1979), and his death was recorded in FWB 13 Jan. 1997, when JHP presented the wine. See also S. Schama, 'Milton's Walk', *CCM* 201 (1976), p. 10; *Guardian*, 15 Jan. 1997.

78. Plumb MSS, CPS to JHP, 8 Dec. 1967; Snow MSS: 166.16, CPS to JHP, 8 Dec. 1967; 166.16, CPS to JHP, 9 March 1978; Snow, *Time of Renewal*, p. 199.

79. Snow MSS 166.16, JHP to CPS, 18, 31 Oct. 1977, 22 June 1978; Plumb MSS, CPS to JHP, 26 June 1968, 17, 24 Oct. 1979; J. P. Kenyon, 'The New Master: J. H. Plumb', *CCM* 203 (1978), pp. 12–13.

80. For JHP's vain pursuit of honours see: Plumb MSS, JHP to CPS, 7 Feb. 1975, 7 June 1976; Snow MSS: 166.15: CPS to JHP, 7 Feb. 1975; JHP to CPS, 8 Feb. 1975; 166.16, JHP to CPS, 8 Jan. 1976, 13 Jan. 1977. In the end, CPS created him a peer, as Lord Ryle, in *In Their Wisdom* (London, 1974). It was an inspired title, for if there was one thing JHP knew well how to do, it was indeed to rile.

81. Pimlott, *Wilson*, pp. 686–90; Ziegler, *Wilson*, pp. 494–8, 504, 509; M. Cowling, *Religion and Public Doctrine in Modern England* (Cambridge,

1980), pp. 389, 394–9; idem, 'The Sources of the New Right', *Encounter*, Nov. 1989, p. 8. See also two reviews of *Essays* i–ii: J. P. Kenyon, *TLS*, 23–29 June 1989; J. C. D. Clark, *English Historical Review* cv (1990), 989–91.

82. JHP, *Essays* i, p. 6; N. McKendrick, 'Sir John Plumb and the Christ's School of History', *CCM* 221 (1996), 22–6; J. Black, 'A Plumb with an acerbic aftertaste', *The Higher*, 16 Aug. 2002. JHP's death was recorded an unprecedented four times in FWB: 22, 24, 28 and 29 Oct. 2002.

83. H. L. Kornberg, 'The Todd Building Inaugurated', *CCM* 213 (1988), pp. 15–17. Within the Todd Building is to be found the Plumb Auditorium: *CCM* 227 (2002), p. 47.

84. CPS, *The Masters*, Appendix; Halperin, *Snow*, pp. 156–7.

85. P. Snow, N. Annan, M. Black, S. Rose, G. Steiner, 'Symposium: The Two Cultures Revisited', *Cambridge Review*, March 1987, pp. 3–14; M. Kettle, 'Two Cultures Still', *Guardian*, 2 Feb. 2002; G. Wheatcroft, 'Two Cultures at Forty', *Prospect*, May 2002, pp. 62–4; W. G. Runciman and R. M. May, *'Two Bodies, One Culture': Speeches Given at the Centenary Dinner of the British Academy, 4 July 2002* (London, 2002); Collini, ed., *Two Cultures*, 'Introduction', pp. xliii–lxxi.

86. *CCM* 208 (1983), pp. 1–2, 8–10.

87. For national coverage, see *The Times*, 23 June and 19 Nov. 1982; *Daily Telegraph*, 19 April 1982; *Sunday Times*, 16 April, 16 May, 27 June and 17 Oct. 1982. For local coverage, see *Stop Press with Varsity*: 24 April, 15 Oct., 12 and 19 Nov. 1982.

PART SEVEN

THE COLLEGE BY 2005

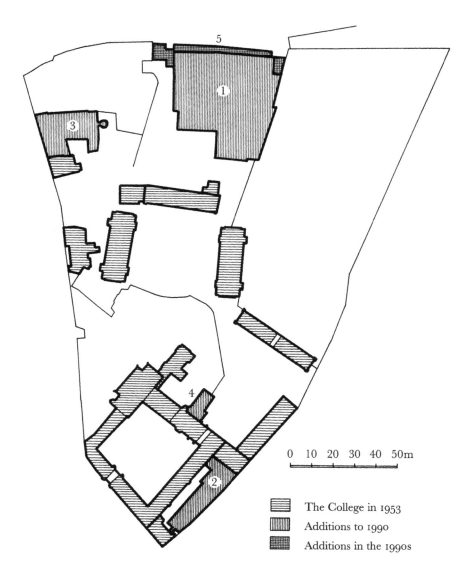

5

3

1

0 10 20 30 40 50m

The College in 1953

Additions to 1990

Additions in the 1990s

4

2

1 – New Court (1970)   2 – New Library (1976)

3 – Todd Building – former County Hall (purchased 1985)

4 – Renovated Fellows' Rooms and Pantry (1990)   5 – Staircase 4 (1993)

THE LAST THIRD of the twentieth century was one of the most prolific periods of building in the College's history. In 1937 the Fellows had shied away from modernism; thirty years on they embraced it more willingly. Denys Lasdun – architect of the University of East Anglia and later the National Theatre on London's South Bank – was commissioned to design New Court (1970) – a complex of sixty-six study bedrooms and six fellows' sets on a stepped terrace at the rear of the College. A new library was opened in 1976, replacing the 1913 bath house off First Court. In 1985 the College purchased the old County Hall, converting it into basement offices, student rooms and a new meeting place for the Governing Body. The Todd Building, topped by the Plumb Auditorium, was formally opened by Prince Philip, Chancellor of the University, in July 1987. And in 1993 the streetward side of New Court was given a friendlier aspect by the completion of Staircase 4 – a series of forty upmarket student rooms built with an eye on the vacation conference trade. These new buildings enabled the College to accommodate more of the student body on-site, rather than in remote lodging houses.

Yet all these physical changes – notable in themselves – were eclipsed by something more fundamental. The College was founded by the mother of a king. It had been kept running by generations of women staff – some of whom, as we saw in the nineteenth century, at times assumed stereotypically male roles. That said, Christ's was an essentially male institution for nearly all of its first five hundred years. All, that is, except the last quarter-century.

The University, as a whole, was slow to admit women, though Fellows of Christ's such as John Seeley and especially John Peile, were in the vanguard of reform. Girton and Newnham were founded in the late nineteenth century, but at a safe distance from the men, and women were not awarded full Cambridge degrees until 1948 – the honorary doctorate conferred on Queen Elizabeth during her visit on 21 October being the first. In the 1950s the expansion of the University continued on single-sex lines, with the establishment of New Hall and Lucy Cavendish (for mature women students). The first mixed colleges came in the 1960s, and only at the graduate level, but then co-residence became a major demand of student reformers and liberal dons. The result was an almost instant revolution, when measured in historical rather than political time. In 1969 no male college admitted women as members; by 1987 all were officially mixed. King's and Churchill were the first to open their doors (in 1972) and Christ's, rather typically, came in the middle.

In November 1974 the Governing Body established a committee to investigate the practical implications of admitting women, stressing that this was in no way a commitment to do so. The committee took account of experience at the first mixed colleges and co-opted a woman tutor from Churchill. The thrust of its report was literally to domesticate the problem, to show that women could be accommodated within College life without drastic change (apart from, say, doors instead of curtains on the showers in New Court). The committee reported in May 1975 but a special Governing Body meeting to discuss the issue of principle was not convened until 9 November 1976 – by which time the momentum across the University had become clear. The vote was thirty-seven in favour and twelve against, with two abstentions. On 14 December the Governing Body formally approved the admission of female graduate students the following autumn and women undergraduates from October 1979.

A velvet revolution, but a revolution nonetheless. Christ's has witnessed several major transformations since 1505. A Catholic chantry converted into a powerhouse of the Puritan Reformation. A backwater of clerical privilege that became an international centre of research. A religious community secularized and invigorated by science. All these were dramatic changes behind the apparently unchanging façade. No less important was the end of male dominion. The working out of this revolution will take many decades. But, when another history of Christ's comes to be written in 2505, the admission of women will surely be deemed one of the most significant innovations of the College's first millennium.

SIMON SCHAMA

Souvent me souvient

FORGIVE ME, SHADE of C. P. Snow, but this is true: I heard Christ's before I ever saw it. An impenetrable December pea-souper shrouded the College as I made my way through the Third Court car-park and up forbidding flights of oak stairs to the room into which, for one night, I would be locked. It was late on a Saturday evening. Rectangles of sallow light were the only evidence of occupancy. Inside the room was an unlit gas fire, a rug which may once have been green or possibly grey and now was both, and a grimly solid, heavily scuffed desk. Volumes on macro-economic policy, as if exhausted by the weight of their own scientific pretensions, leaned against each other for comfort on the sparse shelves. I was trying the mercilessly unyielding bed when I heard, for the first time, the slightly flat clang of the bell in First Court, chiming the hour (eleven). The clangs went on a little longer than seemed natural, as if supported by the density of the fog, each one sustained before the next struck; a canon of the hour. For the next fifteen years that bell would toll the divisions of my Cambridge life: a summons to dine; to be supervised on the hour; to hurry to a College meeting; to mourn a colleague. It was the companion of sleepless nights; a doleful commiserator with adversity, a reluctant celebrator of successes; a melancholy Eeyore of a bell. I still hear it, three thousand miles and an ocean away. I will, I think, always hear it.

It was 1961. I was sixteen, much too young and much too agitated to attempt the College entrance examination. But other, cleverer, historians at my school had gone to Christ's before their A-levels, and had come away with an Exhibition or a Scholarship. I was supposed to do the same. But I was, in those days, an observant Jew: no breakfast bacon; no exams on the Sabbath. The College went out of its way to be helpful. As it happened, the Senior Tutor was in London at a rugby match. (He was generally at a rugby match). En route from Twickenham, I was informed, he would collect me from my house, drive me to Christ's where, briefly incarcerated, I would do the Saturday exam, in my room, on Sunday. The Senior Tutor, a medic, arrived at the Golders Green semi; summed up my likely eligibility for the Third Fifteen (non-existent), sighed a little sigh, and ushered me into the waiting Austin. As his driver (who also functioned as the NCO of the Buttery) tore through a fog that was not so much low visibility as no visibility, and at a speed which periodically sent my stomach for a quick visit to my brain which duly returned the favour, the Senior Tutor offered me a bitterly cheerful guide as to what was in store. '*Tremendously* cold, Cambridge this time of the year. And damp, my goodness me, *very* damp.'

He was right. Later, the clanging bell and the sputtering gas fire did a number in collegiate syncopation, while I shivered beneath blankets which were formidably hairy and the colour of oxtail soup. The next morning, the fog had lifted so that the breakfast tray, covered by a green baize cloth, as if protecting the Eucharist, was revealed in all its brutal glory: a mess of fried eggs cooked by a feverish surrealist, the frilled edges slightly burned, and, nudging up against it, a short bend of greasy sausage and yes, the diabolical rasher, sent to try my Orthodoxy. Flinching, I ate many triangles of cold, burned, pliable toast, drank strong tea and then did the Three Hour Essay, the subject of which I have not the faintest recollection.

The next day, in the Senate House, I not so much passed the exam as passed out, a histrionic meltdown, resulting from misguided late-night swatting up the minutiae of the Diplomatic Revolution. You wanted to know everything about relations between the Duke of Newcastle, the Elector of Saxony, Frederick the Great and Count Choiseul? I was your man. But in the Senate House, turning over the exam paper, I discovered that unfortunately the questions had been written entirely in Swahili, or so it seemed as I stared in glassy incomprehension. A serious but kindly invigilator (and as I discovered many years later a contributor to this volume) attempted to deal with distress verging on hysterics, talked me off the ledge and back into the Senate House where someone had mysteriously translated the paper back into English while the Candidate had been Indisposed.

Dimly aware things were not proceeding according to plan, I reckoned my best chance to redeem myself was the Interview. The interviewer, however, was John Kenyon, (years later, a friend), who sniffed lugubriously at me while I struggled manfully with an interrogation, behind which seemed to lurk the depressing, unspoken assumption that 'you don't really *believe* any of this do you, sunshine?' But, dear readers, I did. I believed in Progress and The Enlightenment, in Rosa Luxemburg, Emiliano Zapata, Charlie Parker, Sartre, CND, and the whole, fabulous, inscrutable but unalterably benevolent onward march of the irresistible, all-harmonizing neo-Hegelian dialectic. From the accelerated tempo of the sniffing, however, I gathered that Kenyon neither shared these enthusiasms, nor wished to hear much about them. Desperate to ingratiate myself, as he ended the interview with the formulaic 'and is there anything you would like to ask yourself?' I blurted out, 'Er, those *animals* over the gateway . . . what *are* they?' A long pause was followed by a deep, brutally dismissive sniff; a thermonuclear sniff, potent enough to annihilate the optimism of an entire generation of undergraduates. 'Those . . . (pause) . . . are . . . (sigh) . . . *Yales.*' 'Oh, I see, thank you *so* much.' I could feel Kenyon's sorrowing gaze follow me all the way down the staircase boring a hole in the back of my neck.

Next year? 1962. A cakewalk. No fog, no bacon, no Senior Tutor, no fainting in coils, no sniffery-dismissery, no problem. Instead, a first sighting of the man who was Christ's history – J. H. Plumb – and who twinkled a smile of almost cherubic Pickwickian benevolence at me, in his rooms, and prematurely welcomed me to the College with one of his high-pitched chuckles of complicity. But I was still only seventeen. I got things wrong. Whatever Jack Plumb was, he was certainly no Mr Pickwick.

Fast forward to 1963, my first year at Christ's. Looking into the Buttery, I seemed to have matriculated into Brobdingnag; for the average size and heft of the regulars was six foot six, usually cubed. Christ's, it dawned on me as I failed to cut a path through the cheerfully roaring scrum, was primarily known and for good reason as The Rugby College. What on earth, then, was I doing there? What were all the other matriculated Lilliputians doing there? There had been, apparently, a change of regime; if not a full-fledged *coup d'état,* then a decidedly New

Direction, heralded by the incoming of small, thin, nervous lower-middle-class suburban adolescents and sundry types whose ticket of admission could only have been as toilers of brain rather than brawn. The engineer of the coup was, of course, J. H. Plumb or rather 'Jack' as we historians were commanded to call him, too soon, we thought, for comfort. And we, along with similarly puny but loquacious undergraduate devotees of the New Criticism or the later Wittgenstein were supposed to be the vanguard of an intellectual reconquest; pint-size Athenians taking on the biggest and best of the Sparta on Hobson's Lane.

Supervisions with different Fellows of the College were our testing-ground and each had their own intellectual micro-climate. Quentin Skinner's supervisions were a whirlwind of analytical intensity; in which lazy, gratuitous anecdotage (rather my forte) was tossed aside to expose the philosophical core of the question at hand. An hour with Quentin and you came out thinking you were far cleverer than you in fact were, benevolently deluded into imagining you had undergone, some-how, an exhilarating exercise in intellectual collaboration, albeit as the very junior partner. In Jonathan Steinberg's supervisions in American history, the tone was more playful (especially when we discovered a common enthusiasm for modern jazz) but in its way artfully exacting since undergraduates were expected to come up with sources and interpretations that circumnavigated the obvious. Transcendentalist utopianism? Read Hawthorne's *Blythedale Romance*, rather than Emerson's *On Nature*. The New Deal? Start, not with Roosevelt, but with Harry Hopkins, the harness-maker's boy from Grinnell, Iowa, and Robert Sherwood's personal narrative of the relationship between the President and his closest adviser. Steinberg's supervisions were perhaps more boogie-woogie than be-bop, the right hand keeping close to the motif while the left hand raced off doing puckish, inventive runs around the Main Issue.

But it was on O Staircase, in Jack Plumb's rooms, of course, between the Sèvres and the Dutch pictures, that the most testing baptism of fire took place. Survival, even commendation, at the end of the hour guaranteed a rush of hard-earned confidence, a tactlessly gleeful entrance into the Buttery where less fortunate casualties of Plumb's coruscating cross-examinations were attempting to reconstitute themselves over pints of bitter. Perhaps surprisingly – though he prided himself, rightly, on the virtuosity of his erudition and the versatility of his teaching – Jack often taught medieval history to the first year undergraduates. In a time when Walter Ullmann at Trinity had made Papal ideology the dominant frame for understanding the great clashes of medieval Europe, Plumb's approach was more anthropological. (In the early 1960s he had already become a great champion of Fernand Braudel and the *Annales*). So while undergraduates grappling with contests between Papacy and Empire were tempted, not unreasonably, to concentrate on the issues of sovereignty implied by Charlemagne's coronation, Jack would want them to think instead of the 'Long-Haired Kings', the Merovingians, the predecessors of the Carolingians, being driven in their chariots long after their power had evaporated, tresses intact, touching for the King's Evil, ritually preserved relics of emptied-out mystery. (He was a great admirer of J. M. Wallace-Hadrill's book on the subject and of Marc Bloch's *Les Rois Thaumaturges*.) Those who didn't get this kind of point, at once acute and creatively perverse, risked dismissive banishment to the outer galaxies of the Ordinary; not a place you ever wanted to be in the cultural universe of J. H. Plumb.

I got him for Tudors and Stuarts into which terra incognita (for at school we seemed to have perpetually recycled Hanoverians and Victorians all the way to A-levels) I plunged with incoherent curiosity. The results were sometimes greeted by Plumb with enthusiasm (an essay on Elizabethan government, such as it was); and as often with incredulity that I had made matters so glaringly simple (why, for example, Charles I had lost his head) so intricate and unpickable a knot of contradictions. It's safe to say that the Civil War and I were not made for each other, not at any rate, in 1964. After a marathon two-week struggle with the one word essay question 'Why?'; after nights of groggy embroilment with everything Christopher Hill, Conrad Russell and Hugh Trevor Roper had ever written (no wonder I was a mess), I cracked, rapping on Plumb's door at nine o'clock one evening, begging for an extension and confessing the whole thing had somehow got Beyond Me. As unsympathetic as he could be to this kind of self-inflicted intellectual wound, Jack suddenly made me feel that a failure to decide between inevitability and contingency in 1640 was not, after all the end of the world. We chatted for an hour or so over a glass of wine, of the Petition of Right and the years of Personal Rule and finally of Van Dyck's great equestrian portrait of the King. Whether it was the Château Léoville-Barton or the message of the baroque painting coming to the rescue, both the assertion and the breakdown of divine-right royal sovereignty suddenly came into crisp focus.

To those taught by him, whether exhilarated or intimidated (and most of us, at different times, experienced both reactions), Jack Plumb was, for all his short, round shape, altogether larger than life. Famously, he liked dividing people into those who, on entering a room raised or lowered the temperature and often he himself sent the mercury right out of the glass. He could bully and goad; he could encourage and sympathize with bursts of gentle understanding; but the raillery was almost always brilliantly witty, and his characterizations of humanity, taken in collective and individual versions, alive and dead, as acute as the best novelists of the human comedy – Austen or Trollope (even though he insisted on mounting a stout defence of Arnold Bennett). It was very clear to us that whatever superior wisdom Jack had as an historian came directly from his full-blooded engagement in the world beyond, as well as within, the academy. There was a touch of Grub Street in him (which would let him grudgingly tolerate my own occasional moonlighting for the *Sunday Times* Magazine when I was a young don), and this feel for the commonplace voice, for the disorderly quotidian mess of history, its protean resistance against the categories convenient to historiography, the arid arrangement of hierarchies of causal significance – all made him perhaps more of a writer about the past than a coherent structural analyst, which was just fine with me. Recognizing this quality he would, when I submitted essays early, take immense and generous pains over an arbitrarily chosen page or even paragraph, going through it sentence by sentence for passages of disfigured style, botched syntax (a lot of that) and adjectival self-indulgence (ditto) all of which would be subjected to one of the most vigilantly corrective editorial hands I have ever experienced. The pruning was severe but the attentiveness sympathetic and sensitive to the nature of the plant. To his great credit, the exercise in disciplined cultivation was not to turn us all into little literary versions of himself – a mere nursery of Plumb-Trees.

Inevitably, though, there were moments of orchestrated gladiatorial combat with Jack's own small but decisive thumb turned (metaphorically) up or down. The most nerve-racking of these performances were his after-dinner seminars, convened in the panelled dining room opposite the sitting room at the top of O Staircase. There, in the candelight (issuing, naturally, from Paul de Lamerie silver sticks of fabulous rococo ornateness), with silver baskets stacked high with fruit, decanters of claret (to be circulated after the paper had been read), all set on a Georgian mahogany table polished so we could see in it our own flustered faces, we faced our several and individual baptisms of fire. Our Falstaff's army, assembled for Jack's inspection, included a startling number of those who subsequently went on to become prolific and distinguished historians – Geoffrey Parker, the authority on Philip II's Spain; Ted Royle, the historian of radical and evangelical Britain; Christopher Green, who switched to art history and ended up writing a great book about Léger and presiding over modern art history at the Courtauld Institute; Andrew Wheatcroft, who has written on the Ottoman and Habsburg Empires and on the culture clash of Islam and Christianity; John Barber, the historian of Soviet Russia; and not least Roy Porter, who even then knew everything about the eighteenth century but was too modest and too shy, yes, *shy*, to say so.

Seemingly always there, at least in my memory, was also the sardonic, elegant Norman Sosnow, the son of the Polish-Jewish economist Eric Sosnow, who had gone from writing about economics to making money, lots of it, in business. Eric had wanted to turn Norman into the perfect hybrid of English manners and Jewish worldly savvy and, despite sending him to Rugby, the transformation had succeeded to an astonishing degree, for Norman appeared at Plumb's seminar in impeccably tailored three-piece Savile Row suits, complete with buttonhole, and proceeded to drop lapidary aperçus on anything from the general frightfulness of Pitt the Younger to the wicked cunning of Zhou En Lai. Jack indulged him and we were slightly in awe of him. He liked to give off waves of indolent *je m'en fichisme*, but the dirty little truth was that, especially in his last year, Norman resolved to become everything his father wanted, and turned into a conscientious, even studious, reader. I once discovered him in his rooms off Maid's Causeway listening to João Gilberto and deep in histories of Indian nationalism. Years later, Norman disappeared aboard a plane flying somewhere over South Africa but no one who was at those Plumb seminars is likely to forget him, not least because he was the only one of us with the insouciance to return some of Jack's fiercer barbs in kind.

The seminar was hardest, of course, on the speaker, since should he ramble on digressively, he risked the censorious twanging of elastic bands mysteriously materializing from – where – Jack's waistcoat pocket? Thus, for instance, Schama: 'and still the debates raged on at Salamanca University...' TWANG! '...on whether or not the Indians of Peru could in fact be enslaved' DOUBLE-TWANG! Schama speeds up and drops to panic-stricken gabble, molto allegro, sotte voce – 'notwithstandingtheneedforabondedlabourforceinthesilvermines-ofHuancavelica ... and so in *conclusion*...' Definitive, satisfactory TWANG!

Most often, in fact, Jack then supplied a few encouraging words and it was the turn of the seminar to comment, in the same direction that the claret was passed. At this point some of us had trouble multi-tasking, wielding the grape scissors (silver again), at the same time as coming up with a comment that would reveal in the properly laconic I don't-want-to-out-foot-note-you manner the breadth of our reading, the depth of our understanding and the penetration of our critical acumen. But it was easy to be intellectually wrong-footed in these discussions precisely because we never were sure which of the two Plumbs were going to show up. There was the Annaliste Plumb, much taken with the historical investigation of social habit, so that the real event of significance in the conquest of America might be not the destruction of the Aztec empire but the discovery of the potato. But then there was the rhetorical Plumb who detested the social determinism of Sir Lewis Namier's reduction of eighteenth-century politics to the war of interests and who (at that time at any rate) insisted on re-asserting the play of ideas amidst the fight of factions. The truth was that both these instincts, the epicurean and the acquisitive on the one hand, and the polemical and the political on the other, cohabited within Plumb's own intellectual temper and the worst thing one could do was to second-guess at any moment what he supposed to be the dominant historical trait governing a particular event or phenomenon. So we tended to tell the truth as the documents had educated us to see it, free from any obligation to toe an historiographical party line. And that intellectual liberty (in a time at Cambridge when party allegiance to sovereign method-ologies reigned at Clare or Peterhouse) was perhaps the richest gift of those memorable seminars.

The last year was different. Failing to give the Tudor and Stuart gobbets the kind of Talmudic reverence they apparently demanded in the canon of English constitutional history, I had crashed to a 2:1 in the Historical Tripos. This seemed no more than just deserts, but Jack took The Great Disappointment personally, ordaining that some sort of miscarriage of justice had been engineered by the examiners and that the College was to pretend that I had, in fact, been robbed of the First that was supposed to have been my birthright. The gesture was extraordinarily generous but also deeply embarrassing, not least in the company of my friends whose own 2:1s and 2:2s were judged to have been perfectly fitting. Taken too seriously, the reprieve could also have reduced me to a wreck as Part II of the Tripos approached and with it a daunting moment suspended between vindication and humiliation.

But what the hell, I was having a ball. Having turned my back on a career in the Law (thank you O *Winfield on Tort*), I read medieval history with dizzy elation. At the top of a staircase in Neville's Court, Trinity, I was ushered into the rooms of Walter Ullmann during Long Vac Term, 1965. His spectacles resembled those of Pope Pius XII and sat perched on the end of the prominent, beaky nose. Ullmann's academic gown glowed with a strange, iridescent verdigris that appeared to be spreading across his shoulders like some ancient fungus. There was a vast mug steaming with some brackish fluid at the bottom and every so often Ullmann would flick ash from his Woodbine so that it fell conveniently into his trouser turn-ups. At the first supervision (on the Emperor Constantine and the Edict of Milan) I read, with understandable nervousness, as Ullmann abruptly rose from his seat, Woodbine still in hand and strode to the window while an improbably savage electric storm banged over the Cam. I stopped reading, expecting a correction to some egregious misunderstanding of the ecclesiastical texts, but after a titanic thunderclap, Ulmann leaned into the livid gloom and declared prophetically as yet another bolt of lightning hit the Backs: 'I HEAR THE DEATH KNELL OF BYZANTIUM!' It was now my turn to be thunderstruck, asking tentatively, after a pause 'Shall I go on?' Ullmann smiled apologetically, returned, albeit reluctantly, to the twentieth century and commanded 'Read, read!' I did as I was told.

It was a good year. There was a Labour government of whom we had high hopes, not yet blighted; Indian history, a lot of it, absorbed in the tiny reading room of the Centre for South Asian Studies in Laundress Lane; punts drifting past as I pondered the political character flaws of Surendranath Banerjea and Motilal Nehru; there were supervisions from the rumbustious, tough-minded Ronald Robinson in St John's who usually needed me to make him a tank of black coffee to jump-start a morning supervision on, say, the Suez Canal; there were heady discussions of the Meiji Restoration and the precise significance of Okubo Toshimichi in the reconstruction of the Japanese state. There were girlfriends and the usual climbing in and out; and there was the editing of the self-effacingly entitled magazine *Cambridge Opinion,* which sent my friend Martin Sorrell and I to America and later to central Europe in the years when Vietnam had suddenly become serious, and whispers about the decline of Antonin Novotny's Stalinist regime could already be heard murmured in the cafés of Prague. And, in the second part of the Tripos there was, I regret to record, in the Indian history paper, projectile vomiting from the unfortunate party immediately behind me, which, such was my enthusiasm for the subject, had no seriously damaging results on my performance.

In 1966, the taught abruptly became the teacher, and the twenty-one-year-old intellectual novice was precociously and outlandishly promoted to a teaching Fellowship at Christ's; stipend £800 plus all the claret I could drink and pay for. This was simultaneously intoxicating and excruciating. I was now supposed to instruct people in the finer points of medieval church history who, but a few months before, had seen me dancing to the Rolling Stones, a spectacle unlikely to enhance my bid for academic authority. At the very moment when the glamour of British pop culture was at its most alluring and febrile, I was supposed to master the protocol of High Table and, in the Senior Combination Room, act as 'Mr Nib', the scribe of the wine book.

Unsurprisingly, behavioural schizophrenia ensued. After a hard day's grind through the Repeal of the Corn Laws and Andrew Jackson's disputes with the Supreme Court (for in good Christ's tradition I was supposed to teach everything to everyone), followed by High Table, Combining and Nibbing, I went back to the house on Chaucer Road which I shared with a geophysicist and a Sudanese Marxist, and reverted to type, alternating Berg and Beethoven with Bob Dylan and Pink Floyd. Jack Plumb began to pass on review assignments from the United States, which may have been counter-productive for my budding sense of scholarly vocation since I got seriously bitten by the journalist bug. A day or so each week, assigned pieces to write by an ex-history undergraduate and friend, then working for the *Sunday Times*, in the golden age of Harold Evans's editorship, I would moonlight in the Gray's Inn Road, doing history vignettes for the magazine. I wrote, most often on art, for anyone who would have me: the short-lived, but spectacularly stoned *Ink*, the child of Richard Ingrams; for the *Times Literary Supplement* and the *New Statesman* and for Tony Elliott's *Time Out*. It was during a particularly ear-splitting, strobe-lit *Time Out* party somewhere in Leicester Square that I was attacked by a contaminated oyster; one of the half-dozen that had been supplied to the College, undergraduates and dons alike, by the owner of Cunningham's Oyster Bars 'in token of his appreciation for Christ's'. Since one in three consumers suffered the same attack of violent food poisoning, exactly thirty-six hours after ingestion, one assumes he had made his point.

Back in Cambridge, I continued, somehow (and to the growing displeasure of Jack Plumb), to nose after journalism, editing the weekly *Cambridge Review* from my ground-floor rooms in the handsomely Palladian Fellows' Building, together with two American co-editors, one destined for Wall Street, the other for a lectureship in English at the University of East Anglia. We hired Clive James to write about films, pontificated mightily on the uproar in the University (for this was now 1968 and *les événements* had come to Cambridge in the shape of sit-ins at the Senate House). We discovered, thrillingly, the typescript poems Sylvia Plath had written for her English Tripos while at Newnham, and we put together a rather grandiose anthology of articles from the *Review*, including essays by Bertrand Russell, J. J. Thompson and Maynard Keynes. We were duly put in our place by a benevolently patronizing review by Hugh Trevor Roper who thought the difference in self-regard on the part of Oxford and Cambridge was perfectly caught by the fact that while we chose to call our collection *The Cambridge Mind*, the corresponding anthology of essays from its counterpart in The Other Place saw the light of day as *The Oxford Sausage*.

By the early 1970s I was seeing a lot of Bedford, Buckingham and Banbury, as I drove regularly to Oxford in search of a graduate seminar devoted to eighteenth-century European history, for, amazingly there was none in Cambridge. I gatecrashed Jack Plumb's graduate seminar on English history, which by now included Linda Colley and John Brewer as well as Roy Porter and which, especially when Quentin Skinner sat in for Jack during a year of his sabbatical, saw methodological sparks fly in a way that caught fire in each of our intellectual imaginations. I was talking to John Brewer a lot about his strongly anti-Namierite work on Wilkes and radical politics, reading Skinner on speech-acts and beginning to think about how what became called 'the turn to language' – the much delayed recognition that ideology could constitute social and political allegiance rather than be constituted by it – could be fruitfully applied to the French Revolution. I may, in fact have taken this new found enthusiasm for the play of rhetoric a bit too far since when I gave one of the course of eight lectures allowed to untenured teaching Fellows by the History Faculty, and did so on the French Revolution, I apparently stood on a table, waved my arms around a lot and bellowed in French, the better to impersonate the body language of Mirabeau, Desmoulins and Georges Danton. Or so some of the audience including Roy Porter later claimed, though, being famous even then for public diffidence, this recollection of a theatrical lecturing style surely seems far-fetched.

Though I was working in the Dutch archives in The Hague as well as the Archives Nationales in Paris, the disputes then roiling the academy of French history, as fierce and unsparing as anything in the Revolution itself, were having an important effect on my own work. The tumbrils weren't carrying denounced profs to the Place de la Révolution, but at least within the Sorbonne and the École des Hautes Études, reputations if not heads were indeed rolling. At stake was the hitherto undisputed thesis passed down from a series of Marxist historians beginning with Albert Mathiez, that the Revolution was to be understood as the work of upwardly mobile bourgeoisie, frustrated by the anachronisms of feudal and absolutist institutions. Sitting in the reading room of the University Library reading room absorbing the impact of François Furet's devastating assault on the nostrums of what he witheringly characterized as the 'catechism' of French Revolutionary history, a cataract fell from my eyes. Following where Furet beckoned, and encouraged by John Roberts at Merton College, and much more surprisingly by Richard Cobb (whose interest in revolutionary ideology was nil), I began to think again about the volumes of revolutionary oratory, which for at least half a century had been discarded and despised as the redundant and disingenuous blather of self-interested windbags. So while Brewer and Colley were tilting at Namier, I began to do the same at the heirs of Mathiez and Lefebvre. In the early Seventies I met Furet himself who became the most generous and warm-hearted mentor.

But all this was taking me, temperamentally and I suppose intellectually, farther and farther from Christ's and indeed from Cambridge. While working away at my research on the fate of the Dutch Republic in the time of the Revolutionary and Napoleonic Wars, I had been assigned as supervisor an eminent economic historian of the Anglo-Dutch world, who, however, seldom showed up for meetings. Our infrequent encounters, though, failed to deter him years later from publishing in the pages of the *New York Review of Books* a mildly critical review of my eventual book – the gist of which was to wonder in print why a young scholar of some promise should have wanted to fritter away all those years in the archives on a subject so self-evidently picayune and dull.

I was in the doldrums. By the mid-Seventies I had published just two articles, each of which seemed to justify the supervisor's pessimism, one on educational reform in the Netherlands; another on the collapse of municipal autonomy in Holland in the Napoleonic Wars. Neither seemed calculated to blaze or even smoulder a trail. Year after year at Christ's I was teaching pupils of rich and original talent – among them Michael Neve and Dominic Lieven – but increasingly I was on cruise control: if it's Monday it must be the Fourth Crusade; if it's Thursday, the rise of the Indian Congress. Junior colleagues elected to Research Fellowships like Geoffrey Parker and Roy Porter did the nibbing now at Christ's, and for a while we remade something of the old scholarly camaraderie we'd had under fire in the heyday of the Plumb seminars. But we were all moving to different places; both methodologically and literally – Geoffrey more and more in the orbit of Fernand Braudel's socially and geographically determined reading of the early modern world; Roy embedded in the history of eighteenth-century geology and feeling his way towards a marvellous marriage of the history of science and the history of social ideas. More crucially, I kept failing to get a job in the Cambridge Faculty of History. My time as a Danton impersonator was clearly running out.

Oxford, in particular Brasenose College, came to the rescue, and it was there that I published my first two books and where I started work in earnest on another, bigger work on Dutch culture, which became *The Embarrassment of Riches*. That long project was, I now realize, and without ever explicitly being so intended, an attempted fusion of the two methodologies which I had explored at Christ's: the anthropological and the rhetorical, as well as between the two skills Plumb had insisted were mutually interdependent, the narrative and the analytical.

So when, almost twenty years later I came back from the United States to Christ's to lecture on 'Landscape and Memory', the landscape of the place carried with it its own freight of memories. There was the wisteria draped over Lady Margaret's oriel window at the Master's Lodge; there were the cobbles of First Court and the eighteenth-century swimming pool in the garden in which I'd swum just once before the foot slipped on some weedy slime and something beneath that, slippery and in motion. There were many of my old colleagues sipping post-prandial wine in the Senior Combination Room who had indulged for so long my often over-colourful construction of what it meant to be a Christ's don. And there, finally, was that bell, the tocsin of my unformed intellect, clanging in salutary reminder that there was still much to learn, and that the College of Milton and Darwin had always been a good place to buckle down, be brave and start afresh.

The Contributors

JOHN BURROW entered Christ's as a Robert Owen Bishop Scholar in 1954 and J. H. Plumb was one of his teachers. He was an undergraduate, graduate student and Research Fellow at the College, before holding teaching positions at the University of East Anglia and the University of Sussex. He was elected a Fellow of the British Academy in 1986. From 1995 until his retirement in 2000 he occupied the Chair of European Thought at Oxford. His books include *Evolution and Society: A Study in Victorian Social Theory* (1966), *A Liberal Descent: Victorian Historians and the English Past* (1981), which won the Wolfson Prize in 1981, *Gibbon* (1985) and *The Crisis of Reason: European Thought, 1848–1914* (2000). He is also editor of the Penguin edition of Darwin's *On the Origin of Species*.

DAVID CANNADINE is Queen Elizabeth the Queen Mother Professor of History at the Institute of Historical Research in the University of London. Educated at Cambridge, Oxford and Princeton, he was a Fellow of Christ's from 1977 to 1988. Like many Plumb protégés, he then crossed the Atlantic to take a Chair at Columbia University, New York, before returning to Britain as Director of the IHR in 1998. His many books include *The Decline and Fall of the British Aristocracy*, *G. M. Trevelyan: A Life in History*, *Class in Britain*, *Ornamentalism: How the British Saw Their Empire*, and *In Churchill's Shadow*. He is Vice-Chairman of the Trustees of the

253

National Portrait Gallery, a Trustee of the Kennedy Memorial Trust, a Commissioner of English Heritage, a member of the Advisory Council of the National Archives, and Vice-Chairman of the Editorial Board of *Past & Present.*

BARRIE DOBSON was Professor of Medieval History at Cambridge and a Fellow of Christ's from 1988 to 1999. A native of Teesdale, he read Modern History at Wadham College, Oxford. After six years as a Lecturer at the University of St Andrews, he joined the Department of History in the then new University of York in 1964. He has written on many aspects of York's medieval past, and was also heavily involved in founding the pioneering York Centre for Medieval Studies. He was Deputy Vice-Chancellor of the University of York from 1984 to 1987. During his eleven years as a Fellow of Christ's, he wrote a series of studies on aspects of late medieval Cambridge, especially its monastic houses and Jewry. After retirement in 1999 he returned to York, where he is currently the Master of the five-hundred-year-old Company of Merchant Taylors.

ROY PORTER was an undergraduate, graduate student and Research Fellow at Christ's between 1965 and 1972, before migrating via Churchill College to the Wellcome Institute in London, where he was Professor in the Social History of Medicine from 1993. A prolific author, his books include *The Making of Geology: Earth Science in Britain, 1688–1815* (1977), *English Social History in the Eighteenth Century* (1982), *London: A Social History* (1994), *The Greatest Benefit to Mankind: A Medical History of Humanity* (1997) and *Enlightenment: Britain and the Creation of the Modern World* (2000), which won a Wolfson Literary Prize. He died suddenly in 2002 at the age of fifty-five, soon after completing his draft chapter for this volume.

DAVID REYNOLDS is Professor of International History at Cambridge. He has been a Fellow of Christ's since 1983 and has held visiting appointments at Harvard and at Nihon University in Tokyo. He is the author or editor of nine books, including two prize-winning studies of World War Two – *The Creation of the Anglo-American Alliance, 1937–1941* (1981) and *Rich Relations: The American Occupation of Britain, 1942–1945* (1995). Other books include *Britannia Overruled: British Policy and World Power in the Twentieth Century* (1991) and *One World Divisible: A Global History since 1945* (2000). His most recent work is a study of Churchill's war memoirs entitled *In Command of History: Churchill Fighting and Writing The Second World War* (2004).

SIMON SCHAMA, CBE, is University Professor of Art History and History at Columbia University, New York. He was an undergraduate and then Fellow at Christ's from 1963 to 1976, before moving to Brasenose College, Oxford (1976–80) and Harvard (1980–93). His books include *Patriots and Liberators: Revolution in the Netherlands, 1780–1813* (1977), which won the Wolfson and Leo Gershoy Prizes; *The Embarrassment of Riches: An Interpretation of Dutch Culture* (1987); *Citizens: A Chronicle of the French Revolution* (1989), awarded the NCR Prize for Non-Fiction and the *Yorkshire Post*'s Book of the Year; *Dead Certainties: Unwarranted Speculations* (1991), which has been filmed for the BBC as 'Murder at Harvard'; *Landscape and Memory* (1995), which received the W. H. Smith Prize for Literature; *Rembrandt's Eyes* (1999); and the three-volume *A History of Britain* (2000–2002) linked to the award-winning BBC TV series.

QUENTIN SKINNER has been the Regius Professor of Modern History at Cambridge since 1996 and a Fellow of Christ's since 1962. He is a Fellow of numerous Academies and has received several honorary degrees. His scholarship has been translated into nineteen languages, and his books include *Machiavelli* (1981), *Reason and Rhetoric in the Philosophy of Hobbes* (1996), *Liberty Before Liberalism* (1998) and *Visions of Politics* (3 vols, 2002). His best-known work is

The Foundations of Modern Political Thought (2 vols, 1978), which won the Wolfson Literary Prize in 1979 and was voted by the *Times Literary Supplement* one of the hundred most influential books of the last half-century.

BARRY SUPPLE is Emeritus Professor of Economic History at Cambridge and a Fellow of the British Academy. He was an undergraduate at the LSE and a research student at Christ's College, 1952–5. He taught at Harvard, McGill, Sussex and Oxford until 1981, when he was elected to the Chair of Economic History at Cambridge and a Professorial Fellowship at Christ's. In 1984 he was elected an Honorary Fellow on assuming the Mastership of St Catharine's College. From 1993 to 2001 he was Director of the Leverhulme Trust. His books include *Commercial Crisis and Change in England, 1600–1642* (1959), *Boston Capitalists and Western Railroads* (1967), *The Royal Exchange Assurance: A History of the British Insurance, 1720–1970* (1970), *The History of the British Coalmining Industry, 1913–46* (1987) and *The State and Economic Knowledge* (1990).

Index

Index

www.panmacmillan.com

www.ingramcontent.com/pod-product-compliance
Ingram Content Group UK Ltd.
Pitfield, Milton Keynes, MK11 3LW, UK
UKHW040640280225
455688UK00002B/42